THE REBIRTH
OF EAST EUROPE

Michael G. Roskin

Lycoming College

PRENTICE HALL, *Englewood Cliffs, New Jersey 07632*

947
R821r

Library of Congress Cataloging-in-Publication Data

Roskin, Michael
    The rebirth of East Europe / Michael G. Roskin.
        p.   cm.
    Includes index.
    ISBN 0-13-763442-0
    1. Europe, Eastern--Politics and government.   I. Title.
DJK42.R67   1991
947--dc20

90-23062
CIP

Editorial/production supervision and
    interior design: Shelly Kupperman
Cover design: Ray Lundgren Graphics Ltd.
Manufacturing buyer: Mary Ann Gloriande
Prepress buyer: Debbie Kesar
Acquisitions editor: Karen Horton
Cover photo: Michael G. Roskin

© 1991 by Prentice-Hall, Inc.
A Simon & Schuster Company
Englewood Cliffs, New Jersey 07632

Printed in the United States of America
10 9 8 7 6 5 4 3

ISBN   0-13-763442-0

PRENTICE-HALL INTERNATIONAL (UK) LIMITED, *London*
PRENTICE-HALL OF AUSTRALIA PTY. LIMITED, *Sydney*
PRENTICE-HALL CANADA INC., *Toronto*
PRENTICE-HALL HISPANOAMERICANA, S.A., *Mexico*
PRENTICE-HALL OF INDIA PRIVATE LIMITED, *New Delhi*
PRENTICE-HALL OF JAPAN, INC., *Tokyo*
SIMON & SCHUSTER ASIA PTE. LTD., *Singapore*
EDITORA PRENTICE-HALL DO BRASIL, LTDA., *Rio de Janeiro*

CONTENTS _____

2   Flunking Democracy: The Interwar Years   26

3   East Europe and World War II   48

8   "Now You Can Choose": The Elections of 1989 and 1990   146

9   The Odds for Democracy   166

PREFACE

This book is not written by an expert on East Europe, nor is it intended for such experts. It grew out of my decision to include East Europe in an introductory comparative politics course. At the time, the upheaval in East Europe was making headlines every day; I could think of no way to make comparative politics more exciting or relevant. I looked for an introductory text and found nothing suitable. Existing works on East Europe tended to be overly specialized studies, sometimes of single countries, which have now been overtaken by events. Many of these studies, prepared with great diligence by careful scholars, are now irrelevant; some were based on mistaken assumptions. Furthermore, the leading edge of political science requires its practitioners to theorize too much. To read some studies, one might think East Europe was populated by theories rather than by humans.

The net package is a literature little accessible to undergraduates, especially to first-time students of East Europe. Many students have never been exposed to the basics that make something like East Europe intelligible. Especially lacking in the specialized literature are geography and twentieth-century history. How many students, for example, can locate Southern Dobrudja on a map? (Even worse, after they've been shown, a few still cannot locate Northern Dobrudja.) Accordingly, an introductory text must fill in many gaps in basic student knowledge.

For classroom instruction, East Europe and its recent upheavals provide some wonderful examples and case studies of legitimacy (or lack thereof), ideology (or lack thereof), the relation between politics and economics, international dependency, political culture, institution building, and party systems. Especially fascinating are the differences between East and West Europe and how rapidly the former will catch up with the latter. The project also gave me the opportunity to return to an area that was of great interest to me many years ago. From 1963 to

1964, I studied at the University of Belgrade, and I had authored an earlier book (*Other Governments of Europe*, Prentice-Hall, 1977) that had included Yugoslavia and East Germany. It was good to get back to an area that in recent years had not attracted the attention it deserves.

In the course of writing this book, it occurred to me that I was engaged in dialogues with three imaginary figures: one a leftist, one a rightist, and the third an optimistic American political scientist. These figures are composites of people I have known over the years. The leftist, while uncomfortable about the actual workings of Communist East Europe, still thinks that Marx was basically right and that some type of socialism—perhaps the alleged "humanist" variety of the young Marx—is the progressive thing to aim for. But East Europe really was socialism in action; what you see is what you get. The later chapters lend support to the Hayekian thesis that socialism—meaning state ownership and control of industry—automatically tends to tyranny.

The rightist, on the other hand, is often little aware of how bad and backward East Europe was before the Communists took over. Now that Communists are out of power (except in the Balkans), rightists tend to think everything will be great. It won't be that simple. The sources of instability are many in East Europe, and attitudes and institutions are little attuned to pluralist democracy and a market system. Some fairly nasty politics may come out of post-Communist East Europe. Ultimately, though, after a long and difficult period of adjustment, I think East Europe will join West Europe as modern democracies and free economies.

The imaginary political scientist—steeped in theories of systems and stability—for some years thought East Europe was headed for some middle way of hybrid regimes in which the Communists shared power with others. After some decades of reflecting on middle ways or third paths between communism and democracy, controlled and market economies (the purpose of my year in Yugoslavia), I have concluded that they do not exist, or, if attempted, they have short life spans. My imaginary scholar also closely analyzes party elites, too closely to notice that the whole system depends on the threat of Soviet intervention. Take away that threat and the game of musical chairs in the Czech politburo is about as significant as arranging deck chairs on the Titanic.

I wish to thank Zsuzsa Kelen, an economist and distant cousin in Budapest, who gave me many insights into the economic difficulties of the transition to a market system. Dr. György Szoboszlai, secretary of the Hungarian Political Science Association, gave me a clear perspective on Hungary's 1990 elections and nascent party system. I also owe special thanks to my Lycoming colleagues. Historian Robert Larson made important comments about and corrections in some of my historical chapters; he saved me from making several misstatements. Mathematician Andrzej Bucki gave me an insider's view of Solidarity and taught me how to pronounce Polish names. Robert Maples of our French department used his computer expertise to turn my electronic manuscript into camera-ready copy on the Laserjet III. Sandra Rife prepared the maps. Additionally, I wish to thank

Donald E. Pienkos of the University of Wisconsin-Milwaukee and Zachary T. Irwin of the Pennsylvania State University-Erie, The Behrend College, for their conscientious and helpful remarks on the manuscript.

Ultimately, of course, full responsibility is mine. I welcome all professional comments and corrections for a possible second edition. They can be sent directly to me at Lycoming College, Williamsport, PA 17701.

MICHAEL G. ROSKIN

EAST
GERMANY

Berlin ●

incorporated
into FRG 1990

POLAND

Warsaw ●

SOVIET UNION

● Prague

CZECHOSLOVAKIA

Vienna ●

● Budapest

AUSTRIA

HUNGARY

ROMANIA

Belgrade ●

Bucharest
●

YUGOSLAVIA

● Sofia

ALBANIA

BULGARIA

Tirana ●

GREECE

East Europe as a Unit of Study

The rebirth of East Europe was inevitable but unpredictable. Sooner or later East Europe was going to escape from the Soviet orbit and from communism, but precisely when no one could know. Upon coming to power in 1989 and 1990, every non-Communist leader of East Europe was stunned with disbelief. Only a few months before, many had been in prison or in the dissident underground. The speed of change was incredible because change was waiting to happen. The weak, unstable Communist regimes of East Europe were waiting for word from the Soviet Union that it no longer wished to retain them. When that word came, Communists were out of power in a matter of months. Communism in East Europe (or, for that matter, probably anywhere) is not a workable system. In East Europe, it lasted only as long as the Soviets were willing to prop it up. Most observers assumed this would be more or less forever.

In 1989, Soviet President Gorbachev pulled the props out and most of the Communist regimes of East Europe quickly collapsed. Transformed Balkan Communist regimes clung to power but probably not for long. Most Western observers greeted the changes with joy. Now at last the lands of East Europe would rejoin Europe and move quickly up to West European levels of prosperity and democracy. This author suspects things won't be quite that simple, and that East Europe will retain its distinctive characteristics for some time. East Europe has long been a backward area and has lagged behind most of West Europe for centuries. The Communists were not the sole culprits. The Communists, to be sure, took a backward area and kept it backward, but they did not invent its backwardness.

This book then is not a starry-eyed view of East Europe. It presents the region with all its problems, and with a few hopes. Ultimately, I am an optimist about

---

Is There Still a Second World?

For the last couple of decades, writers have used the shorthand expressions First, Second, and Third Worlds. The First World designated the market economies and democracies of West Europe and North America. The Second World was the centrally planned Communist economies of East Europe and the Soviet Union. The Third World was almost everything else, namely, Asia, Africa, and Latin America.

Now, suddenly, there seems to be no more Second World, certainly not in East Europe, which has abandoned Communist dictatorship and turned toward market economies. Should we promote them to the First World? There is no international tribunal to place countries in these simplified categories. This book is going to argue that East Europe is still quite different from the First World lands of West Europe. East Europe is poorer, less democratic, and is still experimenting with a market economy. If all goes well, East Europe may some day join the First World. In the meantime, it might qualify as either the Second World or World 1.5.

East Europe. I am convinced that East Europe is going to make it, after much stress and strain, into a new, modern Europe. Not in my lifetime, but perhaps in my grandchildren's, East Europe will reach levels similar to those now found in West Europe. Until then, East Europe will be a fascinating place to study, for it resembles the West Europe of previous decades. Almost like taking a time machine back, in East Europe we can see firsthand the struggle to industrialize, to found stable democracies, and to calm the passions of political extremism. For political scientists, East Europe is a sort of laboratory of democracy, where we can witness in real time experiments we dare not try on our own political systems.

One of the problems in studying East Europe is that East Europeans do not think of themselves as East Europeans. They think of themselves as Poles, Czechs, Hungarians, and so on, and they do not like to see themselves as members of a broader regional entity. West Europeans, on the other hand, increasingly call themselves "Europeans" and think of themselves as members of the European Community, which is slowly turning into a supranational entity they are proud to belong to. There is no such pride of membership in East Europe, for the "East bloc" they were consigned to was not of their making. It was forced on them. And East Europeans, again in contrast to West Europeans, are still rather nationalistic. East Europeans of one country like to look down on East Europeans in neighboring countries.

When you ask East Europeans to generalize about what is happening in their region, it will strike them as an absurd question. They know and care, at most, only about what is happening in their own country. Comparisons among East European nations and generalizations about East Europe as a whole have rarely

What Did We Know and When Did We Know It?

Political scientists have some explaining to do. Some might be a little embarrassed. Most of us failed to anticipate or even conjecture about the collapse of communism in East Europe. Some specialists looked at the Communist regimes of the region as working, more or less permanent structures. Others argued that they would change but not totally; they would reform into "hybrid" regimes that mixed communism with democracy, and centralized economies with market economies.

Why did we underanticipate change in East Europe? Do we tend to underanticipate change in general? Is political science inherently a status quo discipline, one focusing on what is but incapable of detecting the forces for change? By trying too hard to sound scientific, some political scientists embraced formalistic theories of systems and stability that ignored the reality of contrived regimes imposed by foreign bayonets and secret police upon unwilling peoples. In these bloodless, abstract theories, hatred does not compute.

Some political scientists accurately foresaw major upheavals in Vietnam, South Africa, and Central America. These political scientists tend to be liberals or radicals, and they bring with them a critical intelligence that is skeptical of the existing state of affairs and capable of identifying the sources of change. Applied to East Europe, though, these same discerning eyes tended to dim, for they either paid little attention to the region or looked at it through leftist lenses. They liked to study revolution in the Third World, not revolution in the Second World. Some even refused to consider that socialism might be inherently flawed.

About the only people who accurately anticipated the impending collapse in East Europe were the emigrés, those who had fled their native lands to denounce the Communist regimes from exile. They understood the depth of hatred that many theorists missed. But they were often so angry, so nationalistic, and so immoderate in their views that many of us tended to write them off as fanatics. It turned out that many of them had a better handle on reality than some American specialists.

It may be unfair to expect political scientists to anticipate what few others anticipated. Practically no one saw what was coming, including the people making the decisions that made it happen. But political scientists really are supposed to have a handle on reality. If we cannot anticipate political upheavals, what good are we? I do not mean here that we need to make precise predictions about what will happen and when, but we should have a general sense that certain regimes may be headed for breakdown and others for success. "Early warning" is a worthwhile and feasible task for political scientists, and one that would sharpen our analytic skills. A political scientist who accurately anticipates major change also demonstrates his or her mastery of data and of analytical tools. Prediction or at least anticipation should be considered important tests of political science.

occurred to them. They will tell you that comparisons and generalizations about East Europe are not valid, that each East European country is different. This book argues that generalizations about East Europe are not only possible but irresistible. East Europe, while far from uniform, can be profitably studied as a unit. The countries of East Europe share many historical experiences. Notice how one leads to the next.

1. All East European countries were parts of empires, most until this century. Once subjected to one empire, the East European victims usually soon fell into the clutches of another. The Ottoman Turks, the Habsburgs, the Prussians, and the tsarist Russians made East Europe their playground. This kept the countries of the region weak. In sharp contrast, in West Europe strong nation-states emerged early and were able to fight off conquerers and maintain their independence.

2. All East European countries got their independence late, some only at the close of World War I. With the French Revolution, nationalism rippled through Europe, waking up one nationality after another. During the nineteenth century, Romania, Bulgaria, and Serbia pushed out the Turks. By the beginning of the twentieth century, all the subject peoples of East Europe fairly ached to be free and independent. World War I gave them their chance. Their imperial masters— Austria-Hungary and Germany on one side and tsarist Russia on the other—bashed themselves silly and collapsed. From the wreckage rose the subject peoples, the "successor states" to the old empires.

3. All the East European lands except Czechoslovakia flunked their first test of democracy during the interwar years. All were initially set up on a democratic premise, but by the 1930s military coups, royal dictatorships, and the growth of fascistic parties characterized the region. Communist parties, it should be noted, were small and scarcely a problem in the interwar years.

4. Weak and divided, East Europe was a pushover for the Nazis. Czechoslovakia, betrayed by Britain and France in 1938, was taken over without a shot in 1939. Hungary and Romania, under domestic fascistic pressure, joined Hitler's Axis, as did Bulgaria. Poland and Yugoslavia fought but were quickly crushed. By the time the war ended in 1945, the East European lands were weaker than ever and unable to resist becoming Soviet satellites.

5. All East European lands were conquered by Stalin's Red Army in World War II. As the Soviets pushed the Germans back through East Europe, Stalin set up obedient Communist puppets, most of whom had sat out the war in Moscow. Only Yugoslavia's Tito, head of the Partisan army that had liberated roughly half the country, had his own power base. Stalin didn't trust anyone who wasn't his puppet.

6. Stalin ordered all East Europe turned into Soviet satellites. Using his puppets and Communist control of the interior (police) and defense ministries, Stalin moved one step at a time to install Communist regimes modeled on the Soviet system. The

last country to fall was Czechoslovakia, taken over by a Communist coup early in 1948. No Communist regime came to or stayed in power by free elections.

7. The Communist regimes of East Europe, brutally inflicting the Soviet model on captive peoples, had almost no legitimacy. Almost all East Europeans resented and many actively hated their regimes. Over the decades, no Communist regime succeeded in rooting itself into the hearts of its people. Indeed, legitimacy grew

---

The Study of East Europe's Politics

Until recently, East European politics was studied by relatively few specialists. They were trained not only in the languages and histories of their areas but also in the curious logic of Communist systems. To study Communist systems, one had to understand the Marxist-Leninist theory, the importance of party structure and of key party personnel, and the controlled, secretive nature of Communist regimes. Specialists, unable to interview decision makers, developed indirect methods to study East Europe's politics, including a lot of reading between the lines of party and state publications, carefully analyzing speeches for clues about policy, and noting who got fired, retired, or promoted. Using these indirect methods plus some sophisticated intuitions and insights, specialists on East Europe were able to come up with important and accurate analyses. For example, the split of East Europe's Communist parties into conservative and reformist factions was studied well and early by specialists.

Some specialized studies of East Europe, however, have quickly become irrelevant, for things have changed drastically. Closed politics has given way to mass politics. The indirect methods and reading between the lines are no longer particularly worthwhile. Now most of the region's politicians give interviews with reasonable candor. Lesser officials are no longer afraid to talk with visiting Western scholars and journalists. (Under the Communists, officials having any contact—including exchange of letters—with foreigners were subjected to scrutiny and were interviewed by security police.) Free and fair elections can now be studied and analyzed. Election and survey data show a rich political life that was earlier buried under Communist glop.

The study of dictatorships requires a special set of skills, the study of democracies another set. The skills needed to study East Europe are now in large measure the skills long used to study West Europe. This is not to say that the old East Europe specialists are no longer needed. What we need is "cross-training" between East Europe and West Europe specialists. The former must add such approaches as public opinion, interest groups, elections, and legislative behavior, while the latter must add language, historical, and geographic expertise. East European politics has not suddenly become the same as West European politics, but it has started to resemble it, lagging behind it by several decades.

weaker over time. In several East European lands mass discontent erupted in anger and violence against Communist regimes.

8. All the Communist economies of East Europe performed poorly. The socialist economic systems that were to bring a material paradise on earth fell further behind the capitalist systems of West Europe and Japan. By the 1980s, the gaps were glaring and embarrassing, and this produced even more mass discontent.

9. All the Communist parties of East Europe split into liberal and conservative factions. Their confidence shaken by economic failure, the Communists groped for economic answers. The conservative gerontocracies, fearing (accurately) for their jobs and for system stability, offered only the most minor of reforms, reforms that changed nothing. Liberals, generally younger, acutely aware that their economies were becoming laughingstocks, urged major reforms, including large elements of a market system. The liberals sought "middle ways" between socialism and capitalism, between Communist party control and pluralism. They did not realize that a middle way did not exist for them.

10. Amid growing mass clamor, the relatively liberal Communists wrested control away from conservatives and promised major reform. But major reform of a bad, unloved system is not what the people of East Europe had in mind. They wanted an end to communism of any stripe and its replacement by genuine democracy. With their newly won freedom of speech, press, and assembly, they demanded free, multiparty elections. The Communist liberals had unleashed a tiger.

11. Free elections, all with Gorbachev's approval, ousted most Communist regimes in East Europe. The renamed liberal wings of the old ruling Communist parties—they now called themselves Socialists and probably were—got clobbered in these elections with the exceptions of Romania and Bulgaria. Gorbachev was content with the results.

12. Inexperienced, idealistic, centrist regimes took power amid terrible economic problems. Few of the new governments had clear or realistic economic policies. All the new regimes were entering the dangerous, uncharted territory of conversion from centrally planned to market economies. Everyone was scared of runaway inflation and massive unemployment.

These twelve points—and there are others—demonstrate that East Europe forms a unit of study. Let us now consider these points more fully.

CHAPTER ONE _____

Caught between Empires

IS GEOGRAPHY DESTINY?

East Europe was dealt a poor hand and played it even worse. Geography has been unkind to East Europe, but what the political leadership of the region did over the centuries deepened the problems of geography. Human decisions compounded an unfortunate geographic situation into one of weakness, resulting in foreign conquest until most East European lands were reduced to backwater provinces of empires.

East Europe's first geographical problem is its proximity to Asia. Whatever tribes thundered out of Asia, they hit East Europe first and hardest. East Europe can be seen as West Europe's buffer zone and protective barrier, a role East Europe plays to this day. Particularly destructive were the Mongols in the thirteenth century, who left a gigantic swath of destruction that pushed East Europe backward at the very time West Europe was starting to stir culturally, economically, and politically. Then came the Ottoman Turks starting in the late fourteenth century. Unlike the Mongols, they did not destroy for joy, but they implanted a backward system that snuffed out budding kingdoms and cultures and retarded Southeast Europe for centuries.

Consider this: The last invasion of West Europe by non-Europeans began when the Moors crossed into Spain in 711. They reached Poitiers, France, where, in 732 they were beaten by Charles Martel. Thereafter they were slowly pushed back until finally dislodged from Andalusia in 1492. Two peninsulas to the east, at this same time, the Turks were pushing into the Balkans, beating the Serbs in 1389 and the Hungarians in 1526. Three years after that, they were besieging Vienna. While West Europe, free of Muslim invasion or occupation, could develop its states and economies, East Europe (with the exception of Bohemia and Poland) suffered for centuries under the Turkish yoke, a yoke that started to lift only in 1699. The Turks were not fully out of East Europe until 1913. West Europe had a head start in nation building of several centuries over East Europe.

Most of East Europe is on broad plains with few geographical barriers to invasion. The only significant mountains of the region are the Carpathians, running through Slovakia and parts of southern Poland and northern Hungary. But the Carpathians generally run east-west and thus pose few barriers to invasions from east or west. The Balkans, to be sure, are mountainous; *balkan* is Turkish for mountain. But the river valleys in the Balkans run from south to north, straight to Belgrade, the gateway to the Pannonian Basin for the Turks in the fifteenth century.

The region has also been shortchanged on navigable rivers. West Europe has the Rhine, an important trading corridor connecting Switzerland, France, Germany, Belgium, and Holland and emptying into the Atlantic. The magnificent Danube, which flows through Bavaria, Austria, Hungary, Yugoslavia, and Romania, could not play an analogous role. For centuries, the lower reaches of the Danube were in Turkish hands, and it empties into the Black Sea, long a Turkish lake, so its utility for trade was limited by the hostility of the Ottoman Empire. If the Danube had somehow flowed in the opposite direction and emptied into the Atlantic, the history of East Europe would have been quite different.

Trade is an extremely important factor in the growth of national power. Access to the open sea enabled the modernizing regimes of France, Spain, Holland, and England to collect revenues from trade and colonization. Access to the sea was limited for East Europe. Polish access to the Baltic was impeded by the Teutonic knights and then by Prussia. The Dinaric Alps of Yugoslavia cut the Dalmatian coast off from the Balkan hinterland; much of Dalmatia was simply a Venetian colony. The Black Sea, relatively speaking, led nowhere, and for centuries it was Turkish. Compared with West Europe, East Europe was largely landlocked and isolated.

But is geography destiny? Did these geographic disadvantages doom East Europe to slow development compared with West Europe? A cohesive empire running the length of the Danube and able to beat back the Turks might have brought modernization and progess much earlier to the region. Much of the problem has been political. East Europe's curse has been its fragmentation, a problem that continues to this day.

EAST EUROPE'S ETHNIC GROUPS

The formation of a strong empire or kingdom in East Europe was retarded by the multiplicity of the region's very distinct ethnic groups. To this day, most of these groups retain a spiky sense of their uniqueness and resist being amalgamated into larger units. West Europe, in contrast, was generally able to merge smaller peoples into national entities, turning Frisians into Germans, Burgundians into Frenchmen, and so on. The disunity of East Europe's peoples left them vulnerable to conquest and foreign domination.

Let us be careful in what we mean by "ethnic group" here. We do not mean genes or bloodlines. Biologically, the peoples of all Europe, East or West, are so mixed that it is impossible to untangle their genetic origins. Contrary to Nazi (and sometimes more recent) demagogues, there is no "pure-blooded" nation anywhere in Europe. Typically, Europeans are the descendants of peoples who came in waves of immigration that washed into Europe, often from the east.

"Ethnic group" in our context means language, not blood. For example, at one point there were Slavic settlements as far west as Hanover in Germany; these people were soon assimilated into the German language. Many Germans, if you could trace their bloodlines back, are simply German-speaking Slavs. In the early eighteenth century, after the Turks were expelled from Hungary, the Habsburgs settled large numbers of Germans in the depopulated countryside. Their descendants are now Hungarian.

Most East Europeans are of Slavic origin. Like most Europeans, the Slavs orginated as tribes on the borders of Europe and Asia and pushed their way west in the early centuries of the Christian era. Their languages are rather closely related, closer than the Romance languages of West Europe. A Slovak peasant, it is said, can converse with any other Slavic peasant. Slovakia is roughly the hub of the Slavic lands, and peasant speech has not changed that much over the centuries. I found decades ago that I could make myself understood with Serbian in Slovakia, but not in Bohemia (the Czech lands), for Czech has evolved more than Slovak.

Religion deepened the divergences among the Slavic tribes. The western Slavs were Christianized from Rome. Poles, Czechs, Slovaks, Slovenes, and Croats became Catholic and wrote with the Latin alphabet, with some extra marks for peculiarly Slavic sounds. They looked westward and are generally western in outlook. The eastern and southern Slavs were Christianized from Constantinople and became Eastern Orthodox. Their alphabet is Cyrillic, a variation of the Greek that was developed by the Greek monks who converted them to Christianity. Russians, Ukrainians, Bulgars, Macedonians, and Serbs thus developed a more eastward-looking orientation. This was especially a problem when Constantinople (now called Istanbul), the headquarters of Eastern Orthodox Christianity, was conquered by the Turks in 1453 and could no longer serve as a fountainhead of learning and innovation, as Rome served for Catholic Europe.

Splitting the Slavs of East Europe into north and south are the Hungarians. Not to be confused with the Huns who thundered out of Central Asia in the fifth century, the Magyars (as the Hungarians call themselves) drifted from the Volga region of Russia and settled in the fertile Pannonian basin in the ninth centry. Although they accepted Catholicism about the year 1000, Hungarians still stand out for their strange language, which shares few cognates with neighboring tongues. Knowing a Slavic language or German will not help you understand Hungarian, which is distantly related to Finnish.

To the southeast of the Hungarians are the Romanians, descendants of the ancient Dacians and of the Roman soldiers who occupied the area. Romanian is very much a Romance language, and if you know French, Spanish, or Italian, you can figure out some written Romanian. Romanians, though, were Christianized from Constantinople and most are Eastern Orthodox, although they stayed with the Latin alphabet.

Albanians, descendants of the ancient Illyrians, with a Turkish overlay, have a tiny country between Yugoslavia and Greece. Their language is all their own, and they are divided in religion between a Muslim majority and both Catholic and Orthodox Christian minorities. They are further divided tribally between the Tosks of the south and Ghegs of the north.

Complicating matters, East European borders do not neatly demarcate its peoples. Some ethnic groups are settled among other groups, what geographers call "interdigitized." The biggest single problem now is Transylvania, part of Romania but with a large Hungarian population. They are so interspersed that Transylvania cannot be fairly partitioned into Hungarian and Romanian areas. Additionally, there are Hungarian minorities in Yugoslavia and Czechoslovakia. In the south of Yugoslavia, a large Albanian minority has taken over the once-Serbian province of Kosovo, now the scene of violent ethnic clashes.

Dispersed peoples add to the region's complexity. Jews, gypsies, and Germans at one point formed important minorities scattered throughout the region. The Holocaust reduced the Jewish population to a fraction of its prewar numbers. After the war, most Holocaust survivors emigrated. Now there is a significant Jewish community only in Budapest. Gypsies were also victims of the Nazis, but they are still found throughout East Europe. Sizable German colonies, some deliberately planted by the Habsburgs to secure their empire, have greatly shrunk. Millions of Germans fled westward from Poland and Czechoslovakia at the close of World War II. Many of the remaining ethnic Germans of East Europe emigrated to the jobs and prosperity of West Germany, which by law had to take them in, over the decades.

Is the ethnic complexity of East Europe really that different from West Europe? If you go back far enough in West Europe, you find all kinds of ethnic groups. The difference is that most West European monarchies had the political, military, economic, and cultural power to turn divergent ethnic groups into subordinate parts of their kingdoms, in time assimilating them and erasing their languages and cultures. France is the model for this kind of modernizing and centralizing monarchy. Neighboring Spain, unable to turn its Basques and Catalans into Spaniards, exhibits some of the problems of East Europe, especially of Yugoslavia. The point is that almost every country starts with or acquires ethnic groups. The stronger nation-states are able to control, dominate, and sometimes assimilate minority groups. The key is political power, and in this the East European states have been much weaker than their West European counterparts.

East or Central Europe?

Before World War II, the region we are talking about was called Central Europe and the Balkans. After the war, it was called East Europe. There is no tribunal to settle geographic names. Names change over time in response to the political situation. Between the two world wars, Central Europe and the Balkans was the middle area between West Europe (countries which generally touched the Atlantic) and the vast Eurasian power of the Soviet Union. With the Cold War and the division of Europe in two, it seemed more natural to call this middle ground East Europe, to distinguish it from West Europe. During the Cold War, there was no "middle," and the term Central Europe fell into disuse.

Yale historian Michael Howard argues there are religious grounds for distinguishing between Central and East Europe. Central Europe, claims Howard, encompasses the Catholic countries of the former Habsburg (Austro-Hungarian) Empire plus Poland, also Catholic. East Europe, on the other hand, includes the lands of Eastern Orthodox Christianity—Russia, the Ukraine, Serbia, Bulgaria, and Romania. Catholic countries looked to Rome for spiritual guidance and with this came a more western outlook, one still apparent today in art, architecture, and attitudes. For example, Lvov, in the present-day Soviet Ukraine, was for centuries Polish-ruled Lwow and Austrian-ruled Lemberg. It clearly looks different from other Soviet cities. The streets are laid out in square grids and the churches and many other buildings are western in style. In Lvov, you feel you are in Europe.

Eastern Orthodox countries, with the fall of the center of their faith, Constantinople, to the Turks in 1453, essentially had no spiritual capital to look to for guidance and modernization. Moscow claimed to be the spiritual capital of Eastern Orthodoxy, but most branches of the faith paid Moscow no special attention. Cut off by Tatar and Turkish occupation, the Eastern Orthodox countries were bypassed by the invigorating currents that rippled out of Italy with the Renaissance. Whether this was a matter of religious differences or Tatar and Turkish occupation can be disputed.

With the end of Communist regimes in East Europe, the term Central Europe quickly revived; now there was once again a middle between West Europe and the Soviet Union. Perhaps future editions of this book will speak of the region as Central Europe. We will use East Europe here to designate the broad band of countries to the west of the Soviet Union that were or still are Communist. We will also find it useful to split the region into Central Europe—from Hungary north—and the Balkans—lands to the south of Hungary. This is generally accepted geographical usage. Central Europe was largely dominated by the Habsburg Empire, the Balkans by the Ottoman Empire. Each empire left behind different traditions, tastes, and political styles. To this day, the Balkans are backward compared with Central Europe.

WEAK STATES

During the Middle Ages, there were kingdoms in East Europe as developed as any in West Europe at the time. Medieval Poland, Bohemia, Serbia, and Bulgaria attained great strength and respect in their day. Around half a millenium ago, at about the time much of East Europe fell under the Ottomans, a series of changes hit West Europe that moved it to modernity. These changes were generally weaker and occurred later in East Europe and left it relatively backward. The "strong state" developed in West Europe first. Exactly what caused the strong state and which changes came first is disputed, and the changes did not necessarily occur in the following order:

1. *The economy expanded* with trade, new industries, and the opening of the New World. With their access to the Atlantic, most West European monarchs eagerly promoted economic growth and expansion. Relatively isolated, East Europe had slower economic growth.

2. *Monarchs turned absolutist* and developed unquenchable thirsts for national power, both political and economic. Often at war, the ambitious monarchs developed standing armies and navies whose costs escalated. This forced them to modernize their kingdoms and improve administration (especially tax collections), commerce, communication, and education.

3. *The absolutist monarchs thus founded the modern nation-state.* Bypassing the conservative feudal system in which king was balanced by nobles, the new monarchs defined themselves as the last word in law. This gave rise to the notions of sovereignty and nationality. Loyalty to nation became more important than loyalty to locality or to feudal counts and dukes.

4. *The class structure changed as the economy modernized.* Middle classes developed, based on the growth of commerce and industry, in West Europe. They provided a more stable and enthusiastic basis of support for the new nation-state. Better educated, they also made better military officers in time of war. East Europe, still agrarian, stayed feudal with a class structure composed of few nobles and many peasants. Serfdom lasted much longer in East Europe than in West Europe.

Changes such as these added up to what some call the "strong state" or "modern nation-state." East Europe lagged, in part for reasons of geography, but in large measure because it had already been incorporated into empires. Could the East Europeans have avoided it? Only if they had been able to unify, federate, or form alliances among themselves. This they could not—and still cannot—do.

FOUR EMPIRES

At least five distinct empires have dominated parts of East Europe. We will consider four here and save the fifth, the Soviet, for longer consideration in subsequent chapters. Once caught between empires, East Europe tended to stay caught.

The Ottoman (Turkish) Empire

This vast and long-lived, but ramshackle, empire exploded in the fourteenth century as the Ottoman Turks took Anatolia and the Balkans. The Muslim Ottomans beat the Bulgarians at Adrianople in 1361 and the Serbians at Kosovo in 1389, a victory that opened their way into the rich Pannonian basin of Hungary and onto Vienna, which they besieged twice, in 1529 and again in 1683. All Europe trembled until Polish cavalry under Jan Sobieski drove the Turks back from Vienna in 1683 in what is considered one of the most decisive battles of history. At about the same time, the Ottomans took the Arab lands of the Middle East and North Africa. In 1453, the Ottomans cracked the walls of Constantinople, which they had earlier bypassed, with their new cannons and took it over as their capital, Istanbul.

The Ottomans were compelled to keep expanding because much of their revenue was from booty. If they stopped expanding they would have little with which to pay the army. Meritorious soldiers were rewarded on the spot after battles by grants of lands in the newly conquered domain. This gave them a keen edge to fight well. In this way, the Ottomans built up a loyal, landowning class that they could count on to defend both the empire and their individual estates.

How did this gigantic empire, rarely well administered, hold together? There was a kind of Ottoman genius in running their empire; namely, they didn't try to do too much. The Sultan in Istanbul rarely tried to control the whole thing, which, considering the distances involved and poor communications of the time, might

Ottoman Empire at Its Height

have been impossible. Many Sultans were assisted by *viziers*, roughly prime ministers, who were able and vigorous men, some of non-Turkish origin. The Ottomans imposed a "blood tax" on their subject peoples and every few years collected it in the form of young boys plucked from their mothers and packed off to Istanbul to become *janissaries*, the administrators and police of the Ottoman Empire. Forbidden to marry and having no blood ties to the peoples they administered, the janissaries impartially and sometimes brutally imposed order.

Further, in keeping with the hands-off Ottoman governing style, non-Muslim subject peoples of the empire were permitted to largely govern themselves as far as their internal matters were concerned. In what was called the *milyet* (nations) system, Christians and Jews had their own courts and customs. Non-Muslim religions were rarely persecuted; the Turks were tolerant.

The whole empire was loose and sloppy. Hugely corrupt and poorly run, it went into economic decline and slowly fell apart. As the economy and technology of its European Christian foes accelerated, the Ottomans found themselves getting beaten more frequently. In 1687, the Austrians defeated them at Mohács in Hungary. With the Treaty of Karlowitz in 1699, the Ottomans agreed to turn over Hungary and Transylvania to the Habsburgs, Dalmatia to Venice, and Podolia to Poland. They had occupied (and decimated) Hungary for a century and a half. Karlowitz marks the beginning of the slow Ottoman retreat in Europe, as Russia and Austria pushed them back and native Balkan nationalities revolted.

By the early nineteenth century, the Ottomans had lost most of the Balkans. They left behind several small states (see box "Balkanization") and instability. North Africa and Egypt were only nominally part of the empire; powerful local chiefs actually ran them as independent countries. By the late nineteenth century, the Ottoman Empire was widely regarded as "the sick man of Europe." In 1913, the Ottomans were finally expelled from Europe except for the little corner of European Turkey which exists to this day. Allied with Germany in World War I, the Ottoman Empire finally collapsed.

Bear in mind that the Ottoman Empire dominated much of the Balkans for four and even five centuries. This put a distinct stamp on the region that one still notices in foods, architecture, and attitudes. It gives the region a certain Middle East

---

Balkanization

The small countries left as the Turks were pushed out of the Balkan Peninsula gave rise to the derisive term "balkanization," the breaking apart of an empire into small, weak countries. These lands included Serbia and Macedonia (which later became parts of Yugoslavia) and Moldavia and Wallachia (which later became Romania). The word *Balkan* connoted comic-opera countries (such as "Marsovia" in Franz Lehar's *Merry Widow*) that constantly squabbled among themselves.

The Last Ottoman Problem: Palestine

In case you think the problems of the decline of the Ottoman Empire belong to another century, consider present-day Israel. Its conflict with its Arab neighbors and Palestinian inhabitants is also a leftover problem from the Ottoman Empire, for Palestine was a Turkish province for six centuries. As in the Balkans, the Turks were pushed back by a combination of local unrest and great-power intervention, in this case chiefly British.

During World War I, Turkey allied with Germany, and Britain conquered Ottoman holdings in the Middle East, setting up "mandates" from the League of Nations to govern Palestine, Jordan, and Iraq. Britain also permitted large-scale Jewish immigration to Palestine, which increasingly awoke Arab fears that Palestine would be taken from them for a Jewish state. The Holocaust spurred Zionists into pushing Britain out of Palestine, and in 1948 the state of Israel was founded. Arabs and Israelis have been fighting ever since, backed, as in the Balkans, by major outside powers.

---

charm, but it retarded economic and political development. Left behind after the Turks were nationalistic rivalries that started World War I and which continue to this day. Worst of all, the Ottoman Empire prevented the rise of the sort of "strong state" that grew in West Europe. Without such strong states, East Europe was easy pickings for other empires.

The Habsburg (later Austro-Hungarian) Empire

This major dynasty, of German origin, ruled Austria from 1278 to 1918 and Spain from 1516 to 1700. This meant they had numerous other holdings—most of Latin America, the Netherlands, Hungary, Czechoslovakia, and parts of Poland, Italy, Romania, and Yugoslavia. At one point in the sixteenth century, under Charles V, Habsburg military might and New World gold, fighting on the Catholic side, came close to dominating Europe.

It is the eastern Habsburgs that chiefly interest us, for they formed the preeminent East European empire. Every country we are studying in this book (except Albania and Bulgaria) was for centuries, in whole or in part, under the Habsburgs. In large measure, we are studying the Austro-Hungarian "successor states."

In 1620 the Catholic Habsburgs beat the Protestant Czechs and incorporated their lands (known as Bohemia) into the Empire. Late in that century the Habsurgs pushed the Turks out of Hungary and likewise incorporated it into the empire. Hungarian nationalists note that the Habsburgs took their sweet time liberating Hungary from the ravages of Turkish rule. Hungary included Slovakia, Transylvania, and northern Yugoslavia, so all these areas came under the Habsburgs. From 1772 to 1795, with the partitioning of Poland, Maria Theresa of Austria, reluctant to dismember a sister Catholic country, "wept but took her share," the southern part of Poland, known as Galicia. Maria Theresa also began administrative and military reforms that turned the Austrian Empire into a reasonably efficient and rational unit.

Could it have survived? This gigantic and diverse empire was a natural trading zone centered on the Danube. (Vienna, Bratislava, and Budapest are all near each other on the Danube.) One wonders if Habsburg policy had been more flexible and clever whether they would have succeeded in building a cohesive empire in which German, Slavic, and Hungarian speakers would be proud and prosperous citizens. As a trade bloc, the Austro-Hungarian Empire could have become a major economic player and developed all its provinces. If it had stayed together, it would probably have rivaled Germany as an economic power. Broken into weak, small countries after World War I, each separated from the others by hostility, territorial claims, and tariff barriers, the economy of the region stagnated.

But, since the spread of nationalism after the French Revolution and Napoleonic wars, multinational empires are simply not viable. Their component nationalities demand independence. It was the enormous ethnic diversity of Austria-Hungary that finally doomed it. Only a quarter of the population was German. Another fifth was Hungarian, but close to half was of half-a-dozen Slavic nationalities who owed little loyalty to the emperor.

One solution might have been to grant all the nationalities of the Austro-Hungarian empire equal status within a democratic, federal structure, thus transforming the empire into a Danubian federation. Some far-sighted thinkers of the time suggested it, but the Austrian and Hungarian nobles were basically reactionaries who couldn't compromise with the new forces that were rippling through their empire. They wanted to keep things in a mythical golden age. Only in late 1918, two weeks before the empire collapsed in World War I, did Vienna in desperation suggest turning the empire into a federation. Perhaps if they had done it 10 years earlier there would have been no World War I and a "United States of Danubia" would now be a major and prosperous nation.

Even trying to appease a major nationality led to more difficulties for the Habsburgs. Hungarians bitterly resented being treated like second-class citizens and in 1848 rose against Habsburg rule. The tsar sent Russian troops to help put down the uprising. After Austria's disastrous performance in a war with Prussia, in 1867 Vienna granted Budapest equal status within the empire. The emperor of Austria also took on the title of king of Hungary, and the Hungarian parliament, dominated by conservative nobles, ran the Hungarian half of the empire more strictly than the Austrians ran their half. This was called the Dual Monarchy of Austria-Hungary; its symbol was a double-headed eagle.

Now it was the Hungarians' turn to treat subject peoples like second-class citizens, and Slovaks, Croats, and Romanians were forced to obey Budapest and even to learn Hungarian, a policy called "magyarization." Budapest had no intention of granting its subject nationalities equal status. What Hungarians demanded for themselves they denied to others. In East Europe, "freedom" for one

---

"Divide and Rule"

How did the Turks and Austrians run sprawling empires in which they were greatly outnumbered? They practiced the ancient art of imperialism first devised by the Romans, who gave it the Latin name *divide et impera*, divide and rule. Keep your subject peoples divided and hostile to each other; play off one against the other. Then you can easily dominate. For example, since Croats did not like being governed by Hungarians, in the last century Vienna used Croatian troops to suppress unrest in Budapest. The trouble with this clever policy is that it left a legacy of great animosities that now prevent the independent nations from cooperating with each other. Most former Ottoman and Habsburg countries cordially hate each other to this day.

---

nationality meant its dominance over other nationalities.

Another factor doomed the empire: its desire to expand. In a sense, it couldn't help itself. As the Turks were pushed back in the Balkans, Austria-Hungary almost naturally moved into the vacuum. Specifically, in 1878 Austria occupied Bosnia, the mountainous area between Serbia and the Dalmatian coast, which was partly populated by Serbs. Neighboring Serbia, which that same year had won its full independence from Istanbul, didn't like Austria taking what it felt was Serbian territory. Anger grew in Belgrade when Austria annexed Bosnia into the empire in 1908.

In 1914, Bosnian students, equipped with guns and grenades from sympathetic Serbian army officers, assassinated Austrian Archduke Franz Ferdinand in Bosnia's capital of Sarajevo. Austria felt it had to severely punish Serbia to show the Slavic nationalities of its empire that it would not stand for any breakaway movements. Belgrade rejected Vienna's demands to take over Serbia, and Austria attacked. Serbia turned to Russia for help, Austria turned to Germany for help, and World War I was on.

World War I, sparked by terrorism, was the seminal tragedy of the twentieth century, the catastrophe that led straight to communism, nazism, and World War II. Could it have been otherwise? Suppose the Serbian government had given in to Austria's demands. Austria would have occupied Serbia, raised its economic, health, and cultural levels, and given Serbs access to a great empire. Austrian rule, after all, was not so bad; it was vastly better than Turkish rule. Serbs could have worked within the empire with other nationalities to turn the empire into a democratic federation. Such is the nature of nationalism, however, that this suggestion is utterly unacceptable and implausible. Once nationalism gets going, rule by foreigners seems horrible, intolerable, a crime against one's people. In this way, nationalism led to East Europe's fragmentation and vulnerability.

The Tsarist Russian Empire

Throwing off the Mongols in the fifteenth century, the Russian state expanded until, under Peter the Great in the early eighteenth century, it broke through the Turks to the Black Sea in the south and overcame the Swedes in the north to reach the Baltic. Much Russian attention was focused southward, against the Turks. In a long series of wars, Russia pushed the Ottomans back until at one point a Russian army was camped at the gates of Istanbul.

Russian motivation was partly religious but mostly geopolitical. Most of the Christians under the Turks in the Balkans were Eastern Orthodox, and the tsar, as head of the Russian church, felt himself to be their natural protector. In varying degrees, Russian military pressure on the Ottomans allowed Orthodox Christian Serbia, Wallachia, and Moldavia to win their autonomy and then their independence from the Turks. The Russians also dreamed of liberating the historic capital of their faith, Constantinople, from Islamic rule.

The geopolitical motives were probably more important. A Black Sea that belonged securely to Russia offered military protection and a commercial outlet to the Mediterranean. Otherwise, the whole southern part of the tsar's empire was landlocked. To obtain full use of the Black Sea, however, required dominating the Turkish Straits. Otherwise, whoever stood astride the Dardanelles and Bosporus could stop or let pass merchantmen and warships as they wished. Turkey, with a history of centuries of rivalry with Russia, could let in foreign fleets and not let out the Russian fleet. During the Crimean War of the 1850s, Turkey did precisely this, letting the British and French through to fight on Russia's soft underbelly. Control of Istanbul, therefore, became one of the great wishes of Russian and later Soviet foreign policy.

With the partition of the once-large Polish-Lithuanian state between 1772 and 1795, Russia took the eastern territories of the country and after 1815 came to control central Poland, including the capital of Warsaw. These areas Russia ruled

---

Are Lithuania, Latvia, and Estonia Part of East Europe?

No, at least not yet. Between the two world wars, the independent Baltic republics might be included in East or Central Europe, especially Lithuania, which from 1386 to 1795 had been part of the Polish-Lithuanian kingdom. With the partition of Poland in the late eighteenth century, Lithuania came under tsarist Russian rule. Latvia and Estonia had long been part of the tsarist empire but were left largely alone.

Stalin took all three of the Baltic republics in 1940 and had their inhabitants treated brutally. Thousands were deported to Siberia. A big majority of Lithuanians, Latvians, and Estonias fervently wish to be independent. With the possible breakup of the Soviet empire, they may get their wish. Then we can put them under the heading of East Europe.

as its "Vistula provinces" until the end of World War I. In Poland, as elsewhere in the tsarist empire, the Russians tried to "russify" the population by requiring Russian as the official language and discouraging use of local tongues. This policy, of course, created nothing but resentment. Austrian policy in Galicia, its part of Poland, was far more enlightened and permitted a certain autonomy, including the use of the Polish language and an elected assembly.

Russia, too, was a vast multinational empire, but it didn't have quite the same problem as Austria-Hungary, for Russians formed a majority of the population. Nonetheless, World War I wrecked it too. By mobilizing the gigantic Russian army in July 1914, the tsar panicked the German kaiser into doing the same. As the tsarist empire collapsed in the war, its restless nationalities saw their chance for freedom. Lithuania, Latvia, Estonia, and Finland took their independence. The Ukraine nearly did. And Polish independence fighters in the Russian sector of Poland united with colleagues in the German and Austrian zones of the partitioned land to put Poland back on the map of Europe after a century and a half.

The Partitioning of Poland

In three stages, from 1772 to 1795, Austria, Russia, and Prussia, in mutual agreement with each other, took larger slices of Poland until it disappeared from the map of Europe. The weakness and helplessness of Poland in the face of the three empires encapsulates the tragedy of East Europe in general.

Poland was governed by an ancient and unworkable constitution that continued the feudal pattern whereby nobles were more powerful than the king. Recall how in West Europe monarchal absolutism reversed this situation. Poland's nobles, independent and arrogant, met in a council in which each had right of veto over any new law. That is, even one vote against could block any measure. This *liberum veto* (free veto) led to immoderate, insoluble quarrels among factions of nobles. To gain advantage, they turned to outside help, some to the Russians, some to the Prussians, and some to the Austrians. The outsiders simply helped themselves to parts of Poland. Too late, in 1791, Poles produced a modern, reformed constitution inspired in part by the new U.S. Constitution. This effort, however, simply provoked Russia and Prussia into making a second partition in 1793 and abolishing the reform attempt.

Polish patriots hated the partition and rose heroically in 1794, 1830, 1863, and 1905 in unsuccessful attempts to restore an indpendent Poland. Thousands were killed, jailed, or forced into exile. Some of Poland's greatest intellects, such as pianist-composer Fryderyk Chopin and novelist Joseph Conrad, went abroad. Still, the Poles' struggles kept alive the hope that they would one day regain Poland's independence.

The Prussian (German) Empire

During the Middle Ages, Germans pushed eastward along the Baltic, exterminating or enslaving the local populations. These Germans became known as Prussians and their ruling class as *Junkers*, from the German for young gentlemen (*junge Herren*). Frederick the Great of Prussia in the eighteenth century continued the process by seizing Silesia and eagerly participating in the partition of Poland. German colonizers were brought in, Polish landowners were dispossessed, and the Polish language suppressed.

In 1871, under Prussian leadership, Germany unified. The Second Reich stretched from Alsace (now French) to East Prussia (now Polish and Russian). Half of present-day Poland was part of Germany. The Germans, to be sure, brought industry to these territories, but Poles resented them and longed for independence and unification with Russian and Austrian Poland. Deprived of a nation-state, Poles rallied to the Catholic Church, to literature, and to music as a statement of their national identity.

THE EASTERN QUESTION

Where these empires collided, there was war. Notice particularly how the Ottoman Empire at its high point included portions of both Russian tsarist and Austro-Hungarian lands. These areas of overlap were the scenes of fierce battles in which the Turks were slowly pushed back, giving the Russians and Austrians enlarged holdings. What to do with the declining Ottoman Empire was for over a century known as the "Eastern Question."

One may quarrel at length over the net impact of empires. Some bring with them signs of progress. The Austrians in the Balkans, for example, did some good in modernizing backward Ottoman provinces and in bringing them into Europe. In the main, however, empires stifle the freedom, creativity, and economic progress of their subject peoples. The worst thing about empires, though, is that they invariably end, and when they do they leave behind the instability, ambition, and rivalry that lead to new wars.

The retreat of the Ottoman Empire is a case in point. As the Turks were pushed back, by a series of wars and revolts, they left small, dissatisfied states behind—states with undefined borders and exaggerated ambitions. Serbia attempted

---

Is East Germany Part of East Europe?

No, at least not any more. Now unified with the Federal Republic of Germany, the former German Democratic Republic has joined West Europe. Still, because it was very much part of the Soviet bloc for forty years, we will refer to it from time to time as part of East Europe.

Key Treaties of Ottoman Decline

Step by step, Turkish power was pushed back. Each major step was marked by one or more treaties. These are some of the more important ones:

Karlowitz, 1699. Beaten by the Habsburgs, the Ottomans turned over to Austria a vast area that included most of Hungary, Transylvania, and the northern part of present-day Yugoslavia.

Kuchuk Kainarji, 1774. The Ottomans conceded to Russia the right to protect Christians in Wallachia and Moldavia (which later formed Romania). The tsar later grandly claimed the treaty gave him the right to protect all Christians in the Ottoman Empire.

Adrianople, 1829. Confirmed the autonomy of the Serbs, Wallachians, Moldavians, and Greeks, who had revolted against Istanbul. The treaty also awarded Russia the mouth of the Danube.

Unkiar Skelessi, 1833. The weak Ottoman Empire turned to Russia for help in putting down breakaway Egypt. The Treaty of Unkiar Skelessi marked the first time Istanbul had to turn to outside powers to try to hold its empire together.

Straits Convention, 1841. The first of many treaties governing the strategic Turkish Straits, the 1841 agreement put the straits under nominal international control.

San Stefano, 1878. This treaty ended another Russo-Turkish war by giving Russia major gains in the Balkans and by setting up a pro-Russian state of Bulgaria.

Congress of Berlin, 1878. Alarmed that the Russians had gained too much influence in the Balkans in the Treaty of San Stefano, the major European powers scaled back its provisions, set up a smaller Bulgaria, and confirmed Serbian and Romanian independence.

London, 1913. The Ottomans, after five centuries of rule and influence in the Balkans, are pushed out of all Europe except for the present small corner of European Turkey.

to grab a piece of Bulgaria in 1885. (The Bulgarians to this day say that Macedonia belongs to Bulgaria and not to Yugoslavia. Linguistically, they are right, for the Macedonian language is virtually Bulgarian.)

Further, as the Ottoman Empire declined, the other great powers quarreled over who would pick up the spoils. In the nineteenth century, Austria and Britain feared Russia pushing into and taking over Ottoman holdings in the Balkans. The British specifically feared Russian control of the Black Sea and the Turkish Straits, seeing this as a threat to Britain's "imperial lifeline" to India. These concerns led to the curious situation of some of the major Christian powers of Europe propping up the major Muslim power, Ottoman Turkey, against whom in earlier centuries they had conducted crusades. From 1851 to 1856, Britain, France, and Austria fought

Russia in the nasty Crimean War in order to stem Russia's southward advances. (This was the war in which Florence Nightingale founded modern nursing.) These same fears of Russia taking too much territory were apparent in the two treaties of 1878 (see box). With San Stefano, Russia got what the others thought was too much; the Berlin Conference was called to trim back Russian gains in the Balkans.

As the Ottoman grip on the Balkans weakened, these provinces seemed ripe for the picking by other imperial powers. Austria took over Bosnia from the Turks in 1878 and tried to take over Serbia in 1914 (provoked, to be sure, by the Sarajevo assassination of Franz Ferdinand). Russia took territory down to the Danube and set up protectorates with an eye to extending its power to Istanbul and to controlling of the Turkish Straits. The Russian and Austrian empires began to bump into each other as they moved in on the Turkish empire. In the early twentieth century, the rival ambitions of Austria and Russia in the Balkans turned what might have stayed a small Austro-Serbian war in 1914 into World War I.

East Europe in 1914

The Good Soldier Schweik

Czech writer Jaroslav Hasek penned great truth in his satirical novel *The Good Soldier Schweik*. Schweik, a Czech subject of the Austro-Hungarian Empire, is drafted to fight for the empire in World War I. This is the last thing he wants to do. But instead of resisting openly, which would only lead to the firing squad, Schweik uses the tricks of subject peoples. Always appearing to be a "good soldier," Schweik pretends to go along, carrying out orders literally and stupidly, until he bollixes up the Austrian war effort. Schweik became a literary symbol of Czech passive resistance to overlords, first the Austrians, then the Germans, and finally the Russians. Poles and Hungarians historically have resisted more heroically, but the Schweik strategy has served the Czechs well. In Prague today you can drink rich Czech beer in the very tavern frequented by Hasek and described in the novel as Schweik's hangout.

WORLD WAR I IN EAST EUROPE

Both World Wars intimately concerned East Europe. Some thinkers note that both wars started in East Europe, and that is true—the Austrian invasion of Serbia in 1914 and German invasion of Poland in 1939—but the stakes were much bigger than merely control over East Europe. The weak states that succeeded the four empires were tempting targets for conquest, and that struck the sparks that lit the conflagrations of both world wars.

As we have considered, the peoples of East Europe grew increasingly restless under the yokes of their respective empires in the nineteenth century. As Ottoman power receded in the Balkans, Austria and Russia moved into to fill the vacuum, and this rivalry was one important cause of World War I. All four of the empires we have discussed fought and destroyed themselves in the war, including Turkey (which fought on the side of Germany), although by World War I Turkey was effectively out of the European picture.

All East Eurpean nationalities contributed to the war effort, mostly as soldiers in the armies of their respective imperial masters. At first little Serbia held off Austria, but the arrival of German troops put the Serbs to rout. The Serbian army escaped to Corfu and was thence mobilized into the Allied cause to fight under a French general on the Salonika front in northern Greece. Croats, on the other hand, were drafted into the Austro-Hungarian army. Sergeant Josip Broz, for example, joined a German-speaking unit and was captured on the Russian front. When the Bolsheviks took over, he converted to their revolution and later became Tito, the Yugoslav Communist chief. Hungarians, Czechs, Slovaks, Poles, and

---

Woodrow Wilson on East Europe

President Wilson, one of the founders of political science in the United States, brought with him to the Versailles peace conference of 1919 the legalistic and idealistic bent of the subject at that time. Wilson gave his famous "Fourteen Points" address to Congress in early 1918; three of the fourteen points directly concerned East Europe:

"X. The peoples of Austria-Hungary, whose place among the nations we wish to see safeguarded and assured, should be accorded the freest opportunity of autonomous development.

"XI. Rumania, Serbia, and Montenegro should be evacuated [of German and Austrian forces]; occupied territories restored; Serbia accorded free and secure access to the sea; and the relations of the several Balkan states to one another determined by friendly counsel along historically established lines of allegiance and nationality; and international guarantees of the political and economic independence and territorial integrity of the several Balkan states should be entered into....

"XIII. An independent Polish state should be erected which should include the territories inhabited by indisputably Polish populations, which should be assured a free and secure access to the sea, and whose political and economic independence and territorial integrity should be guaranteed by international covenant."

One immediately senses that there would be some difficulty carrying out these grand aims.

Romanians were likewise part of the Austrian armed forces. In 1914, Austrian mobilization orders had to be issued in fourteen different languages.

It was here that Austria-Hungary paid the price for failing to integrate its many nationalities. Why should Czechs and Croats fight for a German dynasty? The subject peoples did not fight enthusiastically; some even wished the empire to split apart. For this, the reactionary Habsburgs had only themselves to blame. They had never defined themselves as anything but a Germanic dynasty with non-German subjects. If over the decades they had converted those subjects to citizens, the empire might have held together.

What was to become of East Europe was not the chief concern of the major powers for most of the war. Then the United States entered the war in 1917—when it was two-thirds over—and President Wilson introduced a new, idealistic set of war aims. These included the liberation of East Europe from its imperial shackles. The aims were wonderful, but were they realistic? The test here is not their lofty intentions but how they worked out in practice. For that, we turn to Chapter 2.

SUGGESTED READINGS

CHIROT, DANIEL, ed. *The Origins of Backwardness in Eastern Europe: Economics and Politics from the Middle Ages Until the Early Twentieth Century.* Berkeley, CA: University of California Press, 1989.

GARTON ASH, TIMOTHY. "Mitteleuropa?" *Daedalus* 119 (Winter 1990) 1.

KANN, ROBERT A., AND ZDENEK V. DAVID. *The Peoples of the Eastern Habsburg Lands, 1526-1918.* Seattle: University of Washington Press, 1984.

JUDT, TONY. "The Rediscovery of Central Europe." *Daedalus* 119 (Winter 1990) 1.

SETON-WATSON, HUGH. *The Decline of Imperial Russia, 1855-1914.* New York: Praeger, 1952.

SETON-WATSON, ROBERT W. *The Rise of Nationality in the Balkans.* New York: Howard Fertig, 1966 (originally published 1917).

TURNOCK, DAVID. *Eastern Europe: An Historical Geography, 1815-1945.* New York: Routledge, 1988.

WOLFF, ROBERT LEE. *The Balkans in Our Time.* Cambridge, Mass.: Harvard University Press, 1956.

CHAPTER TWO _____

Flunking Democracy: The Interwar Years

The nationalities of East Europe were quite old when they at last won their freedom at the end of World War I, but as independent states they were very young. Indeed, as states most of them were artificial creations with unclear boundaries and uncertain popular support. The question of borders looms large in the interwar years. Unsupportable borders both caused and symbolized the turmoil and brevity of East Europe's states between the two world wars. In West Europe, most borders had long been clearly established. The only remaining dispute was over Alsace-Lorraine; it took World War II to settle that quarrel between France and Germany. East Europe was beset by a dozen boundary disputes that were at least as nasty and bitter as the Alsace-Lorraine question. The situation of East Europe between the wars was inherently unstable and had to collapse. This it did, first into the hands of the Nazis, then into the hands of the Communists.

BORDERING ON MADNESS

Each East European nationality had a grand view of its territory. Some romantic nationalists harkened back to the boundaries of ancient kingdoms, as if temporary possession of a piece of real estate conferred permanent title. History gives no such title deeds. Typically, the new states of East Europe that emerged from the peace conferences of 1918-1920 out of the wreckage of the German, Russian, and Austrian empires staked out maximal rather than realistic boundary claims, claims that had to bring them into conflict with neighboring states.

The problem, one found worldwide, is that few nationalities have clearly defined natural borders. If every country could be like Iceland, the world would be spared many wars. Instead, almost everywhere, peoples are dispersed and interdigitized, making clear and fair borders impossible to draw. Drawing borders always includes people of one ethnic group in the territory of another. Between the world wars, an estimated 31 percent of East Europeans were classified as minorities. The solution, if there is one, is to make a state so strong that it can define nationality and inculcate that nationality into all its citizens, so that ethnic backgrounds become irrelevant. Most Alsatians, for example, after centuries of belonging to France, feel, speak, and act French, even though they have Germanic names and also speak German. Rather than change boundaries, you change psychologies.

This solution in East Europe proved difficult if not impossible. The countries were too new, the ethnic identities too strong, and the memories of past hurt or past glory too vivid. Hungarians living in Romania or Slovakia do not willingly turn themselves into Romanians or Slovaks. With this in mind, let us review some of East Europe's interwar border problems.

East Europe in 1930

Poland

The new Poland, reappearing on the map of Europe after more than a century, tried to obtain the borders of the old Poland, the Poland of the seventeenth century. This was done largely by military force, not by negotiation. Poland's new borders were problematic, for the old Poland had included a great deal of Lithuania, Belorussia, the Ukraine, and areas that had become German. The new Poland was beset by boundary disputes on every side.

Germany kept most of its territory—the big butterfly shape of Lower Silesia and Pomerania—but Poland took the most heavily industrialized part of Upper Silesia and Poznan (German: Posen), areas that in earlier centuries had been Polish and still had a Polish majority. Many of the "Germans" of the region, in fact, were of Polish descent; Prussian and German policy had been to Germanize the Polish population. Germany also lost part of Pomerania for a "Polish corridor" to the sea, as Wilson had urged and a friendly Versailles conference had accepted. Poland, after all, was an ally that had suffered greatly during the war, and Germany was a defeated enemy that deserved to be punished. The Polish corridor, however, left East Prussia cut off from the rest of Germany, a loss that many Germans found intolerable. Hitler later played into this longing to recover lost German territory. The largely German city of Danzig (Polish: Gdansk) was declared a "free city" in which Poland had many rights.

To the south, a disputed area on the Czech border, Teschen, was divided between the two new countries, but this left some 140,000 Poles under Czech rule. To the north, Poland also took pieces of present-day Lithuania, including the capital of Vilnius (Polish: Wilno, Russian: Vilna). From 1386 to 1795, Poland and Lithuania had formed one kingdom, and Vilnius had a Polish majority even in the interwar period.

The real problem, though, was to the east, Poland's border with the new Soviet Union. Because ancient Poland had included Lithuania and the Ukraine, the new Poland felt entitled to get at least part of them back. As we noted, history provides no guide to these questions. In two years of fighting between the new Polish army and the new Red Army, the front seesawed back and forth. In May 1920, the Poles were in Kiev, deep within the Ukraine. By June, the Bolsheviks had pushed them out and by August the Bolsheviks were at the gates of Warsaw. It was the Bolshevik dream, especially the dream of Trotsky (who founded and organized the Red Army), that once the Bolsheviks took Poland, spontaneous revolution would spread westwards over all Europe. But the Poles threw the Bolsheviks back, deep into Russian territory, and the two sides settled with the 1921 Treaty of Riga (capital of newly independent Latvia).

This border, though, was not the "right" one, if such a thing is discoverable. It was a hundred or more miles too far east and included lands inhabited chiefly by Lithuanians, Belorussians, and Ukrainians along with a considerable Polish minority. Lwow (Russian: Lvov) had a Polish majority. Some 32 percent of

---

The Curzon Line

In late 1919 an international commission under British Foreign Secretary Lord Curzon came up with an "ethnographic" eastern boundary for Poland, one that took into account which ethnic groups lived where. The Curzon Line, as it was called, placed most Poles to its west and most Lithuanians, Belorussians, and Ukrainians to its east. It was a reasonably fair boundary but never went into effect; both the Bolsheviks and the Poles ignored it. The Polish legions ended up well east of it and were not about to give territory to the Bolsheviks, who had tried to conquer them. The current Polish-Soviet border, seized militarily by Stalin in 1939, approximates the Curzon Line.

Poland's population in the interwar period did not speak Polish as a first language. Was a fair border possible? The Allies at Versailles tried to draw one, and did a pretty good job with the Curzon Line (see box), but Warsaw dismissed the notion of surrendering what it had just conquered. The Polish-Soviet border was fraught with problems and contributed to subsequent events that were disastrous for Poland.

Czechoslovakia

Like Poland, interwar Czechoslovakia was born with some difficult boundary and ethnic problems. Bohemia and Moravia (the Czech lands) were the most advanced and industrialized region of East Europe. The Austro-Hungarian Empire had selected them for industrial development, and the Skoda iron and steel works provided much of the empire's heavy equipment. Educationally and culturally too, Czechs were at least as advanced as Austrians. Slovakia, on the other hand, was a backward region and in 1867 was consigned to the not-so-tender mercies of Hungarian administration. Czechs and Slovaks are two distinct peoples and do not especially like each other. Their languages are related but different. Slovaks, like Poles, are strongly Catholic. Czechs had largely turned to Hussite Protestant ideas after 1410 and were forcibly re-catholicized after their crushing defeat by the Habsburgs at White Mountain in 1620. This left some of them rather secular in outlook. Bohemia had a large German settlement, and many Czechs spoke German. Slovakia had a considerable Magyar population, and Budapest required Slovaks to learn Hungarian. Czechs love beer (and make some of the world's best); Slovaks prefer wine. There is no such person as a "Czechoslovak"; you're one or the other.

To the east of Slovakia stood an even more backward land, Ruthenia, also known as the Carpatho-Ukraine, inhabited largely by Ukrainians. It too had been under the Hungarian crown, and Hungary wanted it back. Ruthenians, like Slovaks, did not like being ruled from Prague.

During World War I, Czech and Slovak representatives agreed in talks in

---

Czechoslovakia or Czecho-Slovakia?

What's in a hyphen? Plenty, if it connotes equality of the two components. Since the founding of the Czechoslovak Republic in 1918, the Czechs always wanted to spell it without a hyphen, the Slovaks with a hyphen. For many Slovaks, seeing Slovakia spelled with a capital S symbolizes Slovak political and cultural autonomy and true federalism. Without the hyphen, they feel, the word symbolizes Czech hegemony. In 1990 the Slovaks gained a symbolic victory in the "hyphen war" when the parliament officially named the country the Czech and Slovak Federative Republic. Most people, of course, still call it Czechoslovakia.

Pittsburgh, Pennsylvania, to form a new country that granted considerable self-government to Slovakia. (Czechs had a long and benevolent American connection. Many had immigrated to the United States. Woodrow Wilson especially liked their American-educated leader, Tomas Masaryk.) The 1920 Czechoslovak constitution, however, created a unitary state, governed by Prague, with Czechs in all the key administrative positions, even within Slovakia. This angered not only Slovaks but the 3 million Germans who lived in a large horseshoe-shaped area around three sides of Bohemia. This area, the Sudetenland, was passed on to the new state of Czechoslovakia with the breakup of the Austro-Hungarian Empire. A Hungarian minority lived in south Slovakia. Thus the brave little Czechoslovak democracy was born with a large percentage of its people resenting the Czechs as the new imperial folk who, many felt, had no business bossing around Germans and Slovaks. These resentments paved the way for Hitler's takeover of Czechoslovakia in 1938 and 1939.

Hungary

Poland and Czechoslovakia were among the East European territorial winners from World War I. Hungary was among the losers, and a major one. The 1920 Treaty of Trianon (so named because it was signed in the Trianon Palace on the gigantic Versailles grounds) gave 72 percent of the prewar Kingdom of Hungary, with 64 percent of its population, to Czechoslovakia, Yugoslavia, and Romania. Although most of the people living in these areas were not Hungarian, a sizable minority was, especially in Transylvania. Altogether, a third of Hungarians now lived outside Hungary's borders, a recipe for extreme Magyar nationalism and revenge. Virtually all Hungarians hated the dismemberment of their kingdom, and "Trianon" became for Hungarians what "Versailles" became for the Germans, an unfair treaty that had to be revised. This climate of bitterness contributed to the rise of reactionary and even fascistic political movements in Hungary. In the free elections of 1990, concern for Hungarians in Transylvania won votes for the conservative Democratic Forum. After 70 years, "Trianon" still echoed in Hungarian politics.

Hungary after World War I

Yugoslavia

Yugoslavia, like Czechoslovakia, was a totally new and somewhat artificial country, born only in 1918. Serbia had won autonomy from the Turks in 1804 and gradually expanded as a small kingdom. Serbs also developed the idea of expelling all foreign occupiers from the region and of founding a "South Slav" state. Using the example of the Piedmont region leading Italian unification, Serbs thought of themselves as freedom fighters for a new monarchy that would gather in and protect the neighboring South Slavic peoples. The flaw in this concept (as with the Hungarians) is that it did not accord equality to the other peoples. As we considered in Chapter 1, Serbian nationalism set off the spark that caused World War I.

During World War I, King Alexander of Serbia obtained the sometimes reluctant agreement of the various nationalities to form a new state. The effort had the support of the Versailles victors, for Serbia had fought on the Allied side. The Croats, the second largest nationality after Serbs, went along with the deal, for they did not like being ruled by Hungary, and their spoken language is virtually identical to Serbian. In December 1918, King Alexander proclaimed the Kingdom of Serbs, Croats, and Slovenes. The name Yugoslavia only became official in 1929.

Yugoslavia was immediately a problem country, one stitched together from former Austrian, Hungarian, and Turkish provinces, with all the cultural and economic differences that implies. In the northwest, the Slovenes were virtually Slavic Austrians, prosperous and Catholic. On the coast, the Dalmatians were sort of Slavic Venetians, fishermen and seafarers. The Croats were heavily influenced by centuries of Hungarian rule (which they disliked). As one moved south, the country got poorer and more backward. Macedonia was nearly a Slavic Turkey, and it was claimed by Bulgaria, for its language really is Bulgarian. Montenegro (meaning "Black Mountain"), nestled in the mountains north of Albania, had never been conquered; it had preserved a backward independence under a prince-bishop and was still dominated by clans. Bosnia had a mixed population of Serbs, Croats, and Muslim Bosniaks (local Slavs who had been converted to Islam by the Turks). Further, there was an important Hungarian community in the north and an Albanian community in the south.

This description of Yugoslavia at its birth requires not one word of change for the Yugoslavia of today. Between the two world wars, as today, Yugoslavia increasingly fell apart due to ethnic strife. As then, only one thing holds it together: fear by the component parts that if they broke apart they would be absorbed by neighboring states.

Yugoslavia Today

Transylvania: Hungarian or Romanian?

In the twentieth century, Transylvania (meaning the "land beyond the forest") changed hands three times. Long part of the Kingdom of Hungary, the 1920 Treaty of Trianon gave Transylvania to Romania, because Hungary had been on the losing side and Romania, nominally at least, on the Allied side.

Hungary joined Hitler's Axis in 1939. Romania came under unbearable pressure from both Germany and Russia—who had agreed to divide East Europe in the 1939 Non-Aggression Pact—and in 1940 Hitler stripped off the northern half of Transylvania and gave it to Hungary in the Vienna Award.

Romania later joined the Axis but dropped out in time to technically be on the winning side in World War II. Because Hungary was again on the losing side, Romania was awarded all of Transylvania in 1945. Romanians and Hungarians are interspersed in Transylvania, making partition impossible. When it belonged to Hungary, the Romanian inhabitants were unhappy. Now that it belongs to Romania, the Hungarian inhabitants are unhappy. There is no solution without leaving at least one side dissatisfied.

Romania

Romania also gained from World War I but was unable to keep its territorial gains through World War II. Romania was neutral at the start of World War I but joined the Allies in 1916. This paid off after the war when Romania was awarded the large area of Transylvania and the Banat region (just south of Transylvania, bordering Yugoslavia) from Hungary, and Bessarabia and Bukovina from the collapsed Russian tsarist empire. Hungary always wanted Transylvania back, and the Soviet Union always wanted Bessarabia and Bukovina back. If there is another war in Europe, it will be between Romania and Hungary over Transylvania.

Suddenly after World War I, Romania more than doubled in size and population. This meant new political problems as the newly acquired minorities, especially Hungarians and Jews, triggered contrary Romanian chauvinist feelings, heightened existing Romanian anti-Semitism, and led to the founding of the fascist Iron Guard party of the extreme Romanian nationalists. This ultimately pushed Romania to the Nazi side in World War II.

Bulgaria

Bulgaria has been one of the losers in East Europe. Harkening back to the large medieval Bulgarian kingdom, Bulgarians in this century have dreamed of a "Greater Bulgaria." In combination with Greece, Serbia, and Romania, Bulgaria succeeded in pushing Turkey back to its present European frontiers in the First Balkan War of 1912-1913. This splendid victory even gave Bulgaria Western

Thrace (now part of Greece) and thus access to the Aegean. But Bulgaria still claimed Macedonia (to which it indeed has historical and linguistic ties), and Serbia and Greece divided Macedonia between them after the First Balkan War. Unable to live with this, Bulgaria attacked them in the Second Balkan War of 1913. Romania and Turkey opportunistically joined in; Bulgaria was at war on all fronts and lost. Macedonia stayed divided between Serbia and Greece; Turkey got back Western Thrace; and Romania took Southern Dobrudja. (Dobrudja is the coastal region south of the mouth of the Danube; most of it went to Romania in 1878.)

The 1913 loss left Bulgaria longing to recover these territories. In 1915, the German side made Bulgaria a better offer than the Allied side, so Bulgaria entered World War I and fought well against Serbia, Romania, and Russia but unfortunately on the losing side. With the 1919 Treaty of Neuilly, Bulgaria again lost its disputed territories. "Neuilly" became for Bulgaria what "Trianon" was for Hungary, a symbol of the fatherland's dismemberment. Poor, agricultural, and now awash with refugees, some Bulgarians still dreamed of a Greater Bulgaria. Bulgarian nationalists sponsored the Internal Macedonian Revolutionary Organization (IMRO), which practiced guerrilla warfare and terrorism in the Macedonian areas of Greece and Yugoslavia. The purpose of IMRO was to recover Macedonia for Bulgaria. Between the world wars, Bulgaria was the wild man of the Balkans, rather like Syria in the Middle East today.

Bulgarian Expansion During World War II

Bulgaria's irredentist aims moved it closer to Germany in the late 1930s, especially in trade. Hitler arranged the return of Southern Dobrudja to Bulgaria from Romania in 1940, and in 1941 Bulgaria joined the Axis. Hitler's victories in the Balkans allowed Bulgaria to take Yugoslav Macedonia and Greece's Western Thrace in 1941 only to lose them in 1944.

Albania

Tiny Albania, the poorest and most backward country of Europe, has been both occupied and occupier. Achieving independence in the First Balkan War, Albania was overrun by five different armies during World War I. Some thought Albania would be divided between Greece and Serbia, but President Wilson wouldn't stand for it, and Albania emerged intact. During the interwar years, Albania fell under Italian control. Since ethnic Albanians also live in Greece and Kosovo (part of Yugoslavia), Albanian forces on the Axis side during World War II attempted to occupy these areas.

East Europe's territorial disputes resemble West Europe's during the Middle Ages and Renaissance. West Europe, after centuries of fighting and the establishment of strong states, worked out most of its boundaries. East Europe, held in a sort of suspended animation by the empires that occupied it for centuries, resumed their boundary quarrels as the empires withdrew or collapsed. We should not poke too much fun at the sometimes crazy way East Europe's borders heaved to and fro. The East European states were making up for lost time, advancing claims to create Greater Serbia, Greater Hungary, Greater Bulgaria, and so on that could not be sustained. By trial and error, they were finding out who had the wealth, power, geography, and allies to get and keep what they claimed was theirs. One hopes that the boundary and ethnic issues are settled; if not it bodes ill for the reborn East Europe of today.

Irredentism

The word *irredentism* is derived from the Italian word for "unredeemed," and it gives us a description of East European border claims. As Italy unified in the nineteenth century, some Italian areas remained under foreign control. Italian nationalists called these places *Italia irredenta*, the parts of Italy not yet redeemed by the Risorgimento. Irrendenta soon came to mean areas outside its borders that a country might claim by virtue of ethnic or historical ties: "It used to be ours. We want it back." Macedonia, for example, might be termed Bulgarian irredenta. A country pursuing such claims is practicing irredentism or has an irredentist policy. East Europe is covered with irredentist claims. The East Europeans, in the phrase of William Safire, see their irredentist twice a year.

POLITICAL INSTABILITY

East Europe's conflicting territorial claims set the stage for political instability. They added one more brick to the already intolerable loads placed on the new democracies of East Europe after World War I. The new systems had little legitimacy to begin with; that is, many citizens doubted the right of the new governments to rule. Further weakening their legitimacy was the massive corruption, at Latin American levels, that pervaded most of East Europe. Irredentism fired nationalist politicians to demand the return of lost territories. Refugees, unfair treaties, and discontented minorities tended to push East European politics between the wars in an extremist and nationalistic direction. Every East European state started out after World War I with a democratic constitution. By the mid-1920s, only Czechoslovakia continued to function as a democracy. All the others were taken over by conservative parties with rigged elections, nationalist generals, royal dictators, or fascistic movements. They quickly flunked their first test as democracies.

In fairness to the the East European states, we should note that numerous other democracies failed during the interwar period. Spain, Italy, Portugal, Germany, Brazil, Japan, Greece, and others went from weak, unstable democracies to dictatorships, some of them bloodthirsty and expansionist. We now see that democracy is not something that can simply be transplanted into a country. However democratic the constitution may be, democracy depends on widespread attitudes of moderation, tolerance, compromise, and restraint. You cannot thrust a democracy on a poor, badly educated population with no experience in self-rule and expect it to work. Democracy takes practice. Without experience and moderate attitudes, democracy becomes chaotic and tumultuous; politicians and parties don't play by the rules; and the democracy soon ends.

We should also note that all East European countries, except Poland and Czechoslovakia, were constituted as monarchies. This, theoretically, could have been a stabilizing factor; a monarch can sometimes give people a unifying and legitimizing figure to focus on. But East European kingdoms were small and weak. In greatly expanding their kingdoms, Yugoslavia and Romania brought their monarchs new subjects who did not feel that the monarchs were legitimate, as did the subjects in the original core area of their kingdoms, respectively, Serbia and the Regat.

It was no accident that democracy worked (and not without problems) in the only East European state with a partly industrialized economy and a rather well-educated population, Czechoslovakia. East Europe on the whole was poor, much poorer than West Europe. The majority of East Europeans were peasants, some landless, others only smallholders. Yields per acre were much lower than in West Europe. Population increases and subdivision of holdings reduced some peasants to the subsistence level on tiny plots; these peasants were called "dwarfholders." Industrial growth was not nearly rapid enough to absorb the population surplus being generated in the countryside. For much of East Europe, poverty in the interwar years grew worse. And one important escape hatch closed in 1924: That year the U.S. Congress passed the Johnson Act that imposed national-origin quotas on immigration, which effectively snipped off immigration from East Europe.

The East European middle class was small and often connected to government bureaucracy. A modern business mentality was alien to East Europe. A disproportionate share of East Europe's business was in the hands of Jews, who, because they had been barred for centuries from farming, had long been merchants and moneylenders. The concept of "going into business" was rare in East Europe and is still something of a novelty today. Instead, a bright young person might aspire for a university degree and a position in the civil service. Unlike Americans, East Europeans (and Europeans generally) assumed that the state should take a leading role and that the private sector should be subordinate to the government. A tiny noble class, some with large land holdings, continued to exercise a disproportionate and overwhelmingly conservative influence in politics.

Anti-Semitism has a long history in East Europe, but between the wars it generally grew worse. Although Jews were rarely more than a small fraction of the population, they were regionally concentrated, especially in the towns. Anti-Jewish feeling ranged from maniacal in Romania to strong in Poland and Hungary. It was often quite regional within one country: moderate anti-Semitism in Croatia and Slovakia, but essentially none in Serbia and Bohemia. Only Bulgaria and Albania developed no anti-Semitic movements.

Anti-Semitism is worth noting for at least two reasons. Its rise indicates that the society is under great stress, and that this stress is pushing people to lash out at handy scapegoats. East Europeans, with new countries and illegitimate regimes, under economic hardship (which got much worse in the 1930s), tended to blame the people who had long been stigmatized on religious grounds. Jews tended to be small shopkeepers; they were visible and somewhat better off than average; they became perfect scapegoats. A rise in anti-Semitism indicates a country is cracking up. (A current example of this can be seen in the Soviet Union.) Second, anti-Semitism feeds the growth of fascistic movements, which both utilize existing hatred of Jews and whip up more. In East Europe between the wars, the rise of anti-Semitism contributed to fascist takeovers and thence to alignment with Nazi Germany.

The Great Depression that started in 1929 hurt East Europe terribly. Farm prices virtually collapsed, and poor peasants got poorer. Industrial growth stopped and sometimes declined. Only Czechoslovak industry weathered the downturn; Austrians used to apply to get into Czechoslovakia for the good factory jobs. But elsewhere, many East Europeans were either indifferent to democracy or welcomed a strong-handed government that would restore order and put some bread on the table. Whatever chance democracy had in East Europe, it went down the drain with the Great Depression.

Poland

Józef Pilsudski fled from the repression of Russian Poland to the relative freedom of Austrian Galicia, the southern part of Poland. A military officer, Pilsudski trained Galician infantry that took part in the Austro-Hungarian war against Russia. His aim, however, was Polish freedom, not Habsburg hegemony. With Russia effectively out of the war by 1917, Poles began to think of fighting Austria. The German army didn't trust Pilsudski and jailed him. Wanting to stir Polish patriotism against the Germans and Austrians, the Allies declared Poland a member of the Allies, so that technically Poland was on the winning side in World War I. In 1918, when the German, Austrian, and Russian empires split their defeat in the war three ways, Pilsudski's rapidly growing Polish legions (they numbered 600,000 by 1920) moved in to fill the vacuum. Pilsudski became the powerful and revered president of a new Poland.

Originally defining himself as a socialist, Pilsudski shifted from democracy to authoritarianism. Admittedly, it would have been awfully hard to have stayed a pure democrat amidst the turmoil of interwar Poland. About a third of the population was non-Polish, and minority nationalities—Germans, Ukrainians, Jews, Lithuanians—formed their own political parties. Further, within the Polish majority, political infighting was immoderate and tumultuous.

Pilsudski, who often governed from the shadows as defense minister, pushed for stronger and stronger presidential rule and obtained it in 1935, shortly before his death. Political parties and the *Sejm* (parliament) were rendered powerless. Pilsudski can be seen as a kind of early version of France's Charles de Gaulle, who also stood on the sidelines until he got a strong presidential constitution in 1958. Both generals disdained parties and parliaments as weakening the country, and each saw a strong presidency—virtually an elected dictatorship—as the only thing that could save the nation.

The mediocre Polish colonels who took over after Pilsudski, however, lacked his vision and charisma. The political parties resented and opposed the presidential dictatorship, which grew repressive, nationalistic, and anti-Semitic. Between the wars, Polish politics resembled those of Argentina.

Czechoslovakia

Symbolically, just as modern Poland was founded by a soldier, Pilsudski, Czechoslovakia was founded and governed by intellectuals, Tomás Masaryk and Dr. Eduard Benes. Politically, Czechoslovakia was, relative to the rest of East Europe, a success story between the two wars. While all the other lands moved to authoritarianism, Czechoslovakia continued as a democracy, with fair elections, a free press, and civil liberties. A major land reform turned millions of peasants into smallholder farmers, and they in turn supported the democratic government. Land reform was easier in Czechoslovakia than elsewhere because many of the large estates had belonged to Austrian and Hungarian nobility, and they were now foreigners without political influence in Prague.

Prague, to be sure, made mistakes. The Czechs, better educated and economically more advanced than the Slovaks, defined themselves as the founders and leaders of the new state. They were slow in according home rule and local administration to the other nationalities. Most of the civil service was Czech. This provided fertile ground for German and Slovak nationalists. With the rise of Hitler in the 1930s, the Sudeten Germans, who lived on the borders of Bohemia, fell under the sway of Nazism and demanded autonomy and then union with Germany. The Slovaks demanded at least genuine federalism and then opted for independence. Czechoslovakia was pulled apart by its nationalities.

Hungary

Interwar Hungary was born angry and stayed that way. Democracy had only the slimmest chance. A brilliant liberal nobleman, Count Mihály Károlyi, tried to set up a democratic system as soon as the Habsburg empire collapsed. Free elections and a free press, civil rights, land reform, and other sweeping reforms were quickly introduced. But a majority of Hungarians, still smarting from defeat and the loss of their gigantic kingdom, failed to rally to Károlyi. The nobles who owned the large estates hated any thought of land reform. Further, Károlyi tried to retain the subject peoples of old in a federation that included Transylvania, something the Allies had no sympathy with. The Allies blockaded Hungary and forced Károlyi to withdraw Hungarian troops from Transylvania in March 1919. Károlyi resigned, and Hungarian democracy died in its cradle.

Into the vacuum moved one of the more bizarre attempts to attain power of interwar Europe, the short-lived Communist takeover of Bela Kun. An officer of the Austro-Hungarian army, the socialist-minded Kun had been captured by the Russians in 1915 and as a prisoner had been converted to the aims of the 1917 Bolshevik Revolution. (Yugoslavia's Tito, also a prisoner in Russia, was likewise converted to communism at that time.) Under Moscow's orders and with Soviet money, Kun returned to Budapest and with local Communist and Socialist supporters seized power and instituted a small version of the Russian Bolshevik Revolution. The Hungarian Socialist Republic was opposed by just about everyone. In August 1919, Romania defeated Kun's Hungarian Red Army and looted Budapest. Kun fled to Russia. (In 1937, amidst Stalin's purges, Kun was arrested and tortured, and then executed in 1939 for alleged espionage.)

Hungary's interwar politics was an uneven struggle between what have been called "populist" and "urbanist" forces. The populists, by far the stronger, were nationalistic, conservative, peasant-oriented, and anti-Semitic. They aimed at getting Transylvania back into Hungary. The urbanists, heavily concentrated in Budapest, were liberal, westward-looking, intellectual, and partly Jewish. Most interesting, exactly the same division reappeared with the Hungarian elections of 1990, again won by the conservatives.

Conservatism and Fascism

These two terms, used to describe the "right" of the political spectrum, need to be clearly differentiated, especially as applied to East Europe. Conservatives want to preserve what is. Sometimes they want to go back to what was; this may earn them the title "reactionary." In East Europe, and indeed in much of West Europe as well, conservatism meant political systems in which democracy was curtailed by means of limited voting rights, the suppression of radical parties, and resistance to economic or social reforms. Political power stayed in the hands of aristocratic or wealthy persons.

Fascism was actually a radical philosophy that called for the revolutionary overthrow of old systems. Some thinkers suggest that fascism doesn't really fit on the right of the political spectrum. Fascists are lunatic nationalists. Nation is everything for them, and they define nationhood in racial terms. Jews are seen as not part of the nation; anti-Semitism is usually one of the building blocks of fascism. Additionally, fascist movements generally include some fake socialism; they talk about jobs and welfare for all. One tip-off of fascist movements: They love to wear uniforms. For them, politics should be structured along military lines: obedience and order!

It is here we may become confused in understanding the difference between fascism and conservatism. A conservative such as Hungary's Admiral Horthy may come from a military background, but he has no interest in militarizing society. Such a leader also wishes to reestablish order, but it is the order of the old days, not of a radical new system. Both conservatives and fascists are firmly opposed to leftists, but the conservatives merely wish to suppress them, the fascists to kill them. Conservatives may also be nationalistic, but they generally practice live and let live with neighboring states. Fascists want to conquer; for them, war proves superiority. Under certain circumstances, as in interwar East Europe, conservatives and fascists may temporarily cooperate, but ultimately they are at odds with each other.

After Kun, conservative forces took over led by Admiral Miklós Horthy. (How could landlocked Hungary have an admiral? Prewar Austria-Hungary did have outlets to the Mediterranean, at Trieste and Fiume.) Horthy was a conservative, maybe even a reactionary, but he was not a fascist, as the Communists later claimed (see box). Horthy occupied a strange office in interwar Hungary: regent, the person who stands in until a new king is ready to take the throne. As conservatives, Horthy and his followers did not want a republic, so they restored the monarchy, but the surviving Habsburg, Karl, was unacceptable as king. Thus interwar Hungary was a monarchy without a monarch, presided over by an admiral without a sea, who served as regent with no expectation of a king.

Conservatives consolidated their hold. Kun's radical forces were brutally suppressed. The leading party became the populistic and conservative Smallholders party (which reappeared in 1990), but the elections were rigged. Horthy was moderately successful at curbing inflation and boosting industry and education. Still, the gap between rich and poor (mainly peasants) remained huge, and anti-Semitism bubbled closer to the surface. Jews, a sizable and better-off minority, were blamed for everything. The Great Depression hit Hungary hard, tensions mounted, and increasingly right-wing governments permitted the rise of the fascistic Arrow Cross movement, paving the way for Hungary's alignment with Germany.

Yugoslavia

Yugoslavia, like Czechoslovakia, was pulled apart by its nationalities. The Serbs, like the Czechs, saw themselves as the founders and leaders of the new South Slav state; the other nationalities were seen as junior partners. The Croats intensely disliked the unitary and centralized Serbian monarchy; they found being governed by Belgrade no improvement over being governed by Budapest. Perhaps, as in Czechoslovakia, a federal system might have calmed the several nationalities.

Matters came to a head in 1928, when a fanatic Serbian nationalist gunned down the top leaders of the Croatian delegation on the floor of the national parliament. Croats, Bosnian Muslims, Macedonians, and even Serbians turned extremist and even fascistic. King Alexander was so exasperated with the turmoil that in 1929 he proclaimed a royal dictatorship. Renaming the country Yugoslavia, Alexander tried to erase the mentality of national areas by setting up artificial districts named after their principal rivers, an old trick of the French revolutionists that survives to this day in France. Alexander was assassinated in Marseille in 1934 by an IMRO gunman with ties to a Croatian fascist movement that in turn was backed by Hungary and Italy. Many forces wanted Yugoslavia dismembered.

Yugoslavia then limped along with a regency until Prince Paul came of age, but every year the country became a little more unstuck. Paul, seeing support from Germany as the only way to hold his kingdom together, drifted in a pro-Axis direction. He was overthrown by pro-British Serbian officers in 1941. Interwar Yugoslavia simply did not jell.

Romania

Romania's interwar politics paralleled those of its neighbors: a monarchy that for a time was a regency, unrest among its minorities, a large agrarian party, a royal dictatorship, and the growth of anti-Semitic and fascist parties. One of the most backward countries in Europe, Romania, by transforming itself into Greater Romania with the addition of Transylvania from Hungary and Bessarabia from Russia, took on problems it couldn't handle.

Under King Ferdinand, a major land reform was politically successful—it calmed millions of landless peasants—but economically counterproductive, as their holdings were too small to be worked efficiently. A soaring birthrate compounded the problem of rural poverty. Romania had one economic trump card: the only major oilfield then known in Europe. Foreign, especially German, capital rapidly began to develop Romanian industry.

The two leading parties were the National Liberal party and the Peasant party, who were elected and governed as a National-Peasant coalition. (Their descendants reemerged in the 1990 election to unsuccessfully challenge the ruling National Salvation Front.) Both these parties were fairly conservative and easily manipulated by large landownders. In 1927, Ferdinand died, but his son Carol abdicated, choosing to live openly with his mistress rather than stay with his queen. Carol's son, Michael (still the pretender to the Romanian throne) was only six at the time, so a regency was set up.

But Carol still had some legitimacy, especially as the Romanian economy suffered under the Great Depression and the National-Peasant regime splintered. Carol returned, ended the regency, and took the throne as Carol II. Building on traditional rabid anti-Semitism, the fascist Iron Guard party grew, and Carol, a conservative of the Horthy mold, could not contain it. In 1938, as chaos grew, Carol declared himself royal dictator. With everything collapsing about him in 1940, he fled with his mistress, and Romania fell into Hitler's clutches.

Bulgaria

Reflecting the peasant economies of East Europe, Bulgaria's leading party between the wars was the Agrarian party. Unique to East Europe at the time, the second largest party (but nevertheless much smaller) was the Communist party, the result of the early spread of Marxism to Bulgaria in the 1880s. The Bulgarian Communist party was founded in 1891, one of the first in the world and well ahead of its Russian counterpart. Bulgaria's Communists staged an uprising in 1923, but were suppressed, decimated, and outlawed. The key conflict in Bulgaria, however, was between the government and IMRO, the revolutionary organization that aimed at the recovery of Macedonia from Yugoslavia and Greece. Agrarian leader Aleksander Stambuliski, with overwhelming electoral support, became prime minister. King Boris had only a weak role. Stambuliski, a far sighted man, recognized that Bulgaria had to make peace with its neighbors, especially Yugoslavia, so he tried to turn off IMRO demands. The IMRO, which regarded any abandonment of their cause as treason, along with nationalist officers, staged a bloody coup in 1923 and gunned down Stambuliski along with thousands of helpless peasant supporters. Bulgaria thus gained a bloodthirsty reputation in the Western press.

IMRO raids into Yugoslavia increased, and Sofia moved closer to Mussolini's Italy, which also wished to dismember Yugoslavia. Another coup in 1934 brought to power officers who had had enough of the IMRO and crushed it. The following year, King Boris, with army support, took over and set up a royal dictatorship. Boris moved Bulgaria closer to Nazi Germany, which established great economic influence in Bulgaria. In 1941, Bulgaria joined the Axis.

Albania

Interwar Albanian politics was a struggle between democratic and authoritarian forces that the latter won. On the liberal side was Fan Noli, a Harvard-educated Orthodox bishop. On the authoritarian side was the son of a Muslim tribal chief, Ahmed Zogu. Zogu gained control in 1921, lost it to Noli in 1924, and regained it in 1925. In 1928, Zogu turned the Albanian republic into a monarchy with himself as King Zog I. Zog did modernize Albania, crushing banditry and building roads and schools. But he drifted closer to Italy, which dominated Albania in the 1930s.

In sum, East European democracy between the wars scarcely had a chance. Struggling from the destruction caused by World War I, the new governments soon faced the disaster of the Great Depression. Untried institutions thrust upon unprepared citizens quickly collapsed into various types of authoritarianism. In every case, boundary and ethnic disputes played a major role in the domestic politics of these lands and helped determine their international alignments.

INTERNATIONAL ALIGNMENTS

Simply by knowing which countries lost territories in World War I we can predict (with one major exception) how they would line up for World War II. The territorial losers, Hungary and Bulgaria, inclined toward the German-Italian Axis. The territorial winners—Poland, Czechoslovakia, and Yugoslavia—fearing revenge and dismemberment at the hands of Germany or Hungary, looked westward for help and thought they had found it in France, which also had a stake in keeping Germany down and retaining newly regained Alsace-Lorraine. The exception is Romania, which won big after World War I but nonetheless inclined toward the Axis as these territories were stripped away in 1940.

France sponsored the Little Entente in 1920-1921. This was a treaty among Czechoslovakia, Yugoslavia, and Romania to keep what they had won against chiefly Hungarian claims. Unfortunately, the Little Entente could not serve as an overall defensive alliance for the region, and for several reasons. Obviously, Hungary was opposed to it. Poland, which had no worries from Hungary but focused on Russia and Germany instead, saw little reason to join the alliance. Furthermore, Warsaw exaggerated the importance of the small Teschen region which Czechoslovakia took but which had a Polish majority. Anger toward Czechoslovakia prevented Warsaw from entering into a defensive alliance with Prague. So the Little Entente started with two major holes in it, Poland and Hungary. Poland did conclude separate treaties with France and Romania. Overall, however, there was no East European alliance.

Overreliance on France was another problem. France was simply not well situated, geographically, militarily, or psychologically, to come to East Europe's rescue. Terribly weakened and embittered by World War I, Paris governments had no stomach for any policy that might seriously lead to war. As early as 1933, Pilsudski suggested joint Polish-French action against Hitler's new government; Paris demurred. Again, in 1936, as Hitler remilitarized the Rhineland, a direct threat to France, Warsaw promised Paris and Brussels support in a showdown with Germany. No response. After a while, the governments of East Europe could see that France was not a pillar of support, and French-sponsored alliances became a dead letter.

The only other power capable of backing up East Europe was the Soviet Union, and it was a nonplayer, with major territorial designs of its own on the region. As far as Stalin was concerned, squabbles between capitalist neighbors were all to the Soviet good; the capitalists would destroy themselves and leave the Soviets alone. Then the Soviets would pick up the pieces. Stalin thus pursued a rather isolationist policy toward East Europe with no interest in joining in a common cause against a German threat.

Economically, Germany penetrated virtually all of East Europe by means of trade. This was in part natural—Germany was and still is the economic giant of Europe and the natural trading partner of the small, poor countries of East Europe—and in part deliberate policy. Especially under the Nazis, Germany arranged major barter deals of East European food and raw materials in exchange for German manufactured goods, effectively tying the economies of East Europe to Germany. (Any resemblance to the current situation is purely intentional.) If East Europe had had other big trading partners, things might have been different, and they might not have ended up in a dependency relationship with Germany. But during the Great Depression trade shrunk, and Germany was the only country willing to work by barter instead of with scarce hard currency.

The main thing Hitler had going for him in East Europe was his understanding of how much the East European states hated each other. He could ply them with trade and territorial promises, working one against the other, and take over all of them when the time came. With no sense of solidarity among themselves, the East Europeans let themselves be picked off one at a time.

"Munich" illustrates Hitler's strategy. Munich, in Bavaria, is widely known as the place where the British and French gave away Czechoslovakia to Germany in 1938 in an attempt to appease Hitler. Munich was that, but it was also more complicated, a multiparty backstabbing arrangement. First, Hitler had a plausible argument that the Sudeten Germans did not wish to be ruled by Prague and did wish to be part of the Reich. It was, of course, more than an ethnographic boundary question, for Czech defenses were well bunkered into the mountains of the Sudetenland. Once Britain and France had pressured Czechoslovakia—which was not even present at the Munich meeting—into giving up the Sudetenland, then with its surrender went Czechoslovakia's main line of defense.

Second, Hitler knew that Slovaks also disliked rule by Czechs. When he moved into the now defenseless Czechoslovakia in the spring of 1939, he handed

The Dismemberment of Czechoslovakia

The Sudetenland was occupied by Germany from 1938 to 1945.

Ruthenia was occupied by Hungary in 1939 and seized by the Soviet Union in 1945.

Teschen

Southern Slovakia and Southern Ruthenia were occupied by Hungary from 1938 to 1945.

Slovaks their independence, and they eagerly took it, becoming a German dependency with a pro-Nazi government too weak to resist Hungarian territorial demands.

Third, other territorially interested states participated in Munich. Poland was awarded the tiny Teschen area that it had long demanded from Czechoslovakia. This enabled Hitler to point out that Czechoslovakia's borders needed correcting for more than just Germans. It also undermined Poland's moral position in standing up to German territorial demands the next year. In a small way, Poland stabbed a fellow Slavic country in the back.

Hungary got in on the deal too. With the so-called Vienna Award of 1938, Hitler let Hungary take Southern Slovakia and Southern Ruthenia with their Hungarian minorities. With the breaking away of Slovakia in 1939, Hungary then took the rest of Ruthenia, snipping off the easternmost 125 miles of Czechoslovak territory. This tied Hungary to German foreign policy, and Hungary joined the Axis. Simply by using East European territorial claims as a diplomatic tool, Hitler thrust German power far to the east in 1939 without firing a shot. Among East European lands there was no sense of solidarity, and this doomed them.

Hungarian Expansion during World War II

Next, Hitler used Soviet claims against Poland to neutralize Stalin. Knowing that Stalin had always wanted the Curzon Line as Russia's border, Hitler gave it to him in the secret protocol of the 1939 Molotov-Ribbentrop pact. (As a sweetener, Stalin turned over to the Gestapo some 500 German Communists who had fled to Moscow.) Seriously misnamed as the Non-Aggression Pact, Hitler was promised Soviet noninterferrence as he invaded Poland on September 1, 1939. On September 17, Stalin invaded Poland from the east, firmly knifing a fellow Slavic state in the back.

As part of the Molotov-Ribbentrop pact, in 1940 Stalin occupied Lithuania, Latvia, and Estonia. Romania was stripped of important territories. In 1940, the Soviet Union took Bessarabia, now the Soviet republic of Moldavia, and Northern Bukovina. With the Second Vienna Award of 1940, Hitler gave North Transylvania to Hungary, and shortly thereafter Southern Dobrudja to Bulgaria. To whom could Romania turn? Russia was the hated Communist land that had taken Bessarabia. With massive fascistic agitation by the Iron Guard, Germany appeared as Romania's only protector against further dismemberment. It was strange: Germany had precipitated Romanian territorial losses and yet Romania had to turn to Germany for help.

The Dismemberment of Romania in 1940

With the German conquest of Yugoslavia and Greece in 1941, their neighbors moved in for the pickings. Hungary took portions of Northern Yugoslavia that had a Hungarian minority. Bulgaria took Western Thrace from Greece (territory that Bulgaria had briefly held in 1913) and Macedonia from Yugoslavia.

Hitler barely had to fight to take over all of East Europe. Only Poland and Yugoslavia resisted, and they were overrun in a matter of days. The rest of East Europe fell into Hitler's hands because he knew their borders were terribly disputed and that they hated each other. Hungary, Bulgaria, and Romania he enrolled as allies. As if in response to Benjamin Franklin's quip to the Continental Congress, "Either we all hang together or we all hang separately," the East Europeans eagerly put nooses around their own necks.

SUGGESTED READINGS

SETON-WATSON, HUGH. *Eastern Europe Between the Wars, 1918-1941.* New York: Harper & Row, 1967.

WALTERS, E. GARRISON. *The Other Europe: Eastern Europe to 1945.* Syracuse, N.Y.: Syracuse University Press, 1988.

CHAPTER THREE _____

East Europe
and World War II

Between the two world wars, the Communist parties of East Europe were generally small. In elections during the 1920s, Communist parties won an average of 10 percent or so for the region as a whole. A temporary high of 20 percent came in Bulgaria in 1920. A Communist vote does not necessarily indicate members or even believers. Much Communist electoral support is a protest vote, cast by people who don't much know or care what the Communists stand for but who dislike the existing system. A great deal of the French and Italian Communist vote is of this nature. French President Mitterrand understood this and, by offering a more attractive way to protest in his Socialist party, has drained off a third of the Communist electoral support.

As R. V. Burks pointed out in his important study, *The Dynamics of Communism in Eastern Europe*, the groups that tended to vote more strongly Communist tell us a good deal about communism and its appeal. The Communists, following Marx's theory of a coming proletarian revolution, always liked to portray themselves as the party of workers. There is little to substantiate this picture in East Europe between the wars. The Communist vote was quite mixed: some workers, many peasants, and surprising numbers of middle-class people. Most of the Communist leadership were intellectuals; few were workers.

Burks finds that Communist voting, membership, and leadership was concentrated among groups with grudges, people who felt they had been treated unfairly and discriminated against. For example, Communist voting was high among the Magyar population that was left outside Hungary's borders by the Treaty of Trianon. Hungarians in Slovakia or Romania could show their resentment against their unhappy national status by voting Communist. Again, a protest vote. Jews in Poland, about 10 percent of the interwar population, were discriminated

Ulbricht: A Stalin Puppet

Typical of the pre-World War II Communist leaders whom Stalin held on ice was the German Communist Walter Ulbricht. His story could be the story of many of East Europe's first generation of Communist leaders, those who were installed by Soviet bayonets after World War II. Ulbricht was born in 1893, the eldest son of a poor Leipzig tailor, who raised Walter as a devout Marxist. Bright but without funds, Ulbricht completed only eight years of schooling before apprenticing himself to a cabinetmaker—a typical German working-class pattern. In 1912, at age 19, Ulbricht joined the Social Democratic party (SPD), then the largest and strongest socialist party in the world. In the Leipzig Workers Educational Institute he picked up a sort of Marxist college education.

As World War I began in 1914, the SPD split. The largest part stayed with the mainstream leaders and supported Germany's war effort. A minority left-wing faction under Karl Liebknecht denounced the war, and Ulbricht aligned himself with this wing. Drafted against his will in 1915, Ulbricht deserted twice and was caught both times. As Germany lurched to collapse in 1918, Ulbricht escaped from military prison to organize soldiers and workers for a short-lived revolutionary takeover attempt. As the new German Communist party (KPD) split off from the SPD in 1919, Ulbricht sided immediately with the KPD and was among its founders. Working his way quickly up through party ranks, Ulbricht was sent as a KPD delegate to the Comintern world congress in 1922, and the following year he was made a member of the KPD central committee. Already he was the party expert on organization. In the mid-1920s he attended a Comintern school in Moscow.

Elected to the Reichstag as a Communist in 1928, in time for the Great Depression, Ulbricht soon was echoing the new Stalinist line of immediate revolution to overthrow the tottering capitalist Weimar Republic. The Social Democrats he reviled as "Social Fascists," no better than the capitalists. The policy was a catastrophe, paving the way for Hitler's rise to power. In 1933, along with many KPD cadres, Ulbricht fled to Paris, where he continued to organize German Communists.

In the late 1930s, Stalin carried out his infamous "purges" of suspected disloyal Communists. These included foreign as well as Soviet party members. Many on the KPD's central committee were summoned to Moscow where they disappeared. Ulbricht, too, was called to Moscow, but he convinced Stalin's police that he was utterly reliable. As the purges executed superiors and rivals within the KPD leadership, they also eased Ulbricht's way to the top.

In 1938, Ulbricht was again ordered to Moscow, this time as the KPD's delegate to the Comintern. With the German invasion of Russia in 1941, Ulbricht organized emigré German Communists and, later, German prisoners of war into a Communist nucleus to take over Germany after the war. In April 1945, as the Red Army pushed into the eastern part of Germany, *Gruppe Ulbricht*, as the Communist group was called, was returned to German soil where it immediately reestablished the KPD and a civilian power structure under Russian military supervision. All over East Europe, trained groups like Ulbricht's were reinserted on their native soil to set up Communist governments as the Germans were pushed out.

In 1949, just after Konrad Adenauer proclaimed a new Federal Republic of Germany in the Western powers' occupation zones, Ulbricht proclaimed a German Democratic Republic in the Soviet zone, and it soon became known as East Germany. Ulbricht was the undisputed boss and president of East Germany through the fiercest years of the Cold War. After watching the GDR's population drain away through West Berlin, Ulbricht built the Berlin Wall in 1961. But Ulbricht was still beholden to Soviet power for his tenure. He was forcibly retired in 1971 for reasons probably having to do with his inflexibility over Bonn's rapprochement with Moscow. Ulbricht didn't like having the Soviet Union deal over his head with West Germany. Although for decades a loyal Stalinist agent, Ulbricht eventually displeased the Kremlin's post-Stalin leadership. His ouster showed how dependent he—and most other East European Communist party chiefs—were on Moscow's support.

Still, it was a remarkable record. By hewing to the right line at the right time, by utterly supporting whatever strategy Stalin proposed, by tireless attention to detail, Ulbricht plodded his way to the top. In contrast to Tito, whom we will consider subsequently, Ulbricht had absolutely no personal charisma. He fought in no battles and led no troops. He came to and retained power on a bureaucratic basis, by loyalty to Moscow and by careful party organizational work. He died in 1973.

against by an anti-Semitic regime, so a higher proportion of them voted Communist. Ukrainians and Belorussians under Polish rule felt the same way, so much of the support for the Polish Communist party was non-Polish. (Ironically, much of Israel's Communist vote now is from Arabs who resent their second-class citizenship but who have few alternatives, for the Palestine Liberation Organization is illegal in Israel. Still, this confirms Burks's thesis that groups with grudges vote Communist in protest, not necessarily out of conviction.)

The point is that there were Communists in East Europe before World War II, but there weren't many. On their own, no East European Communist party would have come to power; they would have stayed minor parties. These small parties did contribute one element to the Soviet takeovers in East Europe after World War II: the initial Communist leadership. Most of the first Communist leaders of East Europe had been active in the small, sometimes underground, Communist parties of the 1930s. With the Nazi takeovers, many fled to the Soviet Union, where Stalin groomed them to set up Communist parties and regimes after the war.

THE STRUCTURE OF COMMUNISM

In 1919, Lenin laid down strict requirements for any party that wished to join the new Communist International he had founded. There was then and still is a Socialist International (called the Second International), a loose grouping of democratic socialist parties. Lenin wished to have nothing to do with that. As far as Communists were concerned, socialists were cowards and fakes. They had long talked about the international solidarity of workers, but in practice they had mellowed into trade unionists and welfarists. Worse, they had cooperated with the capitalist governments' march to war in 1914. German Social Democrats had supported Germany's war effort; French Socialists had supported France's war effort; and British Labourites had supported Britain's war effort. In Bolshevik eyes, the socialsts during World War I were as bad as capitalists.

The Third, or Communist, International—known as the "Comintern" for short—was to be not a debating society but a highly disciplined, centrally controlled network of parties that voluntarily and enthusiastically followed Moscow's every lead. Lenin's purpose was to split off the serious revolutionaries from existing, moderate socialist parties. From 1919 to 1921, virtually every socialist party did split, its left wing becoming the new Communist party and in short order a member of the Comintern. Promising Communist talent was sent to Moscow for training and indoctrination.

The various Communist parties were supposed to have little or no autonomy, but they were to adapt themselves to local conditions. Strategies to achieve this were set by Stalin (Lenin died in 1924). Where communism was suppressed—as in Hungary, after Bela Kun's abortive takeover—Communists were to function underground, organized into small cells. If the police cracked one cell, its members would not be able to reveal more than a few names. In more open circumstances, Communists were to compete in elections, organize unions, and criticize bourgeois governments.

But what if Stalin made a mistake in selecting the strategy? He made many, and it cost Communists a great deal, in some cases their lives. At times, Stalin advised cooperation with bourgeois governments when he should have urged secrecy and a low profile. Once out in the open, Communists could be arrested by conservative regimes. At other times, Stalin ordered Communists to not cooperate with other parties, even against the rise of fascism. This contributed to Hitler's takeover of Germany in 1933 (see box).

However mistaken, Communists were not supposed to question Stalin's strategy. Those who did—or who Stalin suspected did—got taken care of. The Polish Communist party was thoroughly purged in 1938 (and ostensibly dissolved) by simply turning over lists of unwanted members to the Polish police, who in effect did Stalin's dirty work for him. During the Great Purge of the mid-1930s to the late 1930s, East European Communist leaders deemed insufficiently obedient were summoned to Moscow to work at Comintern headquarters and were then arrested,

Stalin and Hitler's Rise

One of the last things Communists liked to talk about was how the German Communist party in the early 1930s helped Hitler rise to power. At that time, Stalin had issued worldwide orders that Communist parties not cooperate with other parties. (Earlier, in the 1920s, the KPD had been instructed to cooperate with other parties.) The theory in the early 1930s was that cooperation with other parties might indicate that they had some merit; this would confuse the masses, who might then vote for a non-Communist party. Communists must avoid compromises and come to power on their own, without partners.

As applied to Germany, Stalin ordered the small but growing German Communist party (KPD) to end its parliamentary alliance with the larger Social Democratic party (SPD), an alliance that might have blocked the takeover by Hitler's National Socialists (Nazis). Stalin evaluated Hitler as essentially a clown (he did resemble Charlie Chaplin), the plaything of sinister but decaying capitalist circles, who was not capable of governing Germany. Even if Hitler did take office, his ridiculous regime would soon collapse. The German Communist phrase of the time was, "Nach Hitler kommen wir" (After Hitler comes us). In other words, the Nazis were the last gasp of a dying capitalism; they would finish off the doomed system and then the Communists would take over.

Hitler did come to power in early 1933, and was soon arresting both Communists and Social Democrats. Some of them paid with their lives for Stalin's monumental misevaluation. In 1935, without ever admitting his error, Stalin cranked out a new line: now all nonfascistic parties— Communists, Socialists, and moderate democrats—were to form a "Popular Front" to block fascism. The operative phrase became that of the French Communists, "Pas d'ennemis a la gauche" (No enemies on the left). In other words, we must all get together to fight this menace. But it was five years too late. In 1941, with the German invasion of the Soviet Union, Russians had to pay with millions of lives for Stalin's blunder. The episode shows both Stalin's limitations in dealing with situations in other countries and the slavish obedience of Communists in following foolish advice.

tried, and executed as spies and foreign agents. Several of the founders and first leaders of East European Communist parties went to the Soviet Union in the 1930s never to return. (See the box on Ulbricht.)

What was Stalin up to? Why would he harm the Communist movements of East Europe? The clue is Soviet national interest, or what Stalin perceived to be Soviet national interest. Stalin didn't give a fig for communism in other countries except insofar as it helped or hurt the Soviet Union. This generally meant a conservative line, especially after Hitler consolidated power in Germany. In the mid-1930s, East Europe started taking on some importance to the Soviet Union.

Stalin did not want East European countries to ally with or be used by Germany as a possible invasion corridor. Under these circumstances, it was unwise to urge local Communist parties to try to overthrow conservative governments, not that any would have been able to. But revolutionary activity would only weaken the none-too-strong governments of East Europe and make it easier for pro-German elements to take over. Accordingly, Communists should generally lay low and not make trouble. Some parties were even formally dissolved, although the leading cadres continued to operate quietly underground. Watch and wait was Stalin's game.

WORLD WAR II IN EAST EUROPE

Stalin did not have long to wait. As we discussed in Chapter 2, Czechoslovakia was the first to go. The 1938 Munich conference in which Britain and France handed Hitler Czechoslovakia's strategic Sudetenland, convinced Stalin that London and Paris were trying to point Hitler eastward, toward the Soviet Union. There is no evidence that they had any such thing in mind, but Stalin was a classic paranoid, quick to believe that others were out to get him. At the same time, Poland and Hungary moved in to pick over the carcass of Czechoslovakia.

World War II, like World War I, started in and over East Europe. In the first war, the problem had been Bosnia and Serbia. In the second war, the problem was Poland, namely German demands to get back territories that Versailles had given to the new Polish republic. In both cases, strong states saw no reason to accommodate weak states. We are strong, said Austria and Germany, respectively, so we will take what we wish. Only one thing made Hitler pause before attacking Poland in 1939: How would the Soviet Union react? Hitler wished no war with the Soviet Union at that time. As we considered in the previous chapter, Stalin made an incredibly cynical pact with Hitler, the 1939 Non-Aggression Pact, a pact that gave Hitler the green light to invade Poland and Stalin permission to annex the eastern part of the Polish state.

What were East European Communists to do as Hitler either lined up the East European states as allies or took them by military conquest? They were to do absolutely nothing, Stalin ordered. Just lay low and wait. Incredibly, Communists were not to resist or plot against German occupiers or fascist puppet governments. That might alarm Hitler, Stalin figured. All that changed on June 22, 1941, for on that date Germany invaded the Soviet Union, and Communists were told that it was suddenly their sacred duty to do everything they could to defeat fascism. Again, the subordination of communism to Soviet foreign policy was evident.

East Europe's Communists liked to boast how they had "fought" the Nazis and local fascists during World War II. This image is accurate only in spots. Here and there, as in Albania, Bulgaria, and Slovakia, Communists organized some guerrilla bands to physically combat the Germans. But most Communist leaders had fled to Moscow where they sat out the war. In Moscow they trained and organized to set

Tito: Not a Stalin Puppet

In many ways Walter Ulbricht and Josip Broz—better known as Tito—were similar. They were almost exactly the same age; Tito was born in 1892, a year earlier than Ulbricht. Both came from modest backgrounds, both worked their way up through their respective Communist parties, served the Comintern in Moscow and elsewhere, and became the post-World War II leaders of their lands. But they gained power very differently and this strongly influenced the courses they took once in power. Ulbricht, a party bureaucrat, was placed in power by Stalin as an obedient puppet. Tito fought his way to power on his own and owed Stalin little. This was the basis for the Tito-Stalin split.

Born in a village in Croatia—then part of the Austro-Hungarian empire—Josip Broz was the seventh of fifteen children, eight of whom died in childhood. Life was harsh under the Hungarian nobles who ruled the area. Broz's father was a Croat farmer, his mother Slovenian. This mixed background later served him well, for he represented two of Yugoslavia's several nationalities. The family lacked money to send the lad to America, so Josip was apprenticed to a blacksmith and mechanic. At night school, he trained himself to become a voracious reader. At age 18, in 1910, Broz began to wander, picking up various jobs, in Austria, in Bohemia, and in Germany, and learning German and Czech. In Zagreb, he joined the Metalworkers Union and the Social Democratic party of Croatia, his first political involvement, a leftist one.

In 1913 Broz was drafted for the standard two-year stint in the Austrian army and he was promoted to sergeant. At the Carpathian front in 1915, Sergeant Broz was lanced in a Russian cavalry charge and captured. (Note that at the same time Ulbricht was busy dodging the German draft.) Broz worked as a mechanic while a prisoner. Hearing of the tsar's overthrow in March 1917, Broz escaped to join the Bolsheviks, who themselves seized power under Lenin in November 1917. By now he was a committed Communist. Marrying a Russian girl (the first of his four wives), Broz returned to the new nation of Yugoslavia in 1920. He had been five years in Russia.

Back in Zagreb, he engaged in union and party activity, working quickly up the ranks of the new Communist party, which was soon declared illegal. In 1928, Broz was arrested and sent to prison for more than five years. (Ulbricht served no prison time.) Tito later reflected that prison was his university, for there he could read and converse with other Communists. Upon release in 1934, Broz went underground as a professional party leader. In 1935, as a Comintern delegate in Moscow, Broz was among the first to receive Stalin's new line of "Popular Fronts"—all left parties against fascism. Part of this line was to help the Republican government in the Spanish Civil War. Traveling around Europe with forged passports, Broz helped organize Comintern volunteers to fight in Spain. Returning to Yugoslavia in 1937, by early 1939 Broz was named general secretary of the Yugoslav Communist party. Several earlier leaders had perished in Stalin's purges.

Taking the *nom de guerre* of Tito, Broz organized and led the Communist-dominated Partisans who battled and outlasted the Germans in the mountains of Bosnia. By 1945, the Partisans had liberated roughly the southern half of Yugoslavia; the Soviet army swept through the northern half. This fact gave Tito an independent power base that no other East European Communist chief had. Tito had his own army, and it had fought heroically and supported him devotedly. The new Communist leaders elsewhere in East Europe had sat out the war in Moscow and had been put in power by Soviet bayonets. This made the difference when Stalin tried to oust Tito in 1948. Stalin could purge other East European Communists with a raised eyebrow, but he could not topple Tito, who stayed president of Yugoslvia until his death in 1980.

Both the situations and the personalities of Ulbricht and Tito were quite different. Guerrilla warfare inside Germany was impossible, and Ulbricht was essentially a bureaucrat with zero charisma. Yugoslavia is largely mountain and forest, perfect for guerrilla warfare. Many Yugoslavs hated the Germans. And Tito was a strong, tough, and charismatic leader. With Ulbricht and Tito, did the situation make the personality or vice-versa? In politics, it's hard to tell.

---

up the first postwar Communist systems in East Europe. Much of East Europe's anti-German resistance, as in Poland, was led by non-Communist nationalists, often at odds with Communist resistance groups. Only one Communist-led outfit really fought the Germans, the Yugoslav Partisans of Tito. For the most part, other Communists organized underground cells in preparation for the arrival of the Red Army.

In the spring of 1941, Hitler conquered Yugoslavia in eleven days. The Yugoslav Communist response? Nothing. That was still the strange period of the Hitler-Stalin pact, and Moscow ordered Communists throughout Europe to not resist. Hitler, knowing that Croats wanted their freedom from Serbia, set up a Croatian puppet state much like Slovakia. Slovenia was incorporated into the Reich. Macedonia was taken over by Bulgaria. Italy occupied the Adriatic coast.

Only with the German invasion of Russia in June 1941 did the Yugoslav Communists swing into action, organizing Partisan forces that practiced guerrilla warfare, mostly in the mountains of Bosnia. The Partisans never beat the German occupiers. In classic guerrilla fashion, they outlasted the Germans, slipping away when outgunned. Much fighting was with other Yugoslavs, the fascist Croatian Ustasha and monarchist Serbian Chetniks. German reprisals against Yugoslav civilians was murderous, but this didn't bother Tito's Partisans. The more civilians the Germans killed, the more recruits for the Partisans. The occupier does the guerrillas' recruiting for them. By the war's end, over 10 percent of Yugoslavia's population had been killed and 3.5 million were homeless.

The Communist-led Partisans were neither the only nor the largest armed group of Yugoslavs. Remnants of the army formed a Serbian guerrilla force called the Chetniks (named after the old anti-Turkish bandits), whose goal was a restoration of the old Serbian-dominated monarchy. As such, the Chetniks were not a viable rallying point for other Yugoslav nationalities. In the 1930s a native fascist movement grew up in Croatia, the Ustasha, which set up a Nazi puppet state, doubling the size of Croatia and slaughtering Serbs. Obviously, the Ustasha could not unite all of Yugoslavia. Only the Communist Partisans were above the old national quarrels; they alone held out the hope of a new system with justice for all national groups. The Chetniks fought for Serbia, the Ustasha for Croatia, only the Communists for all Yugoslavia. It was a potent recruiting device for the Communists, giving them a certain moral authority.

Augmenting this moral authority was the fact that only the Partisans actually fought the Germans. The Partisans suffered some 350,000 dead and 400,000 wounded. During the war, one Yugoslav in ten was killed. Did guerrilla warfare against the Germans do any good? A little. It disrupted communications and tied down several German divisions that were desperately needed elsewhere. By itself, however, it did not defeat the enemy or liberate the country. What it did was secure the Communist guerrilla leaders as their country's next rulers. Partisan chiefs knew they couldn't beat the Germans; they focused on seizing power after the Germans had been beaten by the Allies.

To see how this strategy was attempted and how it failed, let us compare Yugoslavia with Poland. First, under Stalin's orders, the Polish Communist party was purged and ostensibly dissolved in 1938 as Stalin was trying to improve relations with Warsaw. Underground, however, a trimmed-down Polish Workers party continued to exist. Poland was conquered by the Nazis in 1939; most of the Communists who did not flee to Russia were killed by the Germans. Accordingly, the Polish Communists were much fewer in number by June 1941—when guerrilla warfare suddenly became desirable—than the Yugoslav Communists.

Second, there were no nationality quarrels among Poles as there were among Yugoslavs. Offering a solution to the nationalities question was one of the Yugoslav Partisans most important recruiting devices. Poles have a strong sense of national identity, something the Yugoslavs still lack.

Third, especially among Serbs and Montenegrins, Russia still had a favorable image, that of the big Slavic brother who would save them from the Turks. The Russophile Montenegrins, the tiny nationality just north of Albania, used to boast, "Us and the Russians make 200 million." Poles, on the other hand, for centuries had feared and despised Russia, and they had recent memories of the tsarist Russian administration of the central portion of their country. Poles had just gotten rid of the Russians in 1918, and they didn't view the Soviet Union as their savior.

These factors added up to a main Polish underground movement that was thoroughly non-Communist. Forming the Home Army, it answered to the Polish government in exile in London, the so-called London Poles. Thousands of Poles

The Katyn Massacre

As Hitler's Wehrmacht overran the western two-thirds of Poland in September 1939, Stalin's Red Army took the eastern part of Poland as per the dictators' agreement of the previous month. The Soviets captured more than 230,000 Polish soldiers, mostly reservists, without a fight and interned them in Russia. The following spring, all word from about 15,000 of these prisoners—8,000 to 9,000 of them officers, most of the others sergeants—ceased. What had happened to them?

In 1943 the world found out, but some didn't want to believe it. The German invaders unearthed, in the Katyn Forest deep inside Russia, mass graves of thousands of Polish officers and non-coms, each of them shot in the back of the head with a revolver. Gleefully, the Germans showed the graves to the Red Cross and to captured British officers so they might get the word out about what the Russians had done. The London Poles, who had long wondered where the missing officers were, believed the story. The Soviets hotly denied it, blamed the Germans, and huffily broke relations with the London Poles. The following year, Stalin set up his own puppets, the Lublin Polish group, in newly liberated Lublin, Poland.

The facts clearly blame Stalin and his secret police for the Katyn massacre. First, all word of these captured Poles ceased in the spring of 1940. The Germans didn't invade Russia until the summer of 1941. Second, Katyn Forest is deep inside Russia; the Germans did not arrive there until the fall of 1941. Third, the uniforms and boots of the murdered Polish officers showed only moderate wear, as if they had been imprisoned only a few months. Fourth, why would the Germans publicize the horror if they were guilty?

But why would Stalin do such a thing? The Polish officers would have been a welcome addition to the Red Army. They would have fought well against Germans. (Of course, in 1940 Stalin couldn't have known that Germany would invade the next year.) Other Poles were, in fact, recruited into Polish units under overall Soviet command. But the captured Polish officers were not Communists; they would answer only to the London Polish government. After the war, these officers could provide leadership to a non-Communist Poland. In short, if Stalin didn't own them, he didn't trust them. His solution: decapitate a portion of the Polish leadership stratum so they wouldn't give him any trouble after the war. Stalin was perfectly capable of thinking this way.

News of Katyn was officially prohibited in both the Soviet Union and Poland, but by word of mouth not a single Pole was unaware of the massacres. It deepened Polish hatred of Communism and Russians. Finally, in 1990, the Soviet Union handed over to Poland cartons of documents that Soviet President Gorbachev said "indirectly but convincingly" pointed to Stalin's secret police as the culprits. "It is not easy to speak of this tragedy, but it is necessary," he said, trying to establish new and friendly relations with Poland. After half a century of lies, a Soviet leader was admitting what Poles had known all along.

who escaped in 1939 (most via Romania) served under British command. Polish Communists formed a much smaller resistance movement that was commanded from the Soviet Union. Tens of thousands of Polish soldiers who had been captured by the Soviets as they overran eastern Poland in 1939 also served in the Red Army. (Such was the military background of General Wojciech Jaruzelski, later president of Poland.) Thousands of others, though, were murdered under Stalin's orders in the Katyn Forest.

There was some Polish partisan activity in the forests, but in the main the Home Army laid low, knowing that moving too soon against the Germans could be fatal. The Polish underground, for example, offered little help to Jews, who were shipped to Nazi death camps, most of which were on Polish soil. Many Poles were anti-Semitic, and some didn't mind what the Nazis were doing to Jews. (In fairness, it should be noted that some Poles risked their lives to aid Jews. Few Europeans of any nationality stepped forward to save Jews; only Danes and Bulgarians massively resisted the Nazi deportations of Jews to death camps.) When the Warsaw Ghetto at last revolted in 1943, the Polish underground did little, figuring the revolt was a useless gesture. Some Polish guerrilla units did not welcome Jewish partisans; a few even shot them. It was the classic East European story of backstabbing and disunity in the face of adversity.

Perhaps the high point of wartime backstabbing came as the Soviet army pushed the Germans back to Warsaw in the fall of 1944. The Home Army saw this

---

"People's Democracy"

It sounds incredible now, but during the Cold War the Communists claimed that the "people's democracies" and "people's republics" of East Europe were actually more democratic than the ordinary liberal or "bourgeois" democracies in the West. In Communist theory, bourgeois (middle-class) democracy really wasn't very democratic at all, for it left overriding power in the hands of rich capitalists, who structured parties, the press, and politics to protect their own wealth and power. Free speech and opposition parties didn't count for much because they didn't have a chance in competition with the capitalists' money, went Marxist theory.

Real democracy, argued the Communists, came when you got rid of the capitalists. This was "people's" or "popular" democracy, for now the will of the masses, undistorted by the bourgeois parties and media, would stream into political power. Naturally, someone would have to organize and lead the people, and this would be the Communists, who are best equipped to understand what the people really need. Competing parties and opposition viewpoints and media would not be needed since there would now be only one class. Indeed, any attempt to resurrect other parties and news media would indicate the capitalists were trying to sneak back into power and must be squelched. Applying this weird Marxist logic, Stalin justified his "people's republics" in East Europe.

as their chance to liberate Warsaw from the Germans and proclaim a free (i.e., non-Communist) Polish government before the Soviets could set up a Communist government. On August 1, some 35,000 Poles of the "Warsaw Army Corps" rose up with captured and smuggled weapons. Immediately, the Polish fighters called for the nearby Soviet army to help them drive out the Germans. Instead, the Red Army sat on the other side of the Vistula River by Warsaw and let the Nazis get rid of troublesome Polish patriots for them. In 63 days of heroic fighting against five German divisions, the Poles were either killed or fled into the sewers. The Germans turned much of Warsaw into rubble; it was the most damaged city of World War II. After it was over, the Soviets crossed the Vistula and took Warsaw. The Warsaw horror can be seen as a continuation of the Katyn massacre.

Notice how all players in these games, whether Yugoslavs, Poles, or Soviets, whether Communists or non-Communists, have chiefly in mind the seizure of power after the war. Americans are a bit naive on this point; they think wars are fought to beat an enemy. Americans think all should join in selflessly to attain victory and not worry about the postwar situation. The East Europeans were much more cynical; they understood that the big payoff was in who gained power after the war. Fighting the Germans (or simply waiting) were but tactics to this end.

STALIN'S APPROACH TO EAST EUROPE

Stalin was ultracynical about East Europe. Whoever conquered a piece of territory, he said, imposed his political system on it. To him, it was a sort of natural law. The Western Allies did not consult with him in setting up "bourgeois democracies" in Belgium and Italy, and he didn't mind. But neither should Britain or America object to his setting up "people's democracies" in East Europe, he reasoned.

Behind Stalin's Marxist rhetoric stood some plausible geopolitical arguments. East Europe had repeatedly been used as an invasion corridor against Russia. From the Teutonic knights, to the Swedes, to Napoleon, to the Germans in the two world wars, whoever held East Europe was a threat to Russia. That had just been proven by the Hitlerian onslaught, which cost some 20 million Soviet lives. Stalin therefore wished to keep East Europe not on ideological grounds—to spread the Communist revolution—but as a defensive shield for the Soviet motherland. The only way to make sure it stayed a reliable shield was to implant Communist regimes; bourgeois regimes in East Europe would soon incline westward and link up with Russia's enemies. Communism in East Europe was secondary to Soviet security considerations.

By the fall of 1944, the Red Army had liberated the Soviet Union and was pushing the Germans back through East Europe. The Red Army, except for liberating the most and biggest Nazi death camps (which were on Polish soil), did not generally make a good impression. Looting and rape were frequent, and many East Europeans feared and disliked the backward, primitive Russian soldiers, who

The Balkan "Percentages" Deal

One of the war's most cynical geopolitical deals was reached by Stalin and Churchill in Moscow in 1944 as the Soviet army pushed into Romania and Bulgaria. Churchill, a classic British imperialist, wished to outline spheres of influence in the Balkans so that Britain and Russia would "not get at cross-purposes in small ways." Stalin, a classic Russian imperialist, understood exactly what he meant: who was going to own what. Churchill wrote what percentages of predominance the two powers should get in the Balkans:

Rumania	
Russia	90%
The others	10%
Greece	
Great Britain	90%
(in accord with USA)	
Russia	10%
Yugoslavia	50-50%
Hungary	50-50%
Bulgaria	
Russia	75%
The others	25%

Wrote Churchill: "I pushed this across to Stalin, who had by then heard the translation. There was a slight pause. Then he took his blue pencil and made a large tick upon it, and passed it back to us. It was all settled in no more time than it takes to set down."

Did Stalin intend to abide by this partition plan? Probably not, but strangely that is how things approximately worked out. Except for Hungary, which was within a few years a firm Soviet satellite, the note describes the postwar lineup. Stalin did not attempt to take over Greece; he even ordered Greek Communists to give up their guerrilla war (which they nearly won). Yugoslavia from 1945 to 1948 was a strong Soviet satellite, but after Stalin kicked it out of the Soviet camp, it really turned neutral, and Stalin did not invade it. Perhaps Stalin meant what he told Churchill in 1944.

were inclined to "liberate" anything that struck their fancy. After the Red Army had swept through an area, for example, there were few wristwatches left.

Yalta, 1945

As the Allies neared the borders of Germany, the Big Three leaders met at Yalta to set up a postwar world. The series of agreements, some coming before Yalta and some coming after, are sometimes referred to simply as "Yalta." They included the following points, some in writing and some in verbal understandings.

1. **A United Nations was to be set up.** Some of the elements of the UN Charter were mentioned, including the bizarre provision for counting the Ukraine and Belorussia as separate UN members, thus giving the Soviet Union three votes in the General Assembly. Curiously, Roosevelt thought that gaining Stalin's acceptance of the UN was the main thing that had happened at Yalta.

2. **Russia got the Curzon Line** as its western border. As we discussed in Chapter 2, Poland had taken parts of the Ukraine and Belorussia in 1920, well to the east of the Curzon Line recommended by the Western victors at Versailles. Stalin had always wanted this territory back, and had indeed gotten much of it back in his 1939 pact with Hitler. Poland's eastern border was therefore moved about 100 to 200 miles westward, a point that the Allies had agreed to at their 1943 meeting in Tehran, Iran.

3. **Poland got a large chunk of Germany** in compensation for its losses to the Soviet Union. This was confirmed at the Potsdam meeting near Berlin in July. The gigantic butterfly of German territory—Silesia, Prussia, Pomerania—was snipped off at the Oder and Neisse Rivers and handed to postwar Poland. The area had been German for three centuries; millions of Germans fled westward to be replaced by Poles who had been displaced from the eastern part of Poland now taken over by the Soviet Union. Poland was in effect picked up and moved about 100 miles westward. Germany's East Prussia was split in two, the northern half taken by the Soviets, the southern by the Poles. The Soviet portion still exists as the coastal wedge of land between Poland and Lithuania.

4. **Germany was divided into occupation zones**, at first three—British, American, and Soviet—and later four, when France was added. The military occupation was to be temporary. The splitting of Germany into two states, East and West, was not envisioned. Berlin was to be likewise divided but under joint military administration.

5. **Germany was to be disarmed** and kept disarmed and was to pay heavy reparations for the terrible war damage it had inflicted.

6. **The nations of East Europe were to be democratic and friendly to the Soviet Union.** This agreement, admittedly vague, became the snarling point between Washington and Moscow, and it caused much controversy within U.S. domestic politics. The Soviets read "democratic" to mean "people's democracy," which, as we considered earlier, meant Communist control. And "friendly" to the Soviet Union meant occupation by and under the control of the Soviets.

7. The Soviet Union would attack Japan within three months of Germany's defeat. The Soviet Union and Japan had signed a non-aggression pact shortly before the German invasion in 1941 and had scrupulously adhered to it. The Soviets stayed out of the Pacific war until we persuaded them to come in, which they did in July 1945. Yalta provided for the return of Russian territory taken by Japan in the Russo-Japanese War of 1905.

YALTA

Stalin wanted East Europe. Did Yalta give it to him? Critics of President Franklin D. Roosevelt for years lambasted the Democrats as the architects of the giveaway of East Europe. Yalta is a resort town in the Soviet Crimea where in early 1945 the wartime Big Three leaders met—Roosevelt, Stalin, and Churchill. Their attention focused heavily on Poland (Stalin and Churchill having taken care of the Balkans the previous year).

The situation on the ground when Yalta took place in February 1945 did not favor Roosevelt and Churchill. The Western Allies had liberated only France while the Soviets had taken most of Poland, Hungary, and Yugoslavia, half of Czechoslovakia, and all of Romania by that time. A major German counteroffensive had recently taken the Americans by surprise in the Ardennes (the Battle of the Bulge). Soviet forces were about 100 miles from Berlin, the Western Allies about 300 miles from Berlin. No one knew at that time that the Americans would be able to cross the Rhine over the unexploded bridge at Remagen on March 7 and move rapidly across Germany.

There was little Roosevelt or Churchill could do to change Stalin's mind about the territories he had conquered and paid for in Soviet blood. It is possible that the two Western leaders viewed Yalta as a mechanism to keep Stalin from taking any *more* of Europe. Basically, Roosevelt and Churchil conceded to Stalin what Stalin already had in his possession in return for some nice phrases about the United Nations and democracy in East Europe after the war. Notice how much of Yalta concerns boundaries.

At the time, Roosevelt and his assistant Harry Hopkins thought they were getting a pretty good deal at Yalta. Stalin would enter the war against Japan, which at the time was thought to be necessary for victory. Roosevelt didn't know that the atomic bombs, then being frantically developed in the Manhattan Project, would work and that Japan was near surrender anyway. Roosevelt also got Stalin's acceptance of the UN idea, one of Roosevelt's pet projects. Did Roosevelt comprehend the utter cynicism of Stalin and his geopolitical designs on East Europe? Probably not. Roosevelt, who had been an official of the Wilson

Poland Is Moved Westward

administration, carried over some of Wilson's internationalist vision. Roosevelt was personally charming and thought he could persuade Stalin to join in the idealistic open world Roosevelt envisioned. We know now that Stalin regarded Roosevelt not as an idealist but as a crafty imperialist trying to expand U.S. power. Stalin projected his own cynicism onto Roosevelt.

Roosevelt really was a bit naive. Clues to Stalin's behavior were available; some had come from the warning cables of George F. Kennan in the U.S. embassy in Moscow, who noted that our Soviet ally was not a great deal better than our German enemy. Few listened to Kennan at the time. There was a war on, and the Soviet Union was seen as a heroic, embattled ally. U.S. opinion of the Soviet Union during the war was favorable, and Roosevelt shared it. To have said no or to have engaged in tough bargaining at Yalta would have confused and bothered the American people. Stalin's promises on a democratic East Europe seemed fair enough.

Could things have gone differently at Yalta? Only if the United States and Britain had invaded Europe earlier than 1944. If they had taken the chance and invaded France in 1943, they likely would have been able to take large areas of East Europe. (The British and Americans did invade Italy in 1943 but made only slow progress working their way up that mountainous peninsula. Some historians regard the whole Italian campaign as a mistake; others say it was an important gesture to show the Soviets, who had been demanding a second front in the west since 1941, that we were still in the war. Otherwise, some feared, Stalin might have sought a separate peace with Hitler.) Actually, the western area of Czechoslovakia, including Pilsen, was liberated by General George S. Patton's army, but it was turned over to the Soviets as per the Yalta agreement. If the British and Americans had taken an extremely high-risk strategy and invaded the Balkans, they might have been able to liberate most of East Europe. Of course, they might also have gotten bogged down in the Balkans, as they did in Italy.

Another possibility, suggested by famed diplomat-historian George F. Kennan among others, was to have cut off U.S. war supplies to Russia as soon as the Soviet army had liberated its own territory. This would have occurred around August 1944, and such an action could have enabled U.S. and British forces to reach East Europe first. U.S. help to the Soviets was a major factor during the war; many of the trucks hauling fuel for Soviet tanks were American made. Continuing U.S. aid helped the Soviets take over East Europe. But in August 1944, the German army still had plenty of fight left. To have encouraged the Soviets to drop out of the war at that point would have permitted the redeployment westward of the bulk of the German army. Remember, most of World War II in Europe was fought on the eastern front; some 90 percent of the German forces were deployed there. In World War I we called the Bolsheviks traitors and agents of the Germans when they withdrew Russia from the war. Would we have wanted them to withdraw at a similar stage in World War II?

General Dwight D. Eisenhower, supreme commander of the Western Allied forces, did not relish the thought of fighting all the way through Germany to Berlin. He shuddered to think of the American casualties. If Eisenhower had been willing to expend more American lives, Western forces would have liberated most of Germany and the western part of Czechoslovakia ahead of the Soviets. Stalin and his generals shared no such compunctions over sacrificing their young men in order to seize territory and put themselves in a strong postwar position. Remember, the Soviets lost some 20 million citizens during the war. The U.S. lost half a million in both Europe and the Pacific. In short, in 1945 the Soviets were in East Europe, with guns. We weren't, and that made all the difference.

How did Yalta work out in the long sweep of history? Ironically, in 1989 and 1990, Yalta began to be implemented the way Roosevelt envisioned it. The unpopular Communist governments were chucked out, the Soviet troops began to depart, and the Warsaw Pact became a dead letter. East Europe opened to the West. The borders agreed to at Yalta remained. Germany, which was never to have been divided, was reunited. After a 45-year delay, the correct interpretation of Yalta was finally put into practice.

SUGGESTED READINGS

BORSODY, STEPHEN. *The Tragedy of Central Europe: The Nazi and Soviet Conquest of Central Europe.* New York: Collier Books, 1960.

BURKS, R. V. *The Dynamics of Communism in Eastern Europe.* Princeton, NJ: Princeton University Press, 1961.

MACLEAN, FITZROY. *Josip Broz Tito: A Pictorial Biography.* New York: McGraw-Hill, 1980.

ROTHSCHILD, JOSEPH. *Return to Diversity: A Political History of East Central Europe Since World War II.* New York: Oxford University Press, 1989.

CHAPTER FOUR _____

The Communist Takeovers

World War II in East Europe closed with the major shift westward of the Soviet frontiers, in some areas by as much as 200 miles. As well as adding territory to the Soviet Union, the shift changed the geopolitics of East Europe, giving the Soviets direct land access to more countries. Before the war, the Soviet Union on its west bordered only Poland and Romania. Poland and Romania bordered each other at that time, sealing off Czechoslovakia and Hungary from Soviet territory. The Soviet Union even had no border with Lithuania, as Polish territory actually abutted Latvia, effectively insulating Lithuania from Russia.

With the pushing back of Polish and Romanian borders after the war, the Soviet Union gained direct access to Czechoslovakia and Hungary as well as

Stalin Expands the Western Ukraine

Poland and Romania. The Soviet takeover in 1945 of Ruthenia or the Carpatho-Ukraine gave Stalin a Ukrainian salient that extended toward the middle of Europe. Ostensibly, the new government in Prague voluntarily gave Ruthenia to the Soviet Union in 1945. Ruthenia, although it had a Ukrainian-speaking majority, had never belonged to the Russian empire. It had belonged to old Hungary and later to interwar Czechoslovakia. The official Soviet explanation was that the Ukrainians demanded to be united into one country. More likely, Stalin had geopolitical reasons for the annexation. First, it gave him direct access to Hungary. Second, to have left sizable numbers of Ukrainians outside of Soviet control but now directly adjoining Soviet territory could have been a source of infectious ideas about freedom and independence for the long-discontented Ukrainians within the Soviet Union. The border change in this region meant that during the long Cold War period unrest in any four of these East European lands could be crushed by Soviet troops, who did not have to transit any third countries to reach their destinations. A change in borders greatly facilitated Stalin's hold over East Europe.

A series of bilateral treaties between the Soviet Union and each East European state further cemented the region into the Soviet orbit. Under the standard but misleading title of a "treaty of friendship and mutual assistance," these treaties were actually defensive alliances that prohibited the East European country from allying with a Western power. The treaties mentioned Germany by name as a dangerous revanchist (out for revenge) power they must unite against. This is the one area where the genuine national interests of Poland and Czechoslovakia coincide with those of the Soviet Union: rejection of and defense against any German claims to the Oder-Neisse territories, East Prussia, or the Sudetenland. To this day, Warsaw and Prague do not mind this clause in their treaties with Moscow. The treaties also mentioned economic cooperation, thus forming the basis for the Council on Mutual Economic Assistance (Comecon).

SALAMI TACTICS

In general, the Communists did not immediately take over the governments of the newly liberated East European countries. Where they did, in Yugoslavia and Albania, it was because local Communist partisans had fought their way to power against both the German occupiers and local non-Communist forces. Tito saw no reason to wait in communizing Yugoslavia, a point that irritated Stalin and contributed to the later Tito-Stalin split.

In the other countries, Stalin ordered his Communist puppets, most of whom had sat out the war in Moscow, to take over their countries gradually, one slice at a time. Hungarian Communist boss Matyas Rakosi referred to this as "salami tactics." The idea was, first, to not alarm the West, especially the United States. Roosevelt made the tactical mistake of telling Stalin at Yalta (see Chapter 3) that he expected all U.S. forces to be withdrawn from Europe within two years of the war's end. With this bit of information, Stalin knew all he had to do to avoid difficulty with the Americans was to wait two years, until they were gone, before clamping down with full-fledged Communist dictatorships.

Second, a full-fledged and immediate takeover could provoke violent opposition by non-Communist resistance fighters, many of whom distrusted the Communists and had kept their arms. Best to lull them into accepting the mixed regimes, then disarm and isolate them, and finally institute the Stalinist system. Uprisings in East Europe could attract American attention and support, so best to take over slowly and cleverly to head off uprisings. The idea was to make things look confused and chaotic, to blame non-Communist leaders as obstreperous personalities who were standing in the way of national unity and progress for the sake of personal power. The Communists could then claim to be "saving" the country from disunity and reactionary forces. It might be difficult to blame any given incident on the Communists, but when one stood back and looked at the whole process, one saw the unmistakable Communist strategy for seizing power. Unfortunately, for some this recognition came too late.

Could anti-Communists really have done anything about it? Alas, no. Protest, especially armed protest, would simply have been crushed by the local Communist police and army. If supplementary force was needed, the Soviet forces were now never far away. Bloody struggle, with no hope of winning, might have alerted the world a little sooner as to what was happening in East Europe after the war. But by taking over with salami tactics, the Communists were able to lull some people, in both East and West Europe, into accepting the Communist regimes as legitimate and permanent.

We might compare the Communist takeovers with the earlier Nazi takeovers. Both erected essentially fake regimes, but the Germans were much more blunt and direct; they arrested and murdered thousands, in some countries millions of people. They immediately installed either Nazi officials or pliant local quislings into power. The Communists were willing, for appearance's sake, to take a year or two to do the job. They were a bit more clever and subtle than the Nazis; in most countries they arrested only thousands and executed only hundreds. (The bloody exception to this rule was in Bulgaria.) Their victims were mostly leaders who opposed them; they counted on intimidation to cow others into silence. In the long run, of course, it did the Communists little good. The regimes they erected with little popular support could not stand once the Soviet prop was pulled out.

Typically, the first governments immediately after liberation were mixed cabinets containing representatives of all or most prewar parties who had not been tainted with fascism or collaboration with the German occupiers. In almost every East European country, the biggest party was the peasants' party (peasants were called "smallholders" in Hungary). The first stage of the Communist takeovers resembled the old prewar Communist policy of establishing coalitions or "popular fronts" out of all the anti-fascist parties. The presidents and prime ministers were not Communists but generally leaders of revived peasant, liberal, or socialist parties. The press was reasonably free, and most parties were permitted to organize and recruit. It looked like a pretty decent setup, one not too different from many West European countries.

But it was intended as a temporary stage. The Communists always arranged to get themselves or stand-ins named to lead the interior and defense ministries. In the United States, "interior" suggests redwoods and buffalos, but in Europe the interior minister runs the national police. With Communists appointing all the leading personnel of the police and army, soon all means of coercion were in Communist hands. This "mixed stage" lasted from several months to a year or so, depending on the country.

Another important advantage the Communists took in these mixed governments was control of land reform. In some countries this consisted of merely confiscating the great estates of nobles and prewar millionaires and distributing these estates to peasants, thus gaining peasant gratitude and their dependency upon the Communists. This gave the Communists votes and support they would not have otherwise had.

In Poland and Czechoslovakia, though, there was an additional and major element: the lands and dwellings of millions of Germans who fled or who were expelled as World War II ended. Some 7 million Germans were pushed out of the Oder-Neisse territories taken over by Poland, and some 2 million Germans fled the Sudetenland, the area Hitler had gained at Munich in 1938, now returned to Czechoslovakia. This was a rich bounty for Communist officials to distribute, and they used it to insure reliability, like a big-city politician uses patronage jobs. Poles from the eastern territories taken over by the Soviet Union and landless peasants from the crowded central area of Poland were awarded productive farms, houses, and apartments recently vacated by Germans. The people who received these bounties were naturally grateful and a bit worried that their original owners might some day demand them back. Accordingly, the recipients tended to support the Communists who had bestowed these gifts upon them and who were the best protection for keeping them.

The next stage consisted of the gradual tightening of Communist control, slowly enough so that many people were not completely aware of what was going on. Non-Communist parties had trouble organizing and holding meetings, which were sometimes broken up by Communist toughs. The police took no interest in these disturbances. Non-Communist newspapers had difficulty getting published and distributed; shortages of newsprint and trucks hit non-Communist newspapers. Non-Communist leaders, including ministers and prime ministers, who saw the jaws closing and tried to raise alarms, were depicted as reactionaries or imperialist spies and forced to resign. Some died under suspicious circumstances.

Non-Communist parties that grew wary of the Communists found themselves split. One or two leaders, possibly planted earlier by the Communists, would break away and set up a "new" peasant or socialist party, which would then repudiate the parent party as inflexible and mistaken. The new party, essentially a fake, attempted to attract adherents away from the original party. The fake party would

Stalinism

The word "Stalinist" connotes an especially rigid, centralized, cynical, and brutal type of Communist ruling style. Stalin ruled the Soviet Union with a heavy hand from 1927 to 1953, creating the Soviet system that endured until Gorbachev began to significantly alter it in the late 1980s. Stalin also demanded and got strict compliance with his policies from Communists all around the world. They rationalized as follows: Stalin is the leader of the Soviet Union, the world's first socialist country and the path to the future, so by supporting Stalin we are supporting the homeland of socialism and assisting the liberation of humanity from capitalism, imperialism, and fascism. Even if Stalin were a little on the gruff side, he was working for socialism, and that's what ultimately counted, Communists figured. Among the party faithful of the 1930s through 1950s, such attitudes became an almost religious fixation that members refused to question. A word against Stalin was aid to the enemies of socialism. Even after Stalin's crimes and bloodthirsty nature had been abundantly documented, some refused to believe it. Stalinism included the following elements:

1. **Worship of Stalin.** In all Stalinist systems a personality cult was built around the Soviet dictator. Statues of Stalin were built throughout East Europe, as they had been in the Soviet Union. (Now rapidly vanishing, destroyed or melted down, they have become valuable for their rarity.) Boulevards, parks, and factories were named after Stalin. His every public word was elaborately quoted in the media. Policies were justified with Stalin's rhetoric. The heads of satellite states identified themselves with Stalin and copied his political style.

2. **Obedience.** In carrying out policies—economic, political, foreign—individuals were expected to obey. Discussion was held to a minimum and focused only on how to implement the policy, not on overall strategy or goals. Those who opposed or even openly doubted Stalin's wisdom were defined as enemies and dealt with accordingly. Said Stalin of one such doubter: "We will shorten him by a head."

3. **Manipulation.** In Stalinist thinking, politics existed to be manipulated. Public opinion had no life of its own but was to be massaged into shape by lies, provocations, and primitive fright campaigns. Said Stalin on the subject of lies: "The paper will support whatever is written on it." By clever propaganda, Stalinists thought they could manipulate the masses to follow the Communist line. Unpopular, illegitimate regimes could be set up against the will of their citizens, who would soon be brainwashed into supporting them. This type of thinking, of course, is short-sighted. The regimes thus created come tumbling down when their coercive props are removed. Lies achieve only temporary results; eventually the truth comes out.

4. **Centralization of the economy.** Only the smallest of economic activities (e.g., freelance shoe repair) were left out of state control.

Everything else was controlled by a central planning agency, which emphasized heavy industry at the expense of consumer goods. In most countries, farming was collectivized (not in Poland). Production and trade were tied heavily to Soviet needs.

5. **Strict control of the arts and media.** Movies, music, painting, literature, the theater, and so on, were supervised by party hacks to make sure they cranked out the correct messages. Classical materials were left generally untouched, and many educated people sought refuge in them. The themes of new material had to be wholesome, upbeat, heroic, pro-Communist, and easily understandable. Western art was denounced as "bourgeois formalism," and was depicted as a cesspool that reflected the decline of capitalism.

6. **Scrutiny of individuals.** The security forces, usually under the interior ministry, kept tabs on anyone who dissented, had contacts with foreigners, or who traveled abroad. Part-time informers could be in any organization, so people learned to watch what they said. Jail terms were frequent.

"Stalinist" in nonruling Communist parties, as that of France, indicated faithful support for whatever Moscow was doing at that moment. Everything the Soviet Union did was good, from the purges to farm collectivization. When Stalin said unite against fascism, they cheered the Popular Front. When Stalin said stop denouncing fascism, they came up with rationalizations for the Hitler-Stalin Non-Aggression pact.

Stalinist systems outlived Stalin, who died in 1953. How and when Communist countries de-stalinized forms an important part of the story of East Europe. Romania under Ceausescu was essentially a Stalinist system. Albania still is, although it has shown signs of loosening up recently. North Korea, where children worship giant statues of Kim Il Sung, may be the last surviving Stalinist system. "Stalinist" at one point was considered synonymous with Communist. Is it? Or are the two logically separable? Can you have a non-Stalinist Communist system? Or is Stalinism the natural culmination of the system and tendencies Lenin initiated?

enter into the governing coalition and thus enable the Communists to say, "What do you mean, the Peasant party has withdrawn from the coalition? One branch, led by Western capitalist agents, has withdrawn. But the other branch, led by far-sighted progressives, has joined us." This tactic fooled some people for a while.

Virtually all of the Communist parties of East Europe had been small. To boost their apparent numerical strength, socialist or social-democratic parties, which had historically usually been larger, were pressured (or even forced) to merge with the Communist parties. The resulting parties—the United Workers party in Poland, the Socialist Unity party in East Germany—could then claim to speak for the majority of the toiling masses, the true voice of the people, and so on. It didn't fool many.

In the third and final stage the mask slipped away to reveal Stalinist rule. Non-

Communists were dismissed from the cabinets, and only fake non-Communist parties were permitted to exist, usually as members of a united front totally dominated by Communists. Opposition views, both spoken and printed, vanished. All leading positions, in industry, agriculture, education, and so on, were staffed with Communists. Travel and contact with the West were severely circumscribed. The countries of East Europe introduced new constitutions, each modeled on the Soviet Union's 1936 constitution, dubbed the "Stalin constitution." Along with the new constitution, the East European country usually changed its name to "People's Republic of..." or a variation thereof. (See the box in Chapter 3 on "people's democracy.") The Stalin economic model was then put into place.

THE POSTWAR TAKEOVERS

Poland

Stalin used the London Poles' 1943 outcry over the massacre at Katyn as an excuse to break relations with them. Their leader, Gen. Wladyslaw Sikorski, was killed in a plane crash in 1943. His successor, Stanislaw Mikolajczyk (pronounced "me-ko-lye-chick"), head of the important Peasant party, found himself under British pressure to cooperate with the Soviets. After Stalin set up the Polish Committee of National Liberation in newly liberated Lublin (the so-called "Lublin Poles") in 1944, Mikolajczyk joined it. The Warsaw government of 1945 consisted of the Lublin Poles, who were Communist puppets, plus some non-Communists who had been invited in. Seizure of the former German Oder-Neisse territories took place under this government and was quite popular among all Poles, who felt they were entitled to compensation for the German devastation of their country. Resettlement was generally in Communist hands, though, and enabled them to build some Communist sympathies among the recipients of land and houses.

The shift of Polish territory from east to west turned postwar Poland into one of the most ethnically homogeneous countries of Europe. Before the war, the eastern part of Poland contained many Belorussians and Ukrainians; now these lands were Soviet. Poland's three-million strong Jewish community had been largely wiped out by the Nazis; most of the surviving Jews emigrated. The result was a Poland where over 95 percent of the citizens spoke Polish and were Catholic.

Slowly, the Communist noose tightened around Mikolajczyk. His Peasant party was increasingly harassed, even terrorized, and he was accused of being a British agent (he had spent the war in London). The Lublin committee organized a fake Peasant party in competition with Mikolajczyk's. The Communists and their helpers arranged for rigged elections in early 1947, with each party assigned a fixed number of seats beforehand. Had the elections been free, Mikolajczyk and his Peasant party would likely have won, for by then there were no other non-Communist alternatives. In the January 1947 elections, the Communists and their puppets "won" 382 out of the 444 seats of the *Sejm* (pronounced "same"), Poland's parliament. The Peasant party took only 28 seats. The packed Sejm then elected veteran Communist Boleslaw Bierut (who even had Soviet citizenship) president. At that point, it may be fairly said that Poland was officially Communist; it had entered the third stage discussed previously. Seeing no hope for democracy, Mikolajczyk fled to the West in October 1947.

East Germany

At this point East Germany becomes relevant to our study, for during the long Cold War it served as the keystone or plug that locked in much of the rest of the East bloc. When East Germany collapsed in 1989, it was impossible to hold the East bloc together; Gorbachev didn't even try. Starting with Soviet occupation in 1945, East Germany began to take shape as a different country, one very similar in structure to its eastern neighbors. The Soviets did hesitate, however, before setting up a separate East German state.

The Soviet Occupation Zone assigned by Yalta was initially treated like the conquered country it was. The Soviets, who had lost more than 20 million in the German invasion, were vindictive toward Germany. Uppermost in their minds were economic reparations, not setting up an East German Communist state. The Russians immediately began dismantling whole factories in their zone and shipping them home to the Soviet Union. But as in other East European lands, the Soviets also set up a Communist structure. In April 1945, in the wake of Red Army advances into Germany, the "Ulbricht Group" (see Chapter 3) was flown into Soviet-occupied Germany and began setting up a civil administration and reviving remnants of the old German Communist party. At one point (1932) the German Communists had won 13 percent of the German vote, but it had always lagged behind the Social Democrats. In April 1946, Ulbricht persuaded or forced the Social Democrats to merge with the Communists to produce the Socialist Unity party, a Communist party in all but name. By this point or shortly after, we may speak of a Communist regime in East Germany.

But the area was still the Soviet Zone, not a separate country. That came formally only in the fall of 1949. As discussed more fully later in this chapter (see "The Cold War"), conflict between the Soviets and the Western Allies over the fate of East Europe and the treatment of occupied Germany led to the Berlin Blockade and Airlift in 1948-1949. By this time, there were political figures in both Eastern and Western zones working for statehood under, respectively, Soviet and American sponsorship. In the West, Konrad Adenauer urged the founding of the Federal Republic of Germany and achieved it in September 1949. This pushed Stalin to give Walter Ulbricht, just a month later, what he had been wanting, the German Democratic Republic. East Germany was very much a child of the Cold War and did not long outlast the Cold War.

Czechoslovakia

With the only democratic tradition in East Europe that had been carried over from the interwar period, Czechoslovakia held out the longest against a complete Communist takeover. Perhaps the Communists waited in Czechoslovakia because they thought they had a good chance to take over legally and electorally. Many Czechs, including President-in-exile Benes in London, distrusted the Western powers for selling them out at Munich in 1938; they looked with hope to the Soviet Union, the Slavic big brother who liberated them from the Nazis. Czechoslovak Communists built on this feeling. They also gained votes from Czechs who received appropriated German property. In combination with fellow-traveling Social Democrats, the Communists received 38 percent of the vote in reasonably free elections in 1946. That was by far the highest Communist vote they obtained fairly anywhere in East Europe, and that was under the unusual circumstances of postwar uncertainty.

As in Poland, the Communists organized a new government in the eastern part of the country that had been liberated first by the Soviet army, in this case in Kosice. It was a National Front of several parties and was joined by Czechoslovakia's prewar leaders, including Benes. It soon moved to Prague.

Benes was chosen president and, in recognition of Communist strength, he named Communist chief Klement Gottwald prime minister. In turn, Gottwald

---

Masaryk: Murder or Suicide?

Jan Masaryk was the son of Tomas Masaryk, the famed founding president of Czechoslovakia after World War I. Jan Masaryk served as foreign minister of Czechoslovakia after World War II. Like his father, Jan was a devoted democrat and patriot. He saw the Communists taking over power and opposed it. By 1947, all the other East European countries had become openly Communist. Only Czechoslovakia held out, but with a mixed government which the Communists increasingly dominated.

On March 10, 1948, the body of Jan Masaryk was found in the courtyard of the foreign ministry atop Prague's Charles Hill. He had apparently died of a fall from a high window. Or was he thrown out? The official story was suicide, but many believe Masaryk, a hindrance to complete Communist takeover, was taken care of by the Communist-controlled security forces.

"Defenestration" (from the Latin *fenestra*, meaning "window"), the pitching of someone from a window, plays a prominent role in Czech history. The spark that started the Thirty Years War was the Protestant defenestration of Habsburg representatives in Prague in 1618. Masaryk's suspicious death shocked the world and marked the final clanging shut of the Iron Curtain around East Europe.

picked a cabinet with ministers from several parties, with the really important posts going to Communists. Local committees, dominated by Communists, accused opponents of collaboration with the Germans, a charge that was often unfair. The interior ministry, increasingly packed with Communists, announced an alleged conspiracy in Slovakia and arrested many members of the Slovak Democratic party. Most non-Communists in the cabinet, sensing the rigged nature of the police, resigned in February 1948, hoping to topple the government. Instead, the Communists mobilized their police and unions to stage mass demonstrations to make it look like "the people" were supporting Gottwald. The new cabinet was almost completely Communist except for Foreign Minister Jan Masaryk. And he did not last long (see box). What was called the "Prague Coup" of 1948 marked the formal and complete Communist takeover of Czechoslovakia, democracy's last holdout in East Europe.

Hungary

Unlike Poland and Czechoslovakia, Hungary had a fascistic government and was an ally of Germany. There was no government in exile in London. This fact actually made things easier for the Soviets, as the provisional government set up at the end of 1944 under Soviet sponsorship in liberated Debrecen in the eastern part of the country faced no competition. The Soviet army fought its way across Hungary; Budapest was beseiged for seven weeks at the beginning of 1945.

In late 1945 the Soviet occupiers permitted a free election. The results were so disappointing to the Communists—who, with some fellow-travelers, won only 17 percent of the vote—that they never permitted another free election. The prewar Smallholders party was revived to win 57 percent of the votes and a majority of parliamentary seats. Their leader, Ferenc Nagy (pronounced "nadj") became prime minister. The Soviet occupiers, though, would not let the Smallholders fully staff the ministries; key offices, as usual, went to Communists. When the Smallholders complained of the growing Communist takeover, the Communists arrested them as "conspirators" and accused them of being former fascist collaborators. The Peasant party's charismatic second in command, Bela Kovacs, was accused, arrested by the Soviet army, and never seen again.

Under Communist control, new elections were held in 1947. The Peasant party had been broken by arrests, and the electoral franchise had eliminated all persons judged suspicious by the Communists. The Communists still won only 22 percent of the vote, and that was with multiple balloting by Communist toughs. By now Communist domination, in fact if not in name, was nearly complete. Nagy, still prime minister, called for Western help, but there was nothing the West could do. Like another peasant-based party leader, Mikolajczyk in Poland, Nagy fled abroad in 1947. Power was in the hands of Vice-Prime Minister Rakosi, an obedient Stalin puppet who had spent the war in Moscow. In 1948 the Communists, having purged the Social Democratic party of anti-Communists, merged the rump of the Social

Democrats with the Communists to produce the Hungarian Workers party, really just another name for the Communist party.

Yugoslavia

By the end of the war, the Communist-led Partisans of Marshal Tito had liberated roughly half of Yugoslavia. The Soviet army swept the Germans out of the northern portion of the country. The only national political force left was the Partisans, and they saw no need for a gradual takeover. They had fought heroically, taken many casualties, and were impatient to install a Communist system. Prewar politicians, returning from exile or from internal anonymity, were given a few offices but quickly dismissed and sometimes tried as "British agents." The Chetnik leader Mihailovic was hunted down, tried, and shot for allegedly cooperating with the Germans. Democratic newspapers were suppressed after one or two editions.

A People's Front, totally Communist controlled, "won" elections in late 1945 with an alleged 96 percent of the vote. There were no opposition candidates. Industries were quickly expropriated and farms collectivized on the best Soviet model. The 1946 Yugoslav constitution was nearly an exact copy of the 1936 Soviet constitution. The official name of the country was now the Federal People's Republic of Yugoslavia. Tito was president and all ministries were staffed with Communist Partisan veterans.

This was a problem, for the Partisan forces had been composed almost entirely of peasants, people who hated the Germans for the simple reason that the Germans had killed their relatives and razed their villages. The *Partizani* were sturdy and brave mountain fighters, but few were educated and none had experience in governing a country. They mistrusted city people and intellectuals, most of whom had simply stayed in Belgrade or Zagreb and waited out the war. Close to Tito, only Milovan Djilas had attended university. This gave a clumsy, rough-hewn quality to the Communist takeover, which was more brusque and brutal than elsewhere in East Europe.

Stalin did not like the way or the speed of the Yugoslav Communist takeover, even though the Yugoslav leaders aped him with almost embarrassing exactness. Stalin did not want a showdown with the Americans or British, for the Soviet Union was exhausted from the war. Especially difficult for Stalin was Yugoslavia's claim to Trieste, formerly an Austro-Hungarian seaport on the Adriatic, taken after World War I by Italy. Most of Trieste's inhabitants spoke Italian, but most of the surrounding villagers were Slovenians. At the end of World War II, Yugoslav Partisans battled the Germans for Trieste just before the British arrived to claim it. Tension was high. The Yugoslavs swore *"Trst je nas!"* ("Trieste is ours") and demanded Soviet support for their position. An armed conflict with the Western powers over Trieste was the last thing Stalin wanted at that time, and he demurred, urging Tito to take it easy. (Trieste later went to Italy, the surrounding countryside to Yugoslavia.)　The Yugoslavs were quickly becoming a pain to Stalin, who preferred obedience and control.

Romania

Romania, like Hungary, was an ally of Hitler during the war but contributed far more troops to the Russian front than did the Hungarians. The military government of General Ion Antonescu, in league with the fascist Iron Guard, had a major grudge against the Soviets, namely Stalin's seizure of Bessarabia in 1940. In August 1944, as Soviet troops started moving into Romania, the hitherto silent King Michael (who had taken over when his father, Carol, abdicated in 1940) announced that Romania was changing sides and supporting the Allies.

This gesture did little to appease the Soviets, as they followed the general pattern described previously. After a brief period with pro-Soviet Romanian generals as prime ministers, Moscow ordered King Michael to appoint Communist Petru Groza to the office in March 1945 as head of a National Democratic Front composed of several parties but dominated by the Communists.

Elections in late 1946 were rigged. Anti-Communists and other "unreliable" persons were not registered, and the balloting was carried out in a climate of intimidation that gave the bulk of the vote to the National Democratic Front. As elsewhere in East Europe, the large National Peasant party, led by the popular Iuliu Maniu, was harassed and its leaders arrested, including Maniu, on trumped-up charges. A Communist-dominated "Ploughmen's Front" was offered as an alternative to the Peasant party. In late 1947, the mask came off. The Social Democratic party was forced to merge with the Communists. King Michael was ordered to abdicate (he went into exile in Switzerland), and the monarchy was replaced by a Romanian People's Republic.

Bulgaria

Bulgaria, too, was a member of the Axis, but unlike Romania sent no troops to fight in Russia. That would have provoked mass unrest among the russophile Bulgarians, who harkened back to the Russia that liberated them from the Turks. Unlike Romania, Bulgaria developed an armed resistance movement, Communist-led like Yugoslavia's Partisans, but much smaller, totaling perhaps 30,000 fighters. Earlier than Romania, the wartime Bulgarian government of King Boris decided it did not wish to be on the losing side. Boris visited Hitler in 1943 to explain this and mysteriously died. By mid-1944, however, Sofia announced its neutrality. Moscow nonetheless declared war on Bulgaria in September 1944 and Soviet troops swept in. At this same moment a Fatherland Front, composed of Communists and democratic elements, took over in a coup.

As usual, the key positions in the Fatherland Front government were held by Communists. The guerrilla forces of Todor Zhivkov set up people's tribunals that quickly tried and executed some 2,800 wartime political figures, marking

Bulgaria's as one of the bloodiest takeovers in East Europe. Within the Fatherland Front, the Communists arrested the other elements. A 1946 referendum abolished Bulgaria's monarchy, and the boy king, Simeon, left for Spain. Rigged elections later that year gave the Communists a big majority, and they took over totally.

The leader of the Bulgarian Communists—one of the few Communist parties of East Europe to have an early and substantial following—was Georgi Dimitrov, who had fled to Moscow following the abortive Communist uprising of 1923. There, Dimitrov helped direct the Bulgarian Communist party from afar. In 1933 Dimitrov was arrested and tried in Leipzig, Germany, for the infamous Reichstag fire that Hitler tried to blame on the Communists. Defending himself brilliantly and aided by an international outcry, Dimitrov went free. In 1935, Dimitrov was named head of the Comintern, the Moscow-run worldwide Communist organization.

From Moscow, Dimitrov supervised the Communist takeover of Bulgaria until 1945, then he returned to Bulgaria and became prime minister in 1946. He had the leader of the important Agrarian Union, Nikola Petkov, executed on fake charges despite strong U.S. and British protests. Dimitrov paid no notice to reminders that similar protests had saved him from a Nazi noose in 1933. Dimitrov, a perfect Stalinist, then told another opponent: "In this assembly I many times warned Nikola Petkov's group, but they would not listen. They lost their heads, and their leader lies buried. Reflect on your own actions lest you suffer the same fate..." Dimitrov's warning captures some of the cold evil of Stalinism.

Albania

Like Yugoslav Communists, the Albanian Communists fought their way to power, partly against Italian and, later, German occupiers, but mostly they fought against non-Communist Albanians. As the Germans withdrew in November 1944, the Communist-led National Liberation Movement entered Tirana, took over under their chief Enver Hoxha, and shot their rivals in the pro-Western National Front. Again like the Yugoslavs, the Albanian Communists moved quickly with rigged elections and the proclamation of a people's republic in early 1946.

In this way, by early 1948, all of East Europe had been turned into what were called Soviet "satellites," each closely adapted to the Stalin model. An "iron curtain," in the words of Winston Churchill, had fallen across the middle of Europe. It has lifted only in our day.

THE START OF THE COLD WAR

Needless to say, the brutal Communist takeover of East Europe alarmed the West, and that was the crux of the Cold War. If Stalin had observed the letter and spirit of Yalta, there would have been no Cold War. Stalin's behavior in East Europe immediately raised the question: Is this what he intends to do in West Europe as well?

The Cold War

The Cold War was a long period of armed tension between the United States and the Soviet Union that followed World War II. It never erupted into a direct conflict between the two superpowers, but they fought each other indirectly, by means of arms races, alliances, and proxy wars, as in Korea, Vietnam, and Afghanistan. The probable reason why the Cold War was conducted at arm's length was the possession by both superpowers of nuclear weapons. They feared, with good reason, that if they ever started fighting each other directly, the conflict would soon escalate into a nuclear exchange that would devastate both nations.

The precise start of the Cold War is hard to pinpoint. A few writers claim it started with the 1917 Bolshevik Revolution, which the Western Allies strongly opposed. U.S. troops intervened in Russia and fought Bolshevik forces in 1918-1919, confirming the bad will between Russia and the West. More writers say it began as soon as Stalin's designs on East Europe emerged in 1946. By the spring of 1947, Washington was alarmed over Stalin's takeovers in East Europe and announced policies to counter them in the Truman Doctrine, in the Marshall Plan, and in George Kennan's influential "X" article in *Foreign Affairs.* These three moves, coming within weeks of each other, laid down respectively the U.S. political, economic, and theoretical responses to the Soviet threat. Kennan coined the term "containment," the long-term application of U.S. political and military counterforce wherever and whenever the Soviet Union tried to expand until the Soviet empire either mellowed or broke up. Containment was U.S. policy for 40 years. By 1947 the term "Cold War" was in use. The events of 1948—the Prague coup and the Berlin Blockade—confirmed the Cold War.

It is also difficult to pinpoint when the Cold War ended. Some see the Cuban Missile Crisis of 1962 as its dangerous peak; thereafter it slowly subsided. Others think it ended when Nixon turned to a policy of détente (a relaxation of tensions) with Moscow in the early 1970s. Still others claim it didn't end until Gorbachev threw in the towel in the late 1980s.

It is likely that Stalin and his successors never intended expanding westward into West Europe by military force, but in the atmosphere of heightened fear that characterized the Cold War, a Soviet attack was seen as a real possibility. Starting with Truman, American presidents found it convenient to simplify the problem by portraying it in military terms: Get ready for a Russian attack. There were, to be sure, some indications that a Soviet attack might be possible. Communist guerrillas nearly took over Greece. (The West didn't learn until later that Stalin had actually told the Greek Communists to desist and that they operated largely on their own.) The United States quickly sent most of its troops home from Europe after the war and cut its armed forces and defense budget to low levels in the late 1940s. But Stalin kept large numbers of troops in East Europe. Why? He could not have feared Western attack. (Actually, General Patton had urged precisely that.) Therefore, went the reasoning, Stalin must be contemplating an attack of his own. (We now see that Stalin wanted to make sure that East Europe stayed completely under his control, and massive troop strength guaranteed that.)

Compounding the problem was the American tendency after World War II to make a too-exact analogy between Stalin and Hitler. See how Hitler had gobbled up one country after another? Well, Stalin is doing exactly the same thing, went the highly simplified reasoning. The comparison was poor. Hitler was reckless, hot-tempered, and in a hurry. Stalin was cautious, cold-blooded, and felt he had all the time in the world. According to Marxist-Leninist analysis, capitalism would soon crumble. Why start another war when you will be history's winner without one?

What Stalin had in mind for West Europe seems to have been more subtle than military conquest and satellitization, as he had done in East Europe. After World War II, Stalin ordered the West European Communist parties—the most important by far were the large Communist parties of France and Italy—to practice a double strategy of both open political opposition and underground preparation for armed overthrow. Above ground, the French and Italian Communists attempted to attract adherents with a militant pro-labor line of "power for the workers." They organized France and Italy's largest unions and frequently called them out on strike. In parliament, they opposed tenaciously the moderate governments set up after the war. Underground, though, they collected arms from the anti-German resistance (in which both parties had been prominent) and organized for a possible coup.

It seems likely that Stalin sought a weak, fragmented, and neutral West Europe. Some years later, Stalin likely calculated, after the Soviet Union had recovered its strength, a weakened West Europe would fall into his hands. The local Communist parties should prepare and work for that day but not attempt an armed uprising, which would only provoke the U.S. and British imperialists, a point that always obsessed Stalin.

The West did stem Soviet designs on West Europe, but by a combination of economic, political, and military policies, not by armed strength alone. The determination shown by the Berlin Airlift and by the economic aid from the Marshall Plan was more important in the late 1940s than the few thousand American troops still stationed in West Europe. And one of the key factors in stiffening West European resolve was the Iron Curtain itself and what was happening behind it. Except for some committed Communists, few West Europeans wanted to be under Soviet domination.

It was in this political and economic context that the line between the two systems stiffened and solidified in the center of Europe. In Germany, Stalin didn't quite know what to do with his zone, except to loot it for an estimated $20 billion worth of equipment. The Cold War context forced matters to a head in Germany. As Stalin took over the rest of East Europe, the Western occupiers of

Germany—the United States, Britain, and France—grew more alarmed. They decided to build up rather than tear down their zones of Germany and to turn them into a bulwark against the further spread of Communism. Economic revival was the first step. In 1948, millions of Marshall Plan dollars began to arrive in Germany and the currency was reformed, replacing the worthless reichsmarks (German currency from 1924 to 1948), military script, and American cigarettes (a popular currency) with the new deutsche mark. Every citizen got 60 of the new D-marks, and the West German economic miracle began.

The Soviets objected to the currency reform in the Western zones, as they had been flooding the Western zones with reichsmarks as part of their looting campaign. In retaliation, they blocked ground traffic to West Berlin, which was 110 miles inside their occupation zone, figuring the Western Allies, who were assigned zones of Berlin as part of Yalta, would clear out of Berlin. Instead, the Americans and British answered the Berlin Blockade with the Berlin Airlift. For nearly a year, 1948-1949, West Berlin was supplied with everything—food, coal, even animal fodder—by round-the-clock cargo flights. By now the Cold War was clearly in full swing. Stalin solidified his grip over East Europe, and lines that were envisioned as temporary became permanent—or, as things turned out in 1989-1990, semipermanent.

Could things have gone differently? Could the Cold War have been avoided? There were, theoretically, three possibilities, none of them very probable. First, if Stalin had not seized East Europe there likely would have been no Cold War. World War II ends, Soviet troops return home, and both East and West Europe settle down to economic reconstruction with U.S. aid. But Stalin was determined to retain East Europe. With his East European satraps, trained and organized during the war in Moscow, he had been preparing to take over East Europe for years.

A second unlikely possibility might have been for the United States to take immediate U.S. military measures. World War II ends and Allied forces then lay down the law to Stalin to fulfill Yalta and to leave East Europe alone. In such a case, major U.S. forces stationed in West Europe, plus the U.S. monopoly (until 1949) over the atomic bomb, would have backed up Western resolve to get the Soviets out of East Europe. While intriguing, this scenario was psychologically impossible. The American way of war is a massive but brief outpouring of energy to get the war over with; then the boys come home. American politicians had promised to "bring the boys home by Christmas" of 1945, and few American citizens would have stood for a prolonged occupation of Europe. Eventually, of course, that is precisely what happened. In 1945, however, the United States and Soviet Union were allies. When their troops met on the banks of the Elbe River in Germany, they embraced like brothers. How could we suddenly turn on them? And if there had been fighting to dislodge the Soviets, the battleground would have been precisely the East European countries we were trying to liberate. With nuclear weapons, there would have been little worth liberating.

A third possibility would have been to adopt early and publicly a Churchill-like spheres-of-influence policy and divide Europe. Stalin wants East Europe? He gets it, provided he leaves West Europe alone. We leave East Europe alone. Again, psychologically this would have been difficult. Many Americans are of East European descent and care about their homelands. They could not turn their backs on the Stalinist brutalities; therefore neither could American politicians. As mentioned earlier, Americans tended to read into Stalin's actions those of another Hitler. Ultimately, the United States did quietly accept a kind of spheres-of-influence policy. By the late 1960s, busy in Vietnam, Washington lost interest in East Europe. It didn't seem to matter much any more. The Soviets seemed intent on keeping East Europe forever, and we were not about to go to war over it. The futility of the Cold War led to a de facto recognition of East Europe as a Soviet sphere of influence.

Actually, U.S. policy in East Europe was not bad in the long run. Starting with Kennan in 1947, there was the realization in Washington that eventually the Soviet empire in East Europe would collapse. President Eisenhower especially understood that the Cold War was not to be fought but waited out. The wait was frustrating, but it was better than war, and ultimately we won. Few Americans would have understood or accepted this strategy if you had presented it to them in the early years of the Cold War. Americans like to get their wars over with fast; they lack patience.

So the worst was avoided, but the tragedy in this long wait was that East Europe fell so far behind the West. The original Marshall Plan was offered to all of Europe, even to the Soviet Union. The Marshall Plan required open economies and the sharing of economic data, something Stalin would never permit. Traditionally, the Soviet Union has held its economic data as secretly as its military plans. Stalin ordered his puppets in East Europe to not attend the initial Marshall Plan session. Czechoslovakia had been about to attend. Then came the early 1948 Prague coup, and Czechoslovakia too turned its back on the Marshall Plan. To a very considerable extent, we are now picking up four decades later where we left off when Stalin cut East Europe off from the West. The flow of economic aid and trade that would have modernized East Europe is at last underway, and it will eventually make East Europe a part of the global economy.

SUGGESTED READINGS

BURKS, R. V. *The Dynamics of Communism in Eastern Europe.* Princeton, NJ: Princeton University Press, 1961.

GRAEBNER, NORMAN. "Cold War Origins and the Continuing Debate: A Review of the Literature," *Journal of Conflict Resolution.* 13 (March 1969), 131.

SETON-WATSON, HUGH. *The East European Revolution,* 3rd ed. New York: Praeger, 1956.

TURNOCK, DAVID. *Eastern Europe: An Economic and Political Geography.* New York: Routledge, 1989.

CHAPTER FIVE _____

The Hated Regimes

Probably the worst time in the life of East Europeans was the age of Stalinism between the complete Communist takeovers of the late 1940s and the death of Stalin in 1953. Thousands were arrested, tried, and sentenced to long prison terms, merely because they were suspected of opposing the Communists. In some East European countries, thousands were quietly killed. Only recently have their unmarked mass graves been discovered. Within a few years after the tyrant died, things began to ease, slowly and sporadically, in most of East Europe. While Stalin lived, though, the features of Stalinism, discussed in the previous chapter, were laid on with a trowel in East Europe. The governments of the region liked to call themselves either "people's democracies" or "socialist" states, but they clearly qualified as Communist regimes (see box). The "socialism" in East Europe should in no way be confused with the socialism found in West Europe, where it has mellowed into welfarism.

THE STALINIST MODEL

The Party in Power

Perhaps the defining element in a Communist system is that the Communist party overlaps with and very nearly *is* the government. When the two start to split, with government throwing off Communist-party control and direction, you have the end of a Communist system. In these systems, the most powerful figure is invariably the head of the Communist party, usually bearing the title first secretary or general secretary, but referred to in the West as "party chief." In addition, such figures often take on government jobs, namely the presidency. When they lose one

Communism and Socialism: What's the Difference?

There is much confusion and overlap in meaning between these two terms, some of it fostered by Communist regimes themselves. Many of the countries we used to call "Communist" called themselves "socialist." Most of the Communist parties of East Europe in 1990 renamed themselves socialist, and most probably are socialist now. However, the East European governments that existed from the late 1940s until about 1989 were clearly Communist.

Karl Marx, writing in the second half of the nineteenth century, viewed socialism as merely the beginning stage of communism, and the Communist regimes of East Europe followed Marx's notion. Capitalism, Marx predicted, would suffer a series of economic depressions until the impoverished working class could stand it no longer. The working class would turn revolutionary and eventually overthrow the reckless and abusive capitalist system, replacing it with socialism. Socialism, according to Marx, would abolish both private ownership of the means of production and profit, which he regarded as unjust and historically doomed. Marx was vague about socialism, but he suggested that it would mean state ownership of the means of production, a drastic leveling of social-class differences, and material abundance for all. Eventually, when socialism had reached this happy level, it would turn into communism, a utopian society of material plenty and no government or state coercion. It would be perfection, the end stage of human development. Bear in mind that no Communist government claimed to have achieved communism. They had achieved socialism and were working on communism, according to the theory.

Early in the twentieth century, Lenin made some theoretical changes in Marxism so it might apply to a backward economy like that found in Russia. Marx had envisioned socialism growing were capitalism was most developed, as in Britain and Germany. Lenin's main contribution, however, was his theory of tight organization and of control over the Russian Social Democratic Labor party, which at that time was underground or in exile. Lenin, in fact, was living in Switzerland. The party, which was later renamed the Bolshevik, and then Communist party, was not to be a party like others, Lenin wrote. Instead, professional revolutionaries were to be controlled by a disciplined hierarchical structure that reported back to a Central Committee, which Lenin controlled personally. Lenin added the concept of the party as "organizational weapon" to Marx's economic, social, and historical theories about the inevitable collapse of capitalism. The amalgamation "Marxism-Leninism" is another name for communism.

As used in this book, socialism is the broader concept, and communism is a mistaken off-branch of socialism. Socialists have many viewpoints and only one thing in common: All are strongly democratic. Some (a dwindling number) still advocate state ownership of industry, at least certain industries. A few British Labourites still like the nationalization of some industries. Most socialists, however, having noted the failure of state ownership, seek only a certain amount of governmental regulation and control of the economy to correct distortions and abuse. The French Socialists, for example, backed away from state ownership in the 1980s. The mildest socialists, the social democrats, simply urge welfare programs to put a safety net under the poorest and most vulnerable members of society. The German and Swedish Social Democrats could be called "welfarists." And some honest socialists will tell you they no longer know what "socialism" means.

Communists have been the main militant wing of socialism. (There are other militant wings, such as Trotskyists, but they are tiny minorities.) Communists are undemocratic and elitist by nature; they feel that only they know what's best for society. They do not like other viewpoints because, since they already know the answers, they can't stand being challenged. Communists advocate (or advocated) not only state ownership and central control of the economy along with a gigantic welfare state but also the administration and implementation of this by a disciplined "vanguard" party (i.e., the Communist party) that will lead society to a utopia. Under Communism's Stalinist highpoint, Communists around the world had to obey Moscow and follow every twist and turn in the Kremlin line. The standard U.S. State Department rule of thumb for distinguishing Communist regimes from socialist regimes was that the former regimes obeyed and were controlled by Moscow; the latter were independent. This might have been a useful distinction in the 1940s and 1950s, but by the 1960s even hard-line Communist regimes increasingly carved out some space for themselves and sometimes repudiated Moscow's leadership.

or the other position, it usually means they are on their way out. This happened repeatedly in East Europe in 1989: an old Stalinist would be bumped out as party first secretary but keep the presidency. Usually in a few months, he was out of that job too.

As is usual in European governments, a separate prime minister serves under the president to carry out most of the day-to-day governance. In 1989, prime ministers often changed while presidents, usually hard-liners, did not. The prime minister in turn picks a cabinet composed of ministers, who run each branch of government and the economy. All ministers are high-ranking Communist-party members. Some East European systems—Poland, East Germany, Czechoslovakia, and Bulgaria—permitted fake little parties under Communist leadership to have a few seats in parliament, but everyone knew they obeyed the Communists. The Communists never won a free election in East Europe. In coming to and staying in power, they depended heavily on the following institutions.

Warsaw Pact

The Soviets totally dominated the armed forces of their satellite countries through a series of bilateral "friendship and mutual assistance" treaties. Promotions at the higher ranks were reviewed by Moscow, and most generals had been trained, in whole or in part, in the Soviet Union. Until 1956, Poland's defense minister was actually a Russian general, and Soviet officers were laced through the Polish army. Arms and equipment were standardized on Soviet models; tanks and aircraft (rarely the latest models) were purchased from the Soviet Union. In short, East European armies were carefully tied to the Soviet army.

In May 1955, to firm up this arrangement, all the Soviet satellites of East Europe met in Warsaw to set up the eastern equivalent of the North Atlantic Treaty Organization (which had been in existence since 1949). The Warsaw Treaty of Friendship, Cooperation, and Mutual Assistance soon became known as the Warsaw Pact. Like NATO, it attempted to better integrate command and control. It also provided legal grounds for keeping Soviet forces stationed throughout the East bloc or for having Soviet troops enter member countries to conduct "joint maneuvers," which might include the crushing of a breakaway regime, as in Hungary in 1956 and Czechoslovakia in 1968.

The armed forces of East European countries were always a problem for Moscow. They knew they needed allied armies in their struggle with the West. Besides, it wouldn't look right if the Soviets kept their satellites disarmed; that would make the Soviet army look like an occupation force, which is pretty much what it was. On the other hand, arming their satellites too well could mean that someday these weapons could be used against the Soviets. Propaganda notwithstanding, Kremlin leaders knew the Soviet Union was not well liked in East Europe. Trying to strike a balance, Moscow encouraged a modest level of preparedness in East Europe but reserved most powerful and modern weapons for itself.

Ostensibly, Soviet forces were in East Europe to dissuade the imperialist West, especially revanchist West Germany, from invading. In reality, it was to make sure the East European lands stayed firmly in the Soviet camp. The northern tier of East European countries had Soviet troops garrisoned permanently on their soil. The biggest contingent by far was in East Germany—some 22 Soviet armored divisions totaling more than half a million soldiers. Poland, Czechoslovakia, and Hungary had fewer Soviet troops. Soviet forces were kept out of sight, in inconspicuous barracks in the countryside, which the Soviet troops were seldom allowed to leave. Soviet officers, aware of the problems that could grow from the combination of soldiers, alcohol, women, and defection, kept their troops under tight control, which included giving them no local currency. The Balkan lands of Yugoslavia, Albania, Romania, and Bulgaria, since at least the 1960s, have had no Soviet troops on their soil. Yugoslavia and later Albania had gone their own way. Albania dropped out of the Warsaw Pact in 1961, costing the Soviet navy important submarine pens on the Mediterranean, which they could no longer use. Romania exhibited a spiky sense of independence and would not allow Soviet forces on its soil, although it did continue as a Warsaw Pact member. And Bulgaria, a loyal Soviet satellite, didn't need any Soviet forces to ensure its loyalty.

Security Services

The first instrument Stalin's agents in East Europe perfected, even before the final seizure of full power, were internal security services on the Soviet model. Sometimes wrongly called in the West the "secret police" (probably after their Nazi equivalent, the Gestapo), the security services were actually rather public, with uniforms, headquarters, and a presence everywhere. True, they had secret informers and conducted much of their casework behind closed doors. The security forces were neither army nor regular police but a paramilitary force especially trained to do the party's bidding. In 1989, when the security services either couldn't or wouldn't crush anti-Communist protests, the system was doomed.

The leading officers of the various East European security services were trained under careful Soviet supervision, often in Moscow. Most of the top officers thus spoke Russian. In each national organization, many officers reported to Soviet security officials, sometimes secretly, so that the Soviet security organization interpenetrated the local agency. It is safe to say that the Lubyanka, the Moscow headquarters of the KGB, soon knew whatever the East European daughter agencies had learned.

The Communist argument for their security services, starting with the Bolshevik seizure of power in 1917, went like this: We are besieged by hostile capitalist, imperialist, and reactionary forces who want us dead and our revolution demolished. To give them even one inch, to grant them any right to exist inside our country, means they will spread their infection by whipping up discontented elements. They give us no quarter, and we give them none either. Actually, that rationalization is a fairly accurate picture of the Russian Civil War of 1917-1920. It was kill or be killed, defend the revolution or the reactionaries will win. To this end, Lenin had Feliks Dzerzhinsky, of noble Polish origin, set up the dreaded Cheka (Extraordinary Commission) to root out enemies of the revolution. The square in front of the Lubyanka is known as Dzerzhinskaya. The Cheka went through several name changes; under Stalin it was mostly known as the NKVD (People's Commission for Internal Affairs). For some decades it has been the KGB (Committee on State Security), the most powerful Soviet ministry.

Now, every country has a security service. What was different about those of the Communist countries? In democratic countries, security agencies fight against penetration by foreign spies and gather intelligence abroad. They are concerned about their own citizens only insofar as they may be working as foreign agents.

Granted, sometimes security forces in democratic countries exaggerate dangers and harass people on dubious grounds. In the United States an exaggerated Red Scare brought the Palmer raids of 1918-1920. In West Germany in the 1970s, student radicalism plus the Baader-Meinhoff gang (which was supported by East German agents) brought anti-radical decrees that demanded numerous loyalty checks. Typically, though, only a minute fraction of the effort of security services in democratic countries is directed at their own citizenry, for the vast majority of citizens are loyal.

Stalin's Daughters

	Security Service	Party Newspaper
Soviet Union	KGB	Pravda
Poland	UB	Trybuna Ludu
Czechoslovakia	SNB	Rude Pravo
East Germany	Stasi	Neues Deutschland
Hungary	AVH	Népszabadság
Yugoslavia	UDBa	Politika
Romania	Securitate	Scinteia
Bulgaria	DS	Rabotnichesko Delo
Albania	Sigurimi	Zeri i Popullit

In Communist countries, the situation is nearly reversed, with most of the security agencies' attention focused on their own citizens. The agencies suspect (with good reason) that many citizens oppose the Communist regimes, and that foreign contact may indicate espionage or antiregime propaganda activities. The problem, at root, is one of legitimacy. Where legitimacy is high, that is, where most people accept the government as rightful and where most people are generally loyal, as in most Western countries, security services need concern themselves very little with citizen behavior. Where legitimacy is low, where citizens have little respect for the regime, the security services must mount a gigantic effort to oversee vast numbers of citizens. In other words, Communist countries have large, intrusive, and sometimes brutal security services because they need them; their citizens really are disloyal.

Communist security forces, though, make matters worse. Just knowing you are being watched makes people irritable and jumpy. A citizen who has been interviewed for merely exchanging letters with an American relative resents the security forces and the government they represent. A young person who has been denied university admission because of an alleged reactionary family background may turn into a real reactionary. A weekend mountain climber who has trouble getting a passport to climb peaks in another country feels trapped and limited. And of course, anyone who has had a relative killed or imprisoned by security forces will never forget it. Even after the worst excesses of Communist security services subsided after Stalin, they left a bitter taste among people with long memories.

Information Monopoly

As the Communist regimes consolidated their hold over East Europe, they made every effort to choke off alternate sources of information. Communist thinking ran: If we can structure their information world, we can control them. Free media accompanied and hastened the demise of Communist regimes in East Europe in 1989. For party believers as well as the many opportunists, who watched out for the success of their careers, following affairs from the party perspective in the leading party daily could aid in carrying out one's duties and in getting promoted. Each East European country had a party daily newspaper that carried major speeches, policy shifts, and ideological discussions. Distributed nationwide, these party dailies (see earlier box) insured prompt and uniform fidelity to the party line among those who cared, generally only a small percentage of the population.

At a more popular level, daily newspapers for each city and region restrained the amount of policy discussion in favor of sports and local coverage. Still under party control, stories were slanted to emphasize progress, well-being, and national achievements; the tone was up-beat and positive, like the nationwide party daily, but simpler and more eye-catching. Stories reporting on the West emphasized crime, unemployment, poverty, urban blight, and nuclear weapons. There was nothing neutral or objective about Communist news coverage.

The controlled media never worked very well, as many citizens systematically disdained what they read in the press or heard on the radio. Catholic churches, especially in Poland, cautiously offered alternate views from the pulpit, in church-related organizations, and in church-sponsored publications. Further, after a while many developed access to Western news reports, chiefly through radio broadcasts transmitted by Radio Free Europe, Voice of America, Deutsche Welle, or the BBC. Most European radio sets, in both the East and the West, come with a short-wave band, and this proved to be a weak spot in the Communists' information monopoly.

Radio Free Europe (RFE) was set up in Munich, Germany, at first covertly, by the U.S. Central Intelligence Agency to break the Communist party's monopoly on information in East European countries. By means of close readings of the local press, interviews with travelers, and careful analysis, RFE often came up with solid news stories that the local Communist media had tried to bury. By broadcasting such news back into the East European country, RFE sometimes forced the local media to come clean and the regime to admit that something was wrong. Several RFE newscasters were familiar voices; they had been popular on local radio and then fled to Munich. RFE originally broadcast in every East European language but

How Much Did Ideology Count?

Some writers on Communist systems place—or used to place—major emphasis on ideology. They argue that the Communists of these countries really believed in Marxism-Leninism and used its doctrine to build support for the regime, to guide policy making, and to insure discipline and unity of purpose among party members. I see no such thing in Communist countries, especially in East Europe. Accordingly, this book pays little attention to ideology. Communist party members, including those at the very top, were terribly cynical about ideology. Almost uniformly they were opportunists who joined the party only to further their careers and improve their standard of living. Most knew little of Marxism-Leninism and cared less. They mumbled a few Marxist phrases like a badly learned catechism. In fact, serious Marxists in East Europe were likely to become doubters and intellectual troublemakers. If you started applying Marxian analysis to East European societies, you soon discovered a pampered party elite and a ruthlessly exploited working class—a situation worse than anything capitalism had brought about. You were quickly told to shut up and apply your Marxist analyses only to Western societies.

In earlier decades, ideology did play a role in recruiting Communist party members. Horrified by the poverty of their countries and the obvious unfair class differences, the original generation of East European Communists, some of whom came to power after World War II, may have initially been driven by ideological motives. The militant evil of nazism convinced others that communism must be the answer. After these people had been in power a while, though, ideology took second place to retaining power and privilege. Ideology was used as window dressing to justify the latest policy twists, including abrupt about-faces. After a while, even believers stopped believing.

To be sure, all Communist regimes taught Marxism-Leninism to young people in schools, but it soon bounced off them, for young people quickly saw for themselves that the ideology of equality and progress was not being practiced. This deepened the amount of cynicism in society and undermined any effort at building a civic culture of legitimacy and honesty. A few of the more talented young people, however, learned that mouthing the right words along with party membership helped build their careers. By the second generation, 98 percent of the ruling Communist party membership had become opportunists. There could be a few scattered believers, but the regime didn't trust them with anything important. Opportunists are more reliable than believers, because you can closely predict an opportunist's behavior. A believer might start invoking gospel.

Was there ideology in Communist East Europe? Well, the regime shoveled it out, but no one believed it, not even the shovelers. The clincher to my anti-ideological argument, I think, came when the Communist regimes collapsed in 1989. How many citizens were then motivated by Marxist-Leninist considerations? Even former Communists

> abandoned any pretense at ideology—it no longer served their careers—and they announced themselves to be Socialists of a democratic bent. Many Communist managers became enthusiatic capitalist managers. They were, after all, just opportunists. In East Europe, Communist ideology vanished like the smoke-and-mirrors trick that it always was.

later dropped Serbo-Croatian (the chief language of Yugoslavia) and Albanian. Yugoslavia had moved into a nonhostile relationship with the United States, and Albania, RFE research discovered, had too few radios to bother with. RFE broadcasts were often "jammed" by the Communist regimes—simply by broadcasting noise on the same frequency—to try to screen them out. Jamming effectiveness is spotty, however; at different locations the broadcast might get through.

Voice of America (VOA) played a lesser role in East Europe. An official branch of the U.S. government (part of the U.S. Information Agency), VOA concentrates on putting out a favorable image of the United States and its foreign policies rather than detailed news about events in East Europe. VOA broadcast fewer hours in East European languages than RFE; some East Europeans tuned to VOA to improve their English. The authoritative English-language station, though, was the BBC. Starting with its wartime broadcasts to anti-German resistance movements, the BBC developed an enviable reputation for fairness, thoroughness, and restraint.

East Germany (the German Democratic Republic, or GDR) had a special problem with its information monopoly: West Berlin, an island of freedom 110 miles inside GDR territory. With several stations broadcasting from West Berlin in German—perhaps the most famous was RIAS, Radio in the American Sector—East Germany was effectively blanketed with Western radio. Even worse, most of the GDR could pick up West German television. The freer, richer life shown on West German television offered a permanent rebuttal to East German Communist propaganda. In sum, the East European efforts at information monopoly (with the possible exception of Albania) did not work; information got through the Iron Curtain as though it were a sieve.

Russian Language and Culture

As the Communists incorporated East Europe into the Soviet bloc, they tried to strengthen and deepen cultural ties. Russian language instruction became required in most East European high schools. As a Slavic language, Russian should be easy for Poles, Czechs, and Slovaks. The amazing thing is how little Russian most East Europeans know. After several years of study and sometimes visits to the Soviet Union, only a few now speak passable Russian. Given a chance to learn

English (and sometimes German), however, many gained remarkable fluency in two years. What did this indicate? The students were "voting" by studying the English hard, the Russian not. The motivation to study each language, of course, was quite different. The Soviet Union served as an economic, political, and cultural model for very few East Europeans. Traditionally, educated East Europeans looked westward, not to Russia (with the exception of the Bulgarians). English (and German) are useful for foreign trade and tourism, Russian is not. Further, many young East Europeans love rock-and-roll (partly because their regimes tried to ban it), and rock is almost exclusively sung in English.

Soviet-run bookstores offered bargain prices on the collected works of Lenin, Stalin, and Brezhnev, plus other Communist commentaries by lesser lights, both in Russian and in translation. Sales were less than brisk. Better sellers were translations of Russian classics. The Soviets were also big on folk song and dance groups, and there were many tours and exchanges. The Communist theory here is that folk art expresses the genius of the common people, and this genius is fostered and protected by the Communist system. In folk performances, communism and nationalism were to merge. East European countries also cultivated folk song and dance in an effort to gain legitimacy. None of these cultural efforts worked; in their influence on the people, the efforts rolled like water off a duck's back.

Because it is so important, we will explore more fully the impact of socialist or Communist economics on East Europe in the next chapter. Suffice it to say, Stalin generally imposed on East Europe the nationalization of industry and the collectivization of agriculture that he had earlier imposed on the Soviet Union. In both cases, the long-term results were poor and led to gradual economic decay and ultimately to collapse.

The imposition of the Stalinist model on East Europe resulted in very unhappy East Europeans. It is fair to say that in every country the bulk of the population disliked the regime. An unknown portion hated it outright. A basic tenant of Stalinism is that you can force an unwelcome system on a people and they will learn to adjust to it, even to like it. After all, the reasoning goes, you are in tune with history and know that capitalism is dying and communism is the wave of the future. You're just speeding up history a bit. This nonsense was accepted by few people in East Europe, and their numbers grew fewer over the decades.

THE TITO-STALIN SPLIT

One of the most bizarre episodes of the Cold War was the split between Tito and Stalin that burst out in 1948. It was important, for it both reflected what was happening in East Europe at the time, and it contributed to subsequent problems in the Soviet bloc. It showed that under the uniform surface of East European politics lurked personal and nationalistic rivalries that not even Stalin could disguise. We didn't realize it at the time, but the quarrel between the Soviet Union and Yugoslavia was the first and earliest sign that the Soviet bloc would one day break up. The split was one of Stalin's many foreign-policy blunders, all of them related to his very poor understanding of what the people of other countries thought and felt. Stalin thought he knew everything, even what was happening in distant lands.

Tito had been an ultraloyal Stalinist ever since he rose through the party ranks in the 1920s and 1930s. He later remarked that he sensed something was wrong when party comrades were arrested and killed during Stalin's insane purges of the 1930s, but at the time he said nothing. Faint differences emerged during World War II. Stalin was not keen on the Communist-led Partisans; he thought they might alarm the British and Americans. Stalin even urged them to wear the old Serbian monarchist symbol on their caps. Tito insisted they wear the Communist red star, just like Soviet soldiers. In battle, Partisans died with the cry "Stalin! Tito!" on their lips. But the Soviet Union stalled in providing help to the Partisans, and then only a little. The British sent supplies and a team of advisors under the redoubtable Brigadier Maclean.

After the war, the Yugoslav comrades socialized their country faster than Stalin wished. Stalin preferred to go slow to avoid alarming the West. The Yugoslav Communist regime set to work immediately, arresting suspected bourgeois opponents and setting up the above-mentioned artifacts of the Stalinist system, behaving like an overeager younger brother. The 1946 Yugoslav constitution was a word-for-word copy of the 1936 Soviet constitution. It looked as though Yugoslavia were an early and perfect Soviet satellite.

But on June 28, 1948, the Communist Information Bureau, meeting in Sofia, Bulgaria, announced it was expelling Yugoslavia from the Communist camp for alleged deviation and disobedience. The Comintern had been ostensibly dissolved in 1943 as a goodwill gesture to the Western Allies. At the time, it didn't seem right to be fighting a common enemy while one ally was trying to subvert the other. In terms of Stalin's control of the world Communist movement, of course, nothing changed, and in 1947 Moscow announced an ostensibly new organization, the Communist Information Bureau—Cominform for short—that was very similar to the old Comintern.

The comrades of the Cominform made a small psychological blunder in picking that particular date for the expulsion of Yugoslavia, for June 28 is the day of St. Vitus (*Vidovdan*), patron saint of Serbia. Eerily, June 28 also marks the historic (albeit losing) battle of Kosovo Polje against the Turks in 1389 and the Sarajevo visit and assassination of Archduke Franz Ferdinand in 1914. If you are going to do something that will arouse Serbs—the largest nationality and the founding element of Yugoslavia—don't do it on June 28.

But why would the Cominform expel Yugoslavia? No other explanation fits but Stalin's personality. He could not stand what he did not control. Tito may have been completely loyal, but he had his own power base not dependent on Stalin, and that was something the paranoid dictator could not tolerate. All the other

Yugoslavia's Maverick Communism

Yugoslav communism is important not because it worked—over the decades it developed much the same problems as other East European Communist systems—but because it provided an exciting and enticing suggestion throughout the bloc that there could be a socialism not based on the Stalin model. During the 1950s, Yugoslav thinkers, including Tito's right-hand man, Milovan Djilas, who had served as liaison with Stalin during the war, critiqued Soviet-style socialism and found it terribly wanting.

The chief problem, long noted by specialists on Marxism, is that Marx predicted the "withering away" of the state as communism was built. The state, and its coercive apparatus of bureaucrats and police, were needed only to protect the property and privilege of the ruling class, argued Marx. Nationalize property and make all equal, and the state would grow superfluous. But in the Soviet Union, clearly the opposite was happening. Under Stalin, the state was continually growing bigger and stronger. Where was the "withering away" Marx had predicted? Stalin and his hack writers came up with some not very convincing rationales for growing state power: They were surrounded by hostile capitalists; they had to first achieve a considerable material base; history moves in dialectical rather than in straight-line fashion; and so on. Yugoslav thinkers stopped buying these excuses and started calling the Soviet system a mistake, a perversion of Marxism. Actually, Trotsky had developed much the same critique years earlier—"the revolution betrayed"—and this gave Stalin's propagandists a chance to denounce Tito as a Trotskyist, a most improbable charge.

In place of Soviet-style "state socialism," a system that made the state incredibly strong, Yugoslav thinkers proposed a benign "self-managed socialism" in which state power would gradually shrink. This allowed the Yugoslavs to imply that they, rather than the Soviets, were carrying out Marx's designs, a point that made the Soviets very angry, for their way had to be the only way. In a series of reforms during the 1950s, Yugoslavia introduced wide-ranging *decentralization, debureaucratization,* and *worker self-management*. Enterprises were still "socially owned" but run by and for their workers through elected boards. They competed in a partly free market to produce the best products at the lowest prices. The Yugoslavs boasted they had taken the best of capitalism and combined it with the best of socialism. (In later years, some wags chortled that it was the worst of both.)

A close-up view of Yugoslavia was not so rosy. The Communist party, renamed the League of Communists, still monopolized power. The security forces still squelched opposition and jailed dissidents. State interference in the economy was still substantial. State-controlled banks determined who got loans. Government funds subsidized money-losing enterprises. Workers voted themselves wage increases out of line with productivity, and inflation became endemic. Tito, almost like Stalin, was turned into an ikon who could do no wrong.

Still, for a while during the 1950s and 1960s, Yugoslavia became a standing rebuke to the Soviet model. Some thinkers in East Europe were intrigued by the idea of each country charting its own path to socialism. Why should the Soviet Union serve as a model for all countries? In this way, Yugoslavia served as an alternative model and, therefore, as an irritant and destabilizing element in East Europe.

Communist leaders of East Europe were personally and militarily dependent on Stalin; none had come to power on their own. Stalin wrongly presumed that when he signaled his displeasure with Tito by expelling Yugoslavia from the Cominform, loyal Stalinists in the Yugoslav Communist party would quickly depose Tito. Then, thought Stalin, he could pick a puppet to head the Yugoslav party.

To Stalin's chagrin, the Yugoslav Communists ignored Stalin almost to a man and rallied around Tito. A few "Cominformists," the Yugoslav term for a pro-Stalinite, were jailed. Soviet propaganda blasts depicted Tito as a traitor to communism and an American agent. Soviet troops menacingly maneuvered on Yugoslavia's northern and eastern borders (but at no time did they cross over). At first the Yugoslav comrades could not believe what was happening; they had been trained to worship Stalin. For some months Belgrade expected Moscow to cease its obviously insane charges and patch things up. Gradually the Yugoslavs understood that they were outcasts, on their own, that the Soviet Union was as great a threat to their national security as the capitalist West, and that Stalin had constructed a mistaken system. By 1950, the Yugoslavs had resolved to build their own distinctive system, a non-Soviet socialist system. Stalin's paranoia and misjudgment thus created a competing brand of socialism in East Europe that caused Stalin and his successors no end of trouble.

In a rage at not having been able to oust Tito, Stalin, whose paranoia got worse near the end of his life, started seeing "Titoism" throughout East Europe. Political figures—generally those second in command—who might be interpreted as advocating deviations from the Soviet model for building socialism were given rigged trials; most were executed. One suspects that in many cases, the accusations of Titoism were covers for getting rid of political rivals, since no one could say exactly what Titoism meant. It was sort of an all-purpose accusation.

The most famous of these "purge trials" were those of Czech party secretary Rudolf Slansky and several others from 1950 to 1952. In Hungary, Laszlo Rajk, who had been interior minister, was accused of Titoism and executed. In Bulgaria, Traicho Kostov was the comrade most likely to succeed the ailing Dimitrov, but Kostov had voiced some opposition to Soviet economic exploitation of Bulgaria. He was accused of Titoism and executed. In Albania, interior minister and central committee secretary Koci Xoxe represented a pro-Yugoslav faction. He was also a rival for power of Enver Hoxha, who found accusations of Titoism a convenient excuse for executing Xoxe.

Poland was a bit different. In late 1948, Wladyslaw Gomulka, party general secretary and deputy premier, was arrested and accused of "rightist and nationalist deviation," but he was merely fired from his jobs. In 1956, he was suddenly thrust into power as Poland tottered on the edge of revolt. Throughout East Europe, lesser figures were fired, many were jailed, and close to one quarter of the Communist party members were kicked out.

What was Stalin doing? The Communist parties of East Europe had expanded their membership severalfold. Some new members were idealistic fools; most were just opportunists. Stalin, it now seems likely, feared that this rapid expansion of untested members was weakening party control and discipline. For Stalin, any excuse to tighten control was a good excuse. In the 1930s in the Soviet Union it had been "Trotskyism"; now it was "Titoism." And it didn't really matter whether those accused were guilty of any such deviations; most were not. It only mattered that Stalin and his helpers could make an example of someone—anyone—to keep the rest cowed and obedient.

THE RUMBLINGS OF FREEDOM

Needless to say, the inflicting of these foreign, unpopular regimes on the nations of East Europe engendered smoldering, bitter resentment. Direct, open opposition—even verbal—could be punished, but within the confines provided by friends, family, and the church many indicated their continuing discontent. At no time did an East European Communist regime successfully root itself into the hearts and minds of its people. For decades, when there was no hope of change, people got along by going along, although often grudgingly. Hatred of the regime, however, was never far beneath the surface, and from time to time it burst out.

Pilsen, Czechoslovakia, 1953

The western part of Czechoslovakia had been liberated by American forces in 1945. General Patton had gone farther and faster than expected and had arrived earlier than the Soviet army. The U.S. Third Army could have easily taken Prague, but that was left for the Soviets. The Americans meanwhile took Plzen (spelled in German as Pilsen, birthplace of Pilsner beer) amidst great popular acclaim, for Czechs and Americans had a long and close affinity. The American liberation of Pilsen was officially blotted out by the Communist regime, but citizens remembered "the boys from the U.S.A."

It was against this background that a fair-sized worker revolt broke out in Plzen in June 1953. (Stalin had died in March.) The regime imposed higher prices and tighter work rules, and workers strongly objected. Demonstrations spread to other cities. The Communist regime handled the situation carefully, backing down

The Uses of Anti-Semitism

As we considered earlier, there was a great deal of anti-Semitism in East Europe. Their status as unwanted outsiders drove some Jews to see communism as a liberating force that would make all people equal and erase anti-Semitism. As a result, nearly every Communist party in East Europe had a Jewish contingent. These people served Stalin well in the Communist takeovers of East Europe. In the security services, they could be counted on to mercilessly root out anything that smacked of fascism or collaboration with the Nazis. Often included in this group were old-style conservatives and anti-Communists. As a result, Jews, such as Rakosi in Hungary and Ana Pauker in Romania, were sometimes prominent among the tougher (and more detested) Communists.

This suited Stalin just fine. A controlled wave of anti-Semitism provided him with another way to manipulate the population and to deflect discontent from its true cause. When difficulties arose in the communization of East Europe, what handier a scapegoat to blame than Jews? By purging them as Titoists, nationalists, wreckers of socialism, or whatever, he tacitly but clearly communicated to the local population that the real problems were caused by the Jews, not by communism. Stalin knew that many East Europeans were anti-Semitic and that Jewish Communists had done a lot of his own dirty work. Besides, Stalin never fully trusted Jewish Communists; they were too "cosmopolitan," meaning they had international contacts. Hanging Jewish Communists in East Europe thus killed two birds with one stone: It pleased local populations, and it got rid of what Stalin suspected was an unreliable element. The two most prominent Jews to get the rope in East Europe were Slansky of Czechoslovakia and Rajk of Hungary. Since then, most of the Jews who had survived the Holocaust left East Europe. They had gotten the message of how communism uses and then discards Jews.

a bit on their new policies and boosting production of consumer goods. Collectivization of agriculture was suspended, and some farmers were allowed to resume private production. Although not widely noted, the Pilsen revolt marked the first mass outcry against a Communist system in East Europe.

East Berlin, 1953

What happened a short time later in 1953 in East Berlin attracted far more notice than Pilsen, perhaps because Western reporters (and intelligence agents) could move freely between West and East Berlin. East and West Germans were in close proximity and had easy communication with each other, and East Germans could more easily compare their standard of living and of personal freedom with their cousins in West Germany. The East Berlin uprising was bigger, angrier, and bloodier than the Czech one, and it captured the world's attention with a dramatic photograph of unarmed East German workers throwing stones at Soviet tanks.

As in Czechoslovakia, the immediate cause was an economic tightening. In June of 1953, the East German regime issued orders raising work norms in order to boost lackluster economic performance. East Berlin construction workers decided they already were working hard enough and struck in protest against the new norms. Soon other trades joined the protest, which quickly spread to other East German cities. The strikes escalated into antiregime riots. Authorities accused Western agents of stirring up the trouble, but it seems to have been spontaneous. Ulbricht had to call for Soviet help, which was close at hand, as more than 20 Soviet divisions surrounded Berlin. The uprising was quickly crushed. Over 20 demonstrators were killed on the street and another seven executed.

Poznan, Poland, 1956

Since the late 1940s, the old Stalinist, Boleslaw Bierut, had, in various offices, been Poland's paramount leader and general secretary of the United Workers' (Communist) party. But, little appreciated by Westerners at the time, not far beneath the surface of the Polish party grew a split, a point true of most East European Communist parties. The Stalinists of Bierut were in command. These were mostly people who spent the war in the Soviet Union (some in the armed forces and security police) and who enforced a hard-line policy of obedience to Moscow's lead. Other Polish Communists, though, adopted a more "national" approach; that is, they saw things through Polish eyes and envisioned a Polish road to socialism. Some of these people had been in the underground resistance inside Poland during World War II. Others were old-time Polish Socialists who had been forced to amalgamate into the United Workers' party but whose attitudes were more flexible and open than those of the Stalinists.

Khrushchev's moves deepened this split in the Polish party. For one thing, Khrushchev tried to patch things up with Tito; he visited Yugoslavia in 1955 and announced publicly that each Communist party could choose its own path to socialism. This is what the "national" faction of the Polish party had been whispering for years. Its leader, Gomulka, had been dropped as party chief in 1948 for alleged Titoism and had been under house arrest for some years. Suddenly, Titoism was not so bad.

Khrushchev's denunciations of Stalin in early 1956 (see box), further weakened the Stalinist leadership of Bierut, who conveniently died in March. Especially devastating was Khrushchev's admission in the speech of how Stalin had brutally and wrongly liquidated the old Polish Communist party in 1938. Although this was probably unintentional, it severely undermined the legitimacy of the hard-line Stalinists in the Warsaw government.

In June, some 50,000 workers rioted angrily against higher prices and work quotas in Poznan, an important industrial city which lies west of Warsaw. They

Khrushchev's Anti-Stalin Speech

Pilsen and East Berlin were just early rumblings of the discontent that had been smothered under the Stalinist systems of East Europe. What happened in 1956 triggered far greater outpourings. In early 1956, Soviet party leader Nikita Khrushchev gave a stinging, hours-long speech against the "crimes of Stalin" to a party congress of thousands of participants. Khrushchev made the surprise move completely for domestic political reasons. He was at odds, economically and politically, with the Stalinist bureaucrats who still ran the Soviet Union. Trying to prod the system, which was choked with fear and controls, into growth and innovation, Khrushchev went after the chief problem, Stalin's personality cult. He thought he was speaking behind closed doors, but with a little help from the American CIA, copies of the speech soon circulated worldwide.

Around the world, Communists were stunned and shocked. All those terrible things that Western conservatives had been saying about Stalin were now admitted to be true. The purges of the 1930s had murdered loyal party comrades, not British spies or Trotskyist party wreckers. Khrushchev's speech omitted any reference to the millions of ordinary citizens killed in the collectivization of agriculture, for Khrushchev had been one of Stalin's henchmen in that effort. Khrushchev also admitted that Stalin's blunders in World War II cost the Soviet Union millions of soldiers.

In the West, old-time Communists quit the party in disillusionment. In China, Mao Zedong wondered if Khrushchev was rational and reliable; he had rashly smashed the Stalin symbol of Communist unity. And in East Europe, regimes that were still Stalinist and had received no advanced warning of Khrushchev's de-stalinization, trembled with fear that their symbol of Communist resolve had been suddenly dethroned. They had been basing their policies and style for years on Stalin. His pictures were everywhere. Streets and factories were named after Stalin. Now, all of a sudden, he was a villain. Khrushchev, who seems to have given no thought about the likely impact in other countries of his de-stalinization campaign, thus harmed the stability and legitimacy of the East European regimes. Within months of Khrushchev's anti-Stalin speech, Poland and Hungary erupted in anger. With the god destroyed, the people went mad.

cried for "bread and freedom." Soon the workers were joined by students, and the protests spread, taking on a general anti-Communist tone. The Stalinist leadership, frightened that they could be overthrown, called out units of the Polish army to crush the protests. Fifty-four were killed and hundreds were wounded.

Poland tottered on the edge of a major violent revolution. Thoroughly scared, the Warsaw government to save itself turned to the only credible Communist figure, Wladyslaw Gomulka, the alleged Titoist and nationalist who had been fired in 1948 and isolated ever since. Gomulka was named new party chief in October

1956. Khrushchev flew to Warsaw to try to veto the move; he still didn't trust Gomulka. For a while, it looked like the Soviet army would intervene to block the chain of events in Poland. The Polish defense minister at this time was a Soviet general, Rokossovsky, and there were Soviet officers planted strategically throughout the Polish army. Gomulka reassured Khrushchev that Poland would stay Communist and a member of the Warsaw Pact, and Khrushchev acquiesced to the switch in leadership.

Gomulka, unfortunately, was true to his word. He was not quite the reformer that both Poles and Westerners initially celebrated. He denounced Stalinism in the Polish party, released political prisoners, curbed terroristic police power, admitted there was mismanagement and corruption in the Polish economy, and dismissed Rokossovsky and other Soviets from the Polish armed forces. Things relaxed in Poland a bit; life was freer and people spoke rather openly. Censorship lessened and most collective farms disappeared. The regime improved relations with the Catholic Church and gave it considerable autonomy. But Gomulka did little to change the economy, which stayed centralized, state-run, corrupt, and inefficient. He also made sure that Poland followed the Soviet lead, and he allowed no competition to the Polish Communist party. Under Gomukla, Poland adopted some of the symbols of liberalization, but these just whetted Polish appetites for real change.

Budapest, 1956

The real explosion of 1956 came in Hungary just a few days after the "Polish October" installed Gomulka. Emboldened by Khrushchev's de-stalinization, in 1956 Hungarians, especially writers, began to demand the ouster of their longtime dictator, the Stalinist Rakosi. Budapest intellectuals formed the Petöfi Circle, named after a nineteenth-century nationalist poet who had died in the 1848 insurrection put down by Russian troops. The Petöfi meetings grew to include thousands and featured increasingly antiregime speeches. The admission that Bela Kun and Laszlo Rajk had been wrongfully executed did not calm them; instead, it convinced them that the whole Communist package was rotten. Trying further to calm things, in July the Soviet Politboro member Anastas Mikoyan, a crafty Armenian, flew to Budapest to supervise Rakosi's ouster. His replacement, close associate Erno Gero, was no better and calmed no one. Much preferred was Imre Nagy (rhymes with lodge), a relatively liberal Communist leader who had been named prime minister in 1953 but who had been ousted by the Stalinist forces of Rakosi in 1955.

On October 23, a major antiregime demonstration gathered in a square facing the Danube to call for the return of Nagy, free elections, and the removal of Soviet troops. Suddenly security forces fired automatic weapons from buildings, killing several people. That was the signal for the Hungarian Revolution of 1956. Crowds stormed security police headquarters and beat to death security police. A gigantic statue of Stalin in Budapest was pulled down. The revolt spread nationwide. Collective farms were broken up, workers' councils took over their factories, and

Did the U.S. Betray the Hungarian Revolution?

For years, Washington had been talking about liberating East Europe from communism. Eisenhower's Secretary of State John Foster Dulles had issued a famous call to "roll back communism" in East Europe. It was a purely electoral ploy to beat the Democrats, who stood accused of not doing enough against communism, but is it possible that Hungarians took Washington's phrase literally? Radio Free Europe (see earlier in this chapter) had been broadcasting anti-Communist messages to the peoples of East Europe, including the Hungarians. Did these broadcasts encourage Hungarians to throw off the Communist yoke in the expectation of speedy U.S. help? In short, did the United States promise something and not deliver? Did Hungarian freedom fighters die because they were sure the U.S. Army was on the way?

Dulles's rhetoric was revealed as hollow, for there was essentially nothing the United States could do, short of risking World War III with the Soviets. How would Moscow have reacted if U.S. troops had entered Hungary from the west as Soviet forces invaded from the east? Besides, Hungary had no border with a U.S. ally; Austria had been solemnly declared neutral by the Austrian State Treaty of 1955, which the United States had negotiated and signed. We would have had to violate Austrian neutrality to bring U.S. forces to Hungary.

Radio Free Europe affirmed vehemently that its broadcasts had in no way encouraged the freedom fighters to expect U.S. help. To back up this assertion, RFE's Munich headquarters used to eagerly offer visitors a complete replay of their broadcasts of the period. (There is some evidence that a mobile Soviet station broadcast fake RFE promises of help as a way to discredit RFE in particular and U.S. foreign policy in general. The Soviets are no strangers to this sort of "disinformation.") Still, did RFE indirectly encourage an uprising that was certain to be crushed?

There are a couple of morals to the story. The first is that even speeches intended solely for domestic listeners quickly find their way overseas, where they are heard with a different perspective. Dulles shouldn't have talked about a "rollback" unless he was willing to send U.S. troops. And radio messages of hope cannot be too hopeful, for they may give the impression that the United States is ready to jump in and save a country. In late 1956, RFE toned down its militant anti-communism and concentrated on providing accurate news, which in the long run proved more effective. Americans as a whole were a little ashamed for not delivering on their seeming promises.

local committees took over the government. On October 30, Nagy took power and formed a multiparty coalition pledged to fulfilling the demands the demonstrators had made a week earlier. The Nagy government said it sought to build a benign, non-Soviet type of socialism, a middle way between capitalism and communism.

The influence of the Yugoslav example was here apparent. It looked like the Hungarian revolution had triumphed and that soon Hungary would no longer be Communist or part of the Soviet bloc.

Khrushchev played a tricky game. He pretended to withdraw Soviet forces from Hungary, but on November 1 they returned in massive strength to crush the uprising. Nagy declared Hungary's withdrawal from the Warsaw Pact, proclaimed its neutrality on the Austrian model, and appealed for Western help. Ashamed, the Western powers delivered no help, nor could they. On November 4, Soviet tanks entered Budapest to cut down the lightly armed Hungarian soldiers and civilians in several days of street fighting. Altogether, some 32,000 died. With the Austrian border still open, over a quarter of a million Hungarians fled to the West, many to the United States. Nagy and his associates took refuge in the Yugoslav embassy. Moscow promised them safe conduct to leave the embassy and the country. Then it arrested, tried, and executed them in 1958. They were buried in unmarked graves in an overgrown corner of a Budapest cemetery.

From obscurity, Moscow plucked Janos Kadar, victim of an earlier purge who had been imprisoned and tortured, to be leader of Hungary. This gave Kadar a kind of *bona fides* as a non-Rakosi, non-Stalinist Communist. The Kadar government restored order, but it did not reimpose the police terror of Rakosi. Further, Moscow, which took a public-relations beating around the world for its brutality in Hungary, wished no further uprisings, so it treated Hungary with kid gloves, allowing it considerable leeway in developing a Hungarian path to communism and a comfortable standard of living. In a way, the Hungarian rebels won.

SUGGESTED READINGS

BROWN, J. F. *Eastern Europe and Communist Rule.* Durham, NC: Duke University Press, 1988.

BRZEZINSKI, ZBIGNIEW K. *The Soviet Bloc: Unity and Conflict,* rev. ed. New York: Praeger, 1961.

COHEN, LENARD, AND JANE P. SHAPIRO, eds. *Communist Systems in Comparative Perspective.* Garden City, NY: Anchor Books, 1974.

FEHÉRVÁRY, ISTVÁN. *The Long Road to Revolution: The Hungarian Gulag, 1945-1956.* Santa Fe, NM: Pro Libertate, 1990.

FELKAY, ANDREW. *Hungary and the USSR, 1956-1988: Kadar's Political Leadership.* Westport, CT: Greenwood, 1989.

HARASZTI, MIKLOS. *The Velvet Prison: Artists Under State Socialism.* New York: Basic Books, 1987.

HIRSZOWICZ, MARIA. *Coercion and Control in Communist Society.* New York: St. Martin's, 1986.

KOSTRZEWA, ROBERT, ed. *Between East and West: Writings from Kultura.* New York: Farrar, Strauss & Giroux, 1990.

SCHÖPFLIN, GEORGE, ed. *The Soviet Union and Eastern Europe: A Handbook.* New York: Praeger, 1970.

STOKES, GALE, ed. *From Stalinism to Pluralism: A Documentary History of Eastern Europe Since 1945.* New York: Oxford University Press, 1991.

TOMASZEWSKI, JERZY. *The Socialist Regimes of Eastern Europe: Their Establishment and Consolidation, 1944-67.* New York: Routledge, 1989.

WHITE, STEPHEN, JOHN GARDNER, GEORGE SCHÖPFLIN, TONY SAICH. *Communist and Postcommunist Political Systems: An Introduction,* 3rd ed. New York: St. Martin's, 1990.

CHAPTER SIX _____

"We Pretend to Work": The Decay of Communism

MORAL BANKRUPTCY AND MORAL HEROES

By the 1960s, East Europe's Communist regimes were morally bankrupt. Whatever vision they might have been able to offer earlier had vanished amid empty economic promises, police-state repression, and gluttonous opportunism by the party elite. People were resigned and cynical. The Communists controlled the opportunity structure, so if you wanted to go to a university, get a better job, or travel abroad, you got along by going along, usually without enthusiasm. If you publicly opposed the regime, you would have a difficult life. Your writing would not be (legally) published. You would find only menial work. You might go to jail. For most people, there was no point in open defiance. Everyone knew the system was morally bankrupt, but few had the guts to say so openly. It was like the emperor's new clothes: Nobody spoke the obvious. Dictatorship needs not so much enthusiastic believers as a timid and silenced population.

Into this moral vacuum stepped a few cultural and moral heroes, people who, at great personal sacrifice, said no to the regime. They were a diverse lot, ranging from a shipyard electrician to university sociologists to playwrights. Their motivation included religious conviction, humanistic concern over injustice, and the empirical knowledge that communism was a corrupt failure. Their strength was their moral purity; they refused to knuckle under. Through self-published manuscripts (*samizdat*), foreign radio broadcasts, and even being denounced by the regime, these moral heroes gradually became widely known. At the right moment, when the Communist regimes could no longer count on Soviet support, the moral heroes stepped forward to deliver the final puff that collapsed the Communist house of cards.

The context in which these moral heroes became suddenly important and effective is our concern in this chapter. Strength of character by itself did not bring down these police states. It took a series of events that started with the death of Stalin in 1953. After Stalin, things began to loosen up. Could another Stalin have succeeded him, perhaps a dynasty of Stalins? Unlikely. A Soviet Union trapped in the Stalinist mold would have fallen further and further behind the West. A society drenched in fear and routine does not produce or innovate enough to keep up with dynamic free societies. This is what Khrushchev was all about: Get the Soviet economic system moving to catch up with the West. To do this, Khrushchev had to de-stalinize. He permitted the East European countries to do the same.

But with de-stalinization, the several Communist systems, including those of East Europe, began to lose their way. Under Stalin, things had been brutal but clear: push heavy industry, keep the population silent, follow the Soviet model, permit no factions within the party. After Stalin, things were less clear. Separate paths to socialism might now be permitted. After all, Khrushchev had flown to Belgrade in 1955 to apologize to Tito for Stalin's 1948 ouster of Yugoslavia from the Cominform and to affirm Yugoslavia's right to build the kind of socialism it wished in the way it wanted. If Yugoslavia could develop its own path to socialism, why not Poland? And if party members could discuss this possibility, you had automatically allowed a faction of "third way" or "middle way" thinkers to grow up within the party. If you eased up on political controls, you permitted people to criticize the regime. If you eased up on cultural controls, you permitted writers, artists, and performers to come out with cheeky new materials that implicitly rebuked the Communist model.

So you get rid of Stalin in image and structure. Then what do you do? Then does your Communist system start falling apart? As a matter of fact, that seems to be the case, but neither Westerners nor East Europeans understood this at the time. Such were the 1960s in East Europe, an unstable situation in which several regimes had de-stalinized but had not found a new, durable system to replace the Stalin model. This situation showed up in the culture of the period.

Culturally, it was an exciting time, for East European artists lived with an exquisite tension between defective, unpopular political and economic systems and a semifree ability to say they were unjust. In cinema, plays, and literature, East European writers outfoxed low-IQ censors by developing clever, indirect ways of saying things, sometimes by allegory, that scathingly criticized their regimes. It was as if they winked at their audiences to say, "You know what I mean," and the audiences winked back.

These writers played a major role in keeping the spirit of freedom alive. Some were unable to publish legally, but they distributed carbon copies of their stories, plays, and essays among circles of friends, who then passed them on. Some of these were published in the West in emigré journals and broadcast back on Radio Free Europe. In this way, impecunious and suppressed writers often achieved great recognition without ever having been published in their own countries. Some became moral heroes and political leaders, such as playwright Vaclav Havel of Czechoslovakia, who, before he became president, had never had one of his plays legally produced in Czechoslovakia.

ECONOMIC PROBLEMS OF SOCIALISM

The Communist systems of East Europe were doomed mainly because of their laggardly economic performance. For the sake of rapid—if lopsided—industrialization, the Stalin model introduced all manner of dislocations that eventually tripped up economic growth. A relatively short burst of industrial growth in the 1950s was followed by decades of slowing down and falling behind.

By 1950, little private industry was left in East Europe. Only some very small enterprises, employing chiefly family members, were left in private hands. Everything else was taken over by the state, although in some cases it was described legally as "socially owned," that is, owned by the society as a whole. Either way, when freedom came, unclear ownership left behind a difficult legacy of how to privatize firms in the 1990s (see Chapter 9).

There were a number of reasons for nationalization. First, it got rid of capitalists, and capitalists were the enemy. Capitalists deprived of their wealth and power were no longer a threat to the Communist regimes. Second, nationalization of industry gave enormous power to the Communists, increasing their control over society. What got built where, who got hired, who got apartments, and so on, all came under party purview. Third, nationalized industry was, under Stalin, presumed to be more rational and efficient than private enterprise. Although it sounds laughable now, some people honestly thought that socialism outperformed capitalism. They compared the economic decline of capitalist countries during the Great Depression of the 1930s with the rapid growth of the Soviet economy during the same period, the epoch of the Five-Year Plans. Instead of competing enterprises getting in each other's way and having their profits skimmed off by greedy capitalists, a rational, central plan would direct and coordinate all economic activity toward rapid growth.

And there was, to be sure, an ideological element to nationalization, at least at the public-relations level. By doing all of the steps listed previously, the state takeover of industry would show both the local and the world's working classes that socialism was the wave of the future. According to Marxism-Leninism, big state-run industries were an advance over capitalism. Therefore, to have left industry in private hands would have been a sign of doubt and hesitation about the correctness of communism.

A final, and perhaps decisive, point that encouraged the nationalization of industry is that it placed all of East Europe's economy at Stalin's disposal, and he needed it. The Soviet economy was badly damaged by the war, and now a new Cold War was underway. Stalin was desperate for whatever resources he could get

Comecon

In 1949, a year after the Marshall Plan swung into action in West Europe, Stalin set up its eastern equivalent, the Council for Mutual Economic Assistance, called CMEA in the East and Comecon in the West. The Soviet Union, of course, had no aid to give, and in fact collected considerable reparations from its wartime foes of East Germany, Hungary, Romania, and Bulgaria. CMEA had little meaning until after Stalin. Under Stalin, there was much economic duplication and overlap between the various countries, what economists call *autarky*, that is, economic self-sufficiency.

Khrushchev refurbished Comecon as a planning agency that would assign each country production plans and quotas. This, of course, could be more efficient than autarky, but it also took away freedom of choice from member countries. Hungary, for example, built no cars, only buses. Hungary imported cars chiefly from Czechoslovakia, Poland, and the Soviet Union (in descending order of quality). Romania's Communist chief at the time, Gheorghe Gheorghiu-Dej, strongly objected to turning the Romanian economy into an adjunct of the Soviet economy and vetoed Romania's participation in Khrushchev's grand plan, although Romania continued as a Comecon member. Yugoslavia and Albania are not members of the CMEA.

his hands on, and state-run industries controlled by puppet states were a convenient mechanism for making East Europe deliver its goods eastward. A series of "joint companies," partly Soviet and partly local, were set up throughout East Europe, further cementing the East European economies to the Soviet economy. A free-enterprise economy would have largely faced west, for that is where the market and hard currency were (and still are). A state economy faced east and was oriented to Soviet needs.

This Soviet control over East Europe's economy was especially important with the outbreak of the Korean War in 1950. According to Khrushchev's memoirs, believed to be generally accurate, Stalin had not precisely ordered the North Korean invasion of South Korea; rather he had acquiesced to North Korean party chief Kim Il Sung's strong desire to unify his country under communism and Kim's conviction that the United States would not forcibly react to this. American analysts now believe that President Truman's strong reaction—not only in sending a large army to Korea but in greatly stepping up U.S. defense preparations worldwide—surprised and jolted Stalin and forced him to shift suddenly into a gigantic arms-building program. East European industry, especially the metalurgical capabilities of East Germany, Czechoslovakia, and Poland, were extremely valuable to the Soviet arms buildup and, of course, another reason these industries had to be state-run.

With the Korean War came forced industrialization in East Europe on the model of the Soviet Five-Year Plans of the 1930s. The largely agricultural economies of most of the region were rapidly redesigned to favor heavy industry, long a part of Stalinist thinking. Stalin and his helpers argued like this: Heavy industry, namely steel production, is the basis of all economic growth. Locomotives, machine tools, boilers, and so on, are all made out of steel. (Implements of war are also made out of steel.) The more steel you make, the sooner you lay the foundation for a thriving socialist economy, one that will leave capitalism far behind. This kind of economic reasoning, we now see, is extremely dubious—some of the fastest-growing economies are those oriented to consumer goods—but it was accepted without question by East European Stalinists: steel equals good. It is not for nothing, as the Russians like to say, that *stal* is Russian for steel and that Stalin means "man of steel." The results of forced industrialization were mixed. There was rapid industrial growth, but it was temporary, inefficient, environmentally damaging, unrelated to consumer needs, and its products were of poor to mediocre quality.

In the revolts of several East European countries in the 1950s (discussed in the previous chapter) we see another thing that goes wrong with forced industrialization. It squeezes the population unmercifully, giving them little in return, until they rebel. The uprisings of 1953 in Pilsen and Berlin, and of 1956 in Poznan and Budapest came when the industrial output of East Europe was probably showing its fastest increase. Little of it, however, went for consumer needs.

Collectivization of Agriculture

The collectivization of agriculture in East Europe, as in the Soviet Union, was the flip side of forced industrialization. Stalinist reasoning went like this: We are bringing millions of workers from the countryside into the urban areas for our new heavy industries. We are turning peasants into proletarians, who now have to be fed cheaply since we don't pay them much. We've got to squeeze more food at lower cost out of the countryside. Peasant farming is inherently inefficient; the acreage is too small and the techniques too primitive. Besides, peasants are shrewd enough to know when they are being paid too little for their products; then they either stop growing or simply eat up what they have grown. We regard them as nasty little conservative individualists, and we will break them by combining smallholdings into big collective farms. Then we can get greater production with fewer workers and can make sure much of the crop is delivered to the state at a low price.

Collectivization generally took place in the early 1950s. The farmers, of course, felt betrayed. Many had been given acres in the land reforms of the immediate postwar period. Estates owned by Germans and nobles had been confiscated and distributed to peasants. But now what the state had given, the state took away by having small farmers give up their individual holdings to collectives.

The difference between Soviet collectivization in the late 1920s and early 1930s and collectivization in East Europe in the early 1950s was that the latter was not nearly so brutal. For Soviet collectivization, Stalin practiced deliberate mass starvation, deportation, and sometimes the shooting of peasants. An estimated 6 million Ukrainians were starved to death to break their anticollective attitudes. In East Europe, the regimes generally pushed collectivization by taxing individual farmers heavily and by granting better deals on seed, equipment, and marketing networks, including improved health and living standards, to those farmers who joined collectivized units. There was much grumbling but little bloodshed.

In Poland, where even Stalin understood that stubborn peasant resistance was simply too high, the regime let most farmers keep their holdings, but it tied them to state purposes by means of supply and marketing networks that effectively accomplished the same ends as collectivization.

THE LONG-TERM IMPACT OF SOCIALISM

In examining the net result of a socialist—or, if you prefer, Communist—economic system, we should get some things straight. First, a socialist economy does not spell instant catastrophe. The adoption of a Communist economic system one year does not lead to economic collapse the next. Instead, it slowly runs down. At the early stages of industrialization, a Stalinist approach produces impressive, rapid growth. It mobilizes all resources, including unemployed labor, and flings them into the construction of factories, especially those used in heavy industry. Historically, most of East Europe was at a low level of industrialization compared with West Europe. The exceptions in East Europe were certain areas of Bohemia and Poland that had inherited the industries of the earlier German and Austrian empires. By the late 1950s, all of East Europe (with the possible exception of Albania) had a considerable industrial plant and had greatly exceeded their prewar industrial output.

Second, what chiefly concerns us is not *absolute* economic growth but *relative* growth. In almost every year, the economies of East European countries continued to grow. But increasingly, starting in the 1960s, they grew at slower rates than the economies of West European countries. By the 1980s, the economies of East Europe were barely growing at all. This was a painful embarrassment for Communist regimes that had promised the economic collapse of capitalism and the arrival of material bounty through socialism. Everyone in East Europe knew that West Europeans lived better and were moving ahead faster. Even historically backward countries like Spain and Finland were moving into the ranks of prosperous, industrialized countries, and they were doing it without coercion and with improving living standards for their citizens. In the modern age, every country is looking over its shoulder to compare how it is doing with other countries. When East Europeans looked, it hurt. The power of this "jealousy factor" is not to be underestimated.

The Trouble with Statistical Comparisons

Communist countries do not measure their economies the way Western countries do, by Gross National Product (GNP)—the sum total of goods and services produced in a year, usually expressed per capita. The East used material output only. And much of what was reported by the East was lies. Western economists, including a section of the CIA, try to translate East-bloc figures into GNP equivalents, but they are little more than educated guesses and probably too high. But even accurate GNP figures would not tell the whole story. A socialist economy can have a growing GNP but put most of it into investment, thereby shortchanging consumption. This will give it a lower standard of living than a market economy with the same GNP. (A market economy lets consumer demand decide how much and where to invest.) Further, the centrally planned socialist investments may be poor: inefficient factories making junk products that few want. In a given year's economic statistics, these investments may look impressive, but in the long run they will be a drain on the economy and have to be propped up with state subsidies. In the absence of reliable data, perhaps the best indicators are found by visiting and living in East European countries, thereby getting a subjective feel of how they are doing. Good subjective data beat inaccurate objective data.

With these caveats in mind, here are the CIA's per capita GNP estimates for East Europe in 1989:

East Germany	$9,700
Czechoslovakia	7,900
Hungary	6,100
Bulgaria	5,700
Yugoslavia	5,400
Poland	4,500
Romania	3,400

Ahead of the Third World, but behind the First World, East Europe still qualifies as the Second World.

Bearing these two perspectives in mind, we can see that while the Stalinist model was industrializing rapidly, it was also introducing major distortions and dislocations. It paid minimal attention to consumer needs. The Stalinist theory was to disregard consumer needs for at least one generation; this generation was to sacrifice so that future generations could enjoy a utopia. But what then will motivate workers? If they are convinced that they are indeed building a utopia, they may be persuaded to sacrifice. This belief cannot last long, however. All a worker has to do is look around to see that whatever they are building, it is not a utopia. They see dreadful corruption and unfairness, and they start demanding their share of rewards here and now, not waiting for some vague time in the future.

Falling Behind

Hungarian economist Eva Ehrlich gathered data at four points in time to make one of the more sophisticated comparisons of relative economic growth in East and West Europe. American economist Paul Marer then calculated a series of two-country comparisons. Bear in mind that both countries are growing in absolute terms over time, but lower numbers mean that the East European country is slipping behind its Western counterpart. A 100 in the comparison between East and West Germany in 1937 (before Germany was divided), for example, means they were then equal in per capita GNP. A 70 in 1960 means that East German per capita GNP slipped to only 70 percent of West Germany's per capita GNP.

	1937	1960	1970	1980
East/West Germany	100	70	71	64
Czechoslovakia/Austria	90	91	78	70
Hungary/Italy	89	86	70	74
Poland/Spain	105	125	88	77
Romania/Spain	85	85	58	60
Yugoslavia/Greece	87	97	83	81
Bulgaria/Greece	82	122	100	110

In all cases except Bulgaria, the East European country in 1980 was further behind its West European counterpart country than it had been in 1937 or 1960. In some cases, there was a spurt of postwar industrialization in the East European country so that it kept or even improved its position relative to the Western country by 1960 (as in Czechoslovakia, Poland, Romania, and Yugoslavia) only to fall behind in 1970 and 1980. In 1960, some East Europeans could say, "Hey, we're doing pretty well compared with West Europe." Ten and twenty years later, no one could utter such a statement. In the growth race—with the possible exception of Bulgaria, which started from an extremely low level—West Europe beat East Europe.

The system cannot deliver. Geared to heavy industry, it produces too few consumer goods to satisfy mass demand. Wages are held down drastically to prevent inflation, the problem that comes when too many zloty, coruna, or forint chase too few goods. Some goods, even imported electronic treasures from Japan, are in shops, but few have the money to buy them. With such meager rewards, why work?

Lackadaisical work attitudes pervaded East Europe, made worse by the guarantee of jobs for all in a socialist economy. Communists have long insisted that

The Diseducation of East Europe

Over the decades, fewer and fewer East Europeans attended universities, leading to a shortage of highly educated people, another of communism's legacies. Limiting student numbers was not generally the intent of East European regimes. Following socialist doctrine, educated and professional people were deliberately not well paid (unless, of course, they were also Communist party officials). In a system allegedly dedicated to the working class, the salaries of doctors and professors were kept at or below those of workers (who weren't paid very well either). This dissuaded many bright young people from prolonging their education. Instead, they went right into jobs requiring few skills. In some cases, not-so-bright people attended universities, producing what biologists call a "counter-selection," the opposite of skimming off the best and brightest. Years later, this showed up in inept medical care and lackluster scholarship. Education, like everything else, requires incentives, and East European regimes did not provide them.

employment is a constitutional right more important than the bourgeois rights of free speech and a free press. If you can't eat, what good are other rights? Accordingly, economic enterprises were overstaffed and inefficient. Only Yugoslavia, with its experimental mix of socialism and a market economy, permitted unemployment (which grew to be quite huge). Inefficient enterprises were propped up for decades with government subsidies rather than let them go under, for that would mean both an admission of failure and unemployment.

In sum, workers had jobs, but they were poor jobs, with low pay and little chance of advancement. The jobs also put them in a position to judge for themselves the inefficiency of the system, the pervasive corruption, and the unfairness of the big rewards for the bosses and party people. As anger grew, work attitudes declined. This set up a vicious circle. With lackadaisical work attitudes, productivity was low. Discontented workers with inefficient, backward machines and factories turned out few products. With too few products on the market, workers had little to buy and therefore little incentive to produce more. Throughout the Soviet bloc, workers used to say, only half in jest, "We pretend to work, and they pretend to pay us."

The worst problem, found universally through the Soviet bloc, was (and still is) housing. With rapid industrialization came a major influx of workers from countryside to city, and this created a terrible housing shortage, one that continues to this day. Much urban housing in Poland and Yugoslavia had been blown up in World War II, so it was scarce to begin with. Regimes were reluctant to expend their precious resources on apartment construction, for that ate into their plans for industrial growth. The result was a monumental housing shortage, forcing whole families to live in one or two rooms and children to stay with their parents long after their school years. Trying to alleviate the shortage, regimes threw up gigantic prefabricated apartment blocks made of grey concrete slabs at the outskirts of most East European cities. Although small and unattractive by Western standards, East Europeans lucky enough to get the new flats after many years' wait felt triumphant.

In East Europe, in accordance with socialist doctrine, rents were extremely cheap—a few dollars a month—and tenure over an apartment is nearly permanent. Of course there were hidden costs for this socialist bounty. It took years, sometimes decades, on a waiting list to get a small apartment. The money for apartments came not from renters but from the government budget. In effect, taxes went for apartments, so people paid for their cheap flats indirectly in the form of lower salaries. The unfairness with this system is that everybody paid, including people who weren't getting the new apartments. Further, there was little money or incentive for state authorities to build quality new blocks or to maintain the old ones, which often looked shabby.

Perhaps the biggest problem with housing in East Europe was inflexibility. Once you had a flat, you clung to it. This made the system rigid. Instead of a flow of people in and out of apartments—changing as their job, number of children, and ability to pay dictated—you had people staying put forever and passing the apartment on to their children. Desperate East Europeans arranged complicated swaps of apartments in order to get their own rooms or to set up housekeeping as newlyweds. In effect, under a rigid socialist housing program, a "free market" in housing operated in a clumsy, inefficient fashion. Other problems come with housing rigidities. Industry cannot grow and expand if workers can't relocate because new apartments are so hard to find. With young people staying in the parental flat for an unusually long time, there is little incentive for them to work for a place of their own; they are simply not available. Crowding leads to horrendous child-parent fights, and a sense of despair settles over the younger generation, deepening the poor work attitudes.

Other shortages influenced economic growth in East Europe. Desirable consumer goods were scarce. In most of East Europe, few homes had telephones. Customers might have to wait years for a new car, often an obsolete model of an Italian Fiat made under license. Used cars often cost more than new cars, a sure sign of lagging supply. Parts and repair services were scarce, so drivers tried to patch up vehicles themselves. By the 1970s, household appliances became fairly widespread, so homes had refrigerators and televisions. Once consumers had those, the really desirable items became imports from West Europe and Japan, for they were much more advanced in style and technology. Few serious photographers would use a painfully obsolete and poorly made Soviet or East German camera if they could help it; their tongues hung out for new Japanese equipment, which might be brought back by someone who had visited abroad. When video cassette recorders caught on in the 1980s, millions of East Europeans craved them, but few were available; all were imported from Japan and South Korea. In short, what did

The Jealousy Factor

East Europe fell behind West Europe economically, but could the East European socialist systems have endured if their citizens hadn't *known* this? In other words, if they had been kept ignorant of the higher standard of living in the West, would they have been relatively content? Is it comparison with others and jealousy that make people discontent?

East European regimes tried to screen out images of the good life in the West, but, with the possible exception of Albania, they could not. By the 1960s, most East Europeans understood that they lived at a considerably lower standard of living than West Europeans. East European cultural groups performing on tour in West Europe and in the United States brought back stories and gifts of the material abundance capitalism had showered on Westerners. Could the regime have forbidden these cultural exchanges? Only if they wished to stay totally isolated, like Albania. The urge to travel, especially in the West, became an obsession with educated East Europeans. Some people lived to travel. They would carefully save up foreign currency—sometimes from blackmarket exchanges—for a low-budget trip every few years. Could the regime have forbidden travel to the West? Only at the cost of frustration and anger among the educated stratum of people that every regime depends on.

Group trips to the Soviet Union were easier to come by, but most East Europeans saw in the motherland of socialism a system that was poorer and more inefficient than their own. They were generally not impressed, and visits to the Soviet Union often had a negative impact on forming socialist attitudes. After a while, a feeling grew up in East Europe, especially among the more educated, that they had been not only economically deprived but also cut off from their natural ties to West Europe for the dubious advantage of participating in a backward socialist commonwealth of nations. Even hermetically sealed Albania leaked, as we learned when disturbances broke out there in 1990. It turned out that most Albanians all along were aware that they were being held in virtual slavery. In the long run, it was not possible to shield East Europeans from knowledge of the West, and this knowledge bred much discontent.

The tantalizing question remains: What if there had been no West to compare with? Suppose communism had actually triumphed and erected backward, inefficient regimes everywhere? The sources of change would still be present in Communist systems, but the whole thing would have happened much slower. Even without comparing themselves with those in capitalist nations, East Europeans could see gross corruption and inefficiency in their systems. Discontent would still have been high, as average people would still feel relative deprivation when they saw how the party elite lived. Comparison with the West helped things along, though; it served as a catalyst, a small but important chemical boost that speeds up a reaction that would take place anyway. The Cold War was not won by the West having more military might than the East (it didn't); it was won by the West outperforming the East in economic terms.

East Europeans have to work for? Where were the incentives that prompt people to produce more and better goods?

The necessities of life were usually no problem in East Europe. Food and clothing were generally sufficient, although a higher proportion of an East European's budget went to pay for them than would a West European's. And East Europeans might have to wait in lines for them, really inflation in a disguised form. Instead of paying more for something as in Western-style inflation, you pay more for it by spending your time in line. During the 1960s (earlier in Yugoslavia), most East European regimes permitted farmers' markets, areas where producers could bring their foods into town to sell for whatever price they could get. Farmers might still have to deliver quotas to state enterprises, but beyond those they could grow for the market. State stores still monopolized most processed foods at relatively fixed prices. Certain basics, such as bread, were subsidized to sell at low prices. The trouble with subsidizing anything, including the basics of life, is that it encourages people to rely on them rather than raise their sights and work hard to obtain something better. Again, the incentive problem.

LOCKED IN A BLOC

Comecon, the East European trading bloc, had several weaknesses that limited its effectiveness, especially in comparison with West Europe's Common Market, or, as it now prefers to be called, the European Community. No East European currency was convertible; that is, it could not be exchanged for another currency except at set rates by state-run banks. You could not, say, buy Polish zloty in advance in New York for a trip to Poland; that was illegal (although some did it). If you were searched at the border, carrying zloty in or out, you could get in trouble. (Some Polish customs officials shrugged with indifference at smuggled zloty, but you were well advised to not try smuggling East German marks into the GDR; their border guards could be thorough).

Trade accounts between East European Comecon members and the Soviet Union were kept in what were called "transferable rubles," though no rubles changed hands or crossed borders. Countries could accumulate ruble balances but could use them only for purchases of Soviet goods. Hungarian exports of machine tools to the Soviet Union, for example, could be used to purchase Soviet petroleum. Essentially, though, East European lands bartered among themselves: so many Polski Fiats for so many jars of Bulgarian fruit preserves. This, of course, is not nearly as flexible as a system based on convertible currencies, where trading partners use the income from the sale of their goods to buy whatever they wish from any country on the globe.

This arrangement sheltered the countries of the Soviet bloc from competing on the world market and producing world-class products. The various industries of the bloc were not supposed to compete—that was capitalism, messy and duplicative.

The Berlin Wall

Berlin, 110 miles inside East Germany, gave the Communist regime a problem shared by no other East European government: an easy escape hatch. Berlin, although divided into an East and West under the 1945 Allied agreements, remained open to free circulation. All a dissatisfied East German had to do was take a subway to a refugee center in West Berlin, and he or she would be flown out to a new life in West Germany, complete with West German citizenship. From the end of World War II until 1961, some 3 million persons fled through the Berlin escape hatch.

During the 1950s, the GDR was slowly bleeding to death. There were seldom fewer than a fifth of a million emigrating to the West every year, and they were the young, skilled, and productive. The West German *Wirtschaftswunder* (economic miracle) acted as a magnet, drawing East Germans to the West, where they knew they would get better jobs and a higher standard of living. The departure of these same people, on the other hand, severely hindered East Germany's economic growth.

In 1961 old-line Stalinist Walter Ulbricht, in consultation with Khrushchev, dammed the outflow by building the Berlin Wall, a chilling reminder of the GDR's inability to match West Germany's freedom and prosperity. East Berlin propaganda described the Wall as necessary to block "fascist" and espionage penetration from West Berlin, but the real motivation was economic, to stop the manpower loss to the West. When the manpower outflow to the West resumed in 1989—at first through Hungary and Czechoslovakia and then through the reopened Wall—East Germany was finished as a separate country. The Wall had given a temporary life span to a strange, artificial country.

Instead, they were to complement each other by each filling their assigned role in the plan. Quality did not enter into these planning considerations, just gross output. East Europeans figured, "The Soviets will buy anything. So why make it good?" Accordingly, there were very few East European goods (excepting Polish ham and Czech beer) that were good enough to compete against products outside of the Soviet bloc. This has now saddled East Europe with the monumental problem of how to make up for the lost decades and get back into international competition.

Stalin had originally ripped off the East European economies with unfair terms of trade that one-sidedly benefited the Soviet Union. Indiana University economist Paul Marer calculates that after World War II the Soviet Union sucked out some $14 billion from East Europe, about the same amount that the United States was putting into West Europe with the Marshall Plan. In the 1950s, this changed. For one thing, the Polish October and Hungarian Revolution jolted the Kremlin into realizing that East Europeans had to get a better standard of living or there would be more revolts. The terms of trade eased. The Soviets supplied raw materials,

---

The Corruption Factor

Corruption grows at the interface of public and private sectors. The more such interfaces, the more opportunities for corruption. Their economies choked with controls, East Europeans learned that they could make life a little easier by paying off the controllers. East Europeans who know the Soviet Union are quick to point out that the degree of corruption there is much higher. Compared with the Soviets, East Europeans consider their corruption a little harmless greasing of the wheels of commerce. Nonetheless, in East Europe everyone is looking for a deal and is not adverse to cutting a few corners to get it. No one suffers the least pangs of guilt, because all know the system itself is corrupt and not worthy of respect. This severely erodes any sense of civic duty or civic culture that makes democracy possible and is one of the problems communism has left behind for East Europe. It also meant that when the Communist regimes called for citizen support, no one stepped forward. Will they now step forward for the new democracies?

---

particularly petroleum and natural gas, at favorable prices. With the oil price hikes of the 1970s, for a time Soviet petroleum prices to East Europe were way below world prices. And the Soviets took in payment East European products that couldn't make it on the world market. All this served to lock East European economies into the Soviet bloc.

Attempts to break out of this dependency on trade within the bloc were only partially successful. Poland, for example, in the 1970s borrowed a great deal of capital from the West (chiefly from West German banks) to invest in new factories and equipment that would turn out products for the Western market. Much of the investment was thrown away because of inefficient factories, corruption, indifferent workmanship, and the poor choice of products. For example, Poland produced heavy leather luggage in the 1970s when Western travelers had long gone to much lighter plastic and softsided luggage. Poland, which had counted on entering the world market, instead went deeply into debt. By the early 1980s, it was in technical default on its loans; that is, it could not pay, but its creditors, hoping to salvage something, pretended that it eventually would repay. In another example, Volkswagen invested in an East German factory to produce car engines. But their quality was not good enough for the Western market; they could be sold only in East Europe.

With the passing of each year, locked in their bloc, the economies of East Europe fell a little more behind, and it grew a little more embarrassing. By 1980, the per capita GNP of East Europe was roughly half that of the six original Common Market countries of West Europe, and the standard of living was surely less than half. For many East Europeans, including younger party members, this was a potent catalyst for change.

THE BEGINNINGS OF SYSTEM BREAKDOWN

It will be here argued that the East European upheavals that began in 1968 were qualitatively different from those of the 1950s. In 1953 and 1956 we saw the spontaneous anger of workers tired of being squeezed by rapid Stalinist industrialization. In Hungary, of course, there was a considerable intellectual element added to the resentment. In the 1950s, these systems had been Communist only a few years. The Prague revolt in the spring of 1968 marked a more decisive and thought-out attempt to change the system by party people who had come to reject Stalinism.

In Hungary in 1956 we could glimpse the beginning of a split within the Communist party, but it was not the cause of the revolution. In Budapest, after the initial disturbances had broken out, people demanded a return to power of the relatively liberal Communist Imre Nagy, who then proceeded quickly to discard communism. By the mid to late 1960s, you were hearing in East Europe from party members seriously dissatisfied with socialism as it was presently constituted. For want of a better name, we might call them "liberal" Communists. As we shall explore in the next chapter, they were to play a major if short-lived role in East Europe's unsteady march to democracy.

Prague, Czechoslovakia, 1968

In 1968, Czechoslovakia had been Communist for two decades and had the second best economy of the bloc (after East Germany), although since the early 1960s it had shown only sluggish growth. Much of East Europe had moved beyond its original Stalinist leaders of the postwar period, but in Czechoslovakia the old Stalinist hack Antonin Novotny still monopolized power as both party first secretary and president of the country. A malaise of stagnant politics and economics blanketed Czechoslovakia. Increasingly, discussions in party circles blamed Novotny and his associates for staying in power too long. In private conversation with foreigners, Czech and Slovak party members could be amazingly frank about their disgruntlement. This was not the socialism they had worked for or envisioned.

At the beginning of 1968, after much behind-the-scenes debate, the Czechoslovak central committee voted out Novotny as party leader and brought in the relatively liberal Slovak, Alexander Dubcek. In March, Novotny also retired from the presidency. What happened during the next five months, the "Prague Spring," can only be described as wonderful. Quickly, under Dubcek's leadership, the trappings of Stalinism fell away to reveal a vibrant and dynamic Czechoslovakia ready to join the democracies. Conservative Communists were ousted from the central committee to make room for a new breed of relative liberals. Censorship was ended and popular new television programs and newspapers revealed serious economic mismanagement and the misuse of police power. Some police officials, after being interviewed on television about torture, went out and hanged themselves. A New Economic Model brought in many elements of a free market. Delegations visited

Yugoslavia to study the "self-managing" model of socialism. The newly freed labor unions volunteered "Days for Dubcek" of unpaid work, something they wouldn't have dreamed of doing for Novotny. Czechoslovakia saw something it hadn't seen in decades: enthusiasm.

Did Dubcek intend to dismantle communism? He never announced such intentions. Instead, in a parallel with Nagy in 1956, he said his country sought to build "socialism with a human face." But things moved faster than Dubcek anticipated or perhaps even wanted. Like Nagy in 1956, Dubcek found himself at the head of swelling, joyous movement that embraced him as its hero. Conservative Communists both inside and outside Czechoslovkia, though, viewed Dubcek and his program with alarm. If things kept going like this, they reasoned (correctly), Czechoslovakia would soon not be Communist. East Germany's Walter Ulbricht and Poland's Wladyslaw Gomulka feared the Prague Spring could spread. In the Soviet Ukraine, hardline party leader Pyotr Shelest feared that the Ukrainian minority in Slovakia could spread news of the reforms into his fiefdom.

In June, Soviet party chief Leonid Brezhnev met with Dubcek in Slovakia. Dubcek pledged loyalty to the Warsaw Pact and Comecon but defended his reforms. Brezhnev warned him that the Soviet Union would intervene if any Pact member tried to restore a "bourgeois" system—that is, one in which non-Communist parties could compete with the Communists. Conservatives in the Czechoslovak party, in contact with the Soviet ambassador in Prague, continued to denounce Dubcek and plot their own return to power. They finally persuaded Brezhnev, and on August 20, 1968, Warsaw Pact forces swept into Czechoslovakia to "save" socialism. The main forces, of course, were Soviet, but token Polish, Bulgarian, and East German troops were ordered to participate in order to show it was an all-bloc effort.

There was no armed resistance and little bloodshed. Two-thirds of the Czechoslovak Communist party central committee condemned the intervention. The population was near to unanimous in its condemnation and proudly placed pictures of Dubcek everywhere. Dubcek was arrested and taken to Moscow for talking to by Brezhnev, but Dubcek wouldn't back down. Brezhnev, knowing the world was watching, let Dubcek return to office but greatly curbed his reforms. In April 1969, Dubcek was formally ousted and made a minor forestry official in his native Slovakia with instructions to not speak to the media. Conservative Communist Gustav Husak, also a Slovak, was named party first secretary and proceeded to purge reformist elements at every level. Husak called it "normalization," in effect, a partial return to the Stalin model but with greater attention to consumer needs. This brought a temporary improvement in the standard of living, but Czech enthusiasm for work, which flowered under Dubcek, evaporated, and the economy slowed.

The seeds of Husak's later downfall, though, were planted. The liberal and reformist Communists who carried out the Prague Spring were either purged from the party or quit. Some joined with anti-Communist dissidents in 1977 to found

---

The Brezhnev Doctrine

One of the most interesting points of the 1968 Soviet invasion of Czechoslovakia was the way Soviet party chief Leonid Brezhnev rationalized it. Once a country had turned Communist, it would be against Marx's laws of history to let capitalists and imperialists sneak back in and take it over again. History proceeds only onward, to socialism. So, argued Brezhnev, if fools and traitors try to make a Communist country non-Communist, it is the internationalist duty of other Communist states to rescue their threatened brother. The Brezhnev Doctrine—it was so named in the West, not the East—in other words said, once Communist, always Communist.

    Underneath the Marxist mumbo jumbo, the real meaning of the Brezhnev Doctrine was that the Soviet Union still evaluated East Europe as its protective shield against the West. A non-Communist Czecho-slovakia—which is what the country would have soon become with Dubcek's far-reaching reforms—would drop out of the Warsaw Pact or become an uncooperative member. Looking at a map, Czechoslovakia stretches like a dagger from West Germany to the Soviet Ukraine. Stalin, you will recall, seized Ruthenia in order to have a border with Czechoslovakia. Geopolitics rather than ideology provides a better explanation for the Brezhnev Doctrine.

Charter 77, an organization for civil rights that was rudely suppressed. Among the original 242 signers of Charter 77 were 140 ex-Communists. Charter 77, although many of its members were jailed, kept alive the spirit of opposition and served to produce the political seeds and the leadership for Civic Forum, which brought down the Communist regime in 1989.

Gdansk, Poland, 1970

Within a few years of his elevation to power during the Poznan uprising of 1956, Gomulka had proved himself to be generally conservative. Under his relatively relaxed police and cultural controls, there was a great deal of intellectual ferment in Poland, all pointing in the direction of greater freedom. Gomulka, however, rejected suggestions for political and economic liberalization. Basically, Gomulka was afraid that such reforms could both weaken the party's control and bring Soviet intervention. Actually, he was right on both counts. But without economic reform, the Polish economy began to run down. The Prague Spring entranced Polish students. Discontent and disturbances grew in the late 1960s. Police beat and dispersed student demonstrators.

An example of the Communist use of anti-Semitism for political infighting came in Poland in 1968 from the man in charge of Poland's police. Brutish interior minister Mieczyslaw Moczar, leader of the party's conservative and nationalistic

Partisan faction (so named because some had fought in the underground during the war), blamed the disturbances on Jews still serving the Communist regime. Moczar called their presence a "Zionist plot." Poland's Jews, by that time reduced to fewer than 30,000 and mostly elderly, were a handy scapegoat. Moczar attempted to use traditional anti-Semitic feelings as a lever to pry Gomulka from power so that he could take over himself. Brezhnev, fearing Moczar's nationalistic tendencies, backed Gomulka. Gomulka stayed in power; he purged Jewish officials and encouraged Jews to emigrate; most of the able-bodied did.

Such distractions did nothing for Poland's worsening economic situation. In December 1970, the desperate Gomulka government simultaneously raised prices and cut wages, and did this just in time for Christmas. Street demonstrations and violence broke out all along the Baltic seacoast in reaction to the price hikes. At the Lenin Shipyards in Gdansk (formerly the German city of Danzig) on the Baltic, workers struck, occupied the shipyards, and refused to leave. Troops moved in, killing 45 and injuring nearly 1,200. Workers put up three giant steel crosses in Gdansk to commemorate the massacre. As the protests started to spread, Gomulka, who suffered a stroke or heart attack upon hearing of the violence, resigned. His replacement, party administrator Edward Gierek, was no better.

The Rise of Solidarity

Like Gomulka, Gierek proved to be a temporary calmer-downer rather than a finder of long-term solutions. He was more responsive to worker demands. He even held an open dialogue when Baltic workers threatened another strike. Gierek blamed Gomulka, rescinded the price hikes, and boosted wages and fringe benefits. He allowed and recognized worker committees outside of the officially controlled Communist unions. He eased out Moczar and his unsavory Partisans. All of this was well and good, but it did nothing for the Polish economy.

Gierek's plan for the Polish economy, if indeed there was one, was to borrow heavily from the West for the purchase of modern imported technology, which would then be used to manufacture goods for export. It didn't work; in fact, it didn't work anywhere in East Europe. The Polish goods could not compete on the world market; some were completely the wrong product and were too expensive. The oil price hikes of the 1970s were reflected in higher costs for Soviet energy (which were still below world prices), and this increased costs for Poland's energy-inefficient factories. Poland, tied more than ever to the Soviet economy, produced much of its ships, locomotives, computers, and construction equipment for the Soviet rather than for the Western market. The foreign loans, much of them West German, were largely wasted, and by 1980 Poland's international debt topped $20 billion, one of the highest per capita debts in the world.

Polish farm production stagnated, and food shortages started appearing. The regime, always unhappy about the largely independent Polish farmers, was still trying to encourage them to form larger units for greater productivity. Polish peasants, smelling a trick, continually refused; they saw no reason to cooperate with the regime.

In 1976, new strikes broke out, but this time with a twist that proved to be decisive. Worker discontent was one thing. Workers had specific demands related to the cost of living and their wages. The regime might be able to handle these demands by giving in a little, applying force here and there, and keeping the strikes isolated. Intellectual discontent was something else and had to be handled differently. Intellectual demands were not so specific or easy to compromise as worker demands, for intellectuals wanted not a few more zloty but major reforms. Unstated, of course, many of them wanted the end of the entire Communist system. They rejected the system not just on grounds of material deprivation, but also on moral and philosophical grounds. In Poland intellectuals were sheltered and aided by the Catholic Church, which had been left largely autonomous by the regime. The Communists knew better than to take on the Polish Catholic Church. Intellectuals could be somewhat controlled by prison terms, by the loss of their jobs, by a lack of publishing resources, and by encouraging them to emigrate.

Revolutions, it has been said, must be based on the coming together of mass discontent and elite discontent, the numbers being provided by the workers and the brains being provided by the intellectuals. Kept separate, the two forms of opposition are weak and controllable. When the two streams of discontent form an alliance, however, they gain greatly in strength, sometimes enough to overthrow the regime. In Poland, numbers and brains combined effectively for the first time in East Europe, eventually leading to the first ouster of communism in the region.

The 1976 Polish strikes inspired a group of dissident intellectuals, with sociologist Jacek Kuron and historian Adam Michnik prominent among them, to form the Workers' Defense Committee, known by its Polish initials as KOR (*Komitet Obrony Robotnikow*). KOR investigated police brutality against strikers and offered legal aid for those arrested. In this way, intellectuals bridged the gap that had separated them from workers. Next, university students formed a Committee for Student Solidarity that published underground many antiregime pamphlets. Combining with KOR, they formed a "flying university" that held seminars and alternative courses in private apartments, free of the surveillance of Communist education officials.

By 1980, the ingredients were in place for a major antiregime movement that had both numbers and brains. The trigger came that year when the regime, in desperate economic straits, moved to raise meat prices. Worker opposition again flared at the Lenin Shipyards and quickly spread along the Baltic coast. Its leader was a modest but tough electrician, Lech Walesa, a man of little formal education but of firm Catholic and worker-rights convictions who had been fired from the shipyards in 1976 for his role in strikes. Worker committees soon banded together under the name Solidarity (in Polish, *Solidarnosc*), and the movement spread like wildfire nationwide in late 1980. Within a year, Solidarity had an amazing 7 million members, nearly a fifth of the Polish population. Eventually, it totalled 10 million.

Communist Praetorianism

It used to be theorized that Communist countries were immune to military coups because the party was so strong and controlled everything, including the armed forces. We now see this is inaccurate. A Communist regime is as vulnerable to praetorianism—the tendency to military takeover—as any other type of regime. A weak government, as in much of the Third World, has little to rely on. Its legitimacy is low or nonexistent; its parties are just puppets of the regime; and, being corrupt and inefficient, it usually does a bad job making the economy grow. In times of crisis—a wave of strikes, a mounting guerrilla war, an outbreak of urban terrorism—the military often pulls a coup with the stated intention of saving the country from chaos. The generals do not necessarily relish the idea of seizing power, but they become convinced that they are the only organized force left in the country—and sometimes they are right. Praetorianism is therefore not just a problem of a power-mad military but of system breakdown in which the military is about the only structure left. Later, of course, the military may become power-mad and stay in power for decades. Such was the pattern in Brazil and Chile.

We now see that Communist countries can suffer system breakdown too. Into the vacuum may step the army, and for exactly the same reasons as have been demonstrated in the Brazilian or Chilean military coups. In the late 1960s, as the ragtag Red Guards of the Cultural Revolution ravaged all authority in China, including the authority of the Communist party, the Chinese army quietly took over and gradually restored order. In 1981, Poland, in effect had a military coup. The Polish generals saw themselves as the only ones who could restore order and save Poland. Any country, Communist or not, that comes under severe stress with weak political institutions is likely to fall into the praetorian pattern of the military stepping forth to "save" the country from chaos. This, of course, is a possibility in the Soviet Union too.

In addition to the usual worker demands for more pay and less work, Solidarity demanded to be officially recognized as a legal trade union, something the Warsaw regime was reluctant to do, for it already had a puppet Communist union that it used as an instrument of control. The regime also understood that something as big and angry as Solidarity had more than worker rights in mind; it threatened their very rule. And soon enough, Solidarity also began to demand worker self-management on the Yugoslav model, with elected committees in each factory to name directors and guide financial and production decisions. Solidarity, with its intellectual and Catholic input, saw itself as far more than a labor union. It was a movement to save Poland by introducing democracy. To calm the Soviets, at its first national conference in the fall of 1981, Solidarity said it had no intention of pulling Poland out of the Warsaw Pact.

The Soviet Union, then under the aging conservative Leonid Brezhnev, the same man who had invaded Czechoslovakia in 1968, did not trust Solidarity. The Gierek regime, unmasked as corrupt and incapable, was by now totally illegitimate in the eyes of its citizens. Communist party members were resigning in droves. A power vacuum was starting to build. Before Solidarity could fill it, the Polish army took over on December 13, 1981, reportedly with the Kremlin's approval. For Moscow, a Polish military takeover was cheaper and easier than the sending in of Soviet troops. The commander of Poland's armed forces, General Wojciech Jaruzelski, who began his military career in Polish units organized by the Soviet army in World War II, named himself Communist party first secretary and prime minister. Thousands of Solidarity activists were arrested, including Walesa. Strikes were put down by armed coercion. Solidarity went underground. The only plausible argument Jaruzelski could offer—and he never said it in public—was, "Better me than the Russians." It was one of the few things the Warsaw military regime and the Polish people could reluctantly agree on.

SUGGESTED READINGS

BATT, JUDY. *Economic Reform and Political Change in Eastern Europe: A Comparison of the Czechoslovak and Hungarian Experience.* New York: St. Martin's, 1988.

BUGAJSKI, JANUSZ. *Czechoslovakia: Charter 77's Decade of Dissent.* Westport, CT: Praeger, 1987.

_____, and MAXINE POLLACK. *East European Fault Lines: Dissent, Opposition, and Social Activism.* Boulder, CO: Westview, 1989.

CARRÈRE D'ENCAUSSE, HÉLÈNE. *Big Brother: The Soviet Union and Soviet Europe.* New York: Holmes & Meier, 1987.

KITTRIE, NICHOLAS, AND IVAN VOLGYES, eds. *The Uncertain Future: Gorbachev's Eastern Bloc.* New York: Paragon House, 1988.

LINDEN, RONALD A. *Communist States and International Change: Romania and Yugoslavia in Comparative Perspective.* Boston: Allen & Unwin, 1987.

MARER, PAUL. "The Economies and Trade of Eastern Europe." William E. Griffth, ed. *Central and Eastern Europe: The Opening Curtain?* Boulder, CO: Westview, 1989.

SCHÖPFLIN, GEORGE, ed. *The Soviet Union and Eastern Europe: A Handbook.* New York: Praeger, 1970.

SCHWARTZ, HARRY. *Eastern Europe in the Soviet Shadow.* New York: John Day, 1973.

WESCHLER, LAWRENCE. *The Passion of Poland: From Solidarity to the State of War.* New York: Pantheon, 1984.

CHAPTER SEVEN _____

1989: The Gorbachev Factor

The Prague Spring of 1968 marks the appearance of open splits in the ranks of the Communist elites of most East European countries, splits that eventually brought liberal Communists to power for very brief tenures. By 1990, liberal Communists had in turn been voted out of power by non-Communists in all but the Balkan countries; their turns for non-Communist governments will come with genuinely free elections. However brief their time in office, it will be argued here that these liberal Communists played an important role in bringing down Communist regimes.

At first the term "liberal" or "reform" Communist may sound a little funny. We can define a *conservative* Communist as one who wishes to generally preserve the Stalinist system, and a *liberal* Communist as one who wishes to reform it in a more open and flexible direction. Historically, no Communist party has permitted formal factions, liberal or conservative. Informally, of course, factions often formed around personalities and programs, but no one admitted this or attached a public label to themselves. That could have been fatal, for any identifiable faction could serve as a scapegoat, "an antiparty group," and get purged. So factions in ruling Communist parties were always low-profile, discerned only by the diligent research of Western analysts. Now, of course, even in the Soviet Communist party, there are fairly clear factions, but they have gone public only recently. It is probably safe to say that all Communist parties contain factions just waiting to come out of the closet. In East Europe, over the course of a generation, liberal Communists increasingly stepped forward.

Already in the late 1950s, faint stirrings could be heard among some East European economists about the need to explore non-Stalinist alternatives. The limits and imbalances of the Stalinist model were slowly becoming clear, and growth was starting to slacken. Khrushchev's 1955 apology to Tito emboldened some East

---

The Poisoning of East Europe

East Europe is the world's most polluted region, the result of four decades of Stalinist industrialization. The very heart of Europe, where Poland, Czechoslovakia, and East Germany border one another, is described by experts as an "ecological disaster." For Communists who were trying to boost industrial production, the environment counted for absolutely nothing. Capitalist countries have vastly better controls against pollution. This is because pluralist Western systems are responsive to protest by concerned groups; Communist systems aren't. Visitors had long noticed the terrible air in most East European cities, much of it from the unlimited burning of cheap brown coal, lignite. Most Western countries control the burning of lignite (named after Legnica, Poland, formerly Liegnitz, Germany), which produces little heat and much pollution, especially sulfur dioxide. Many East European cities have a distinctive, acrid smell from the burning of poor-quality coal.

The growth in number of private automobiles in East Europe made the air much worse by adding another acid, nitrous oxide. Soviet and East European motor vehicles are inefficient consumers of fuel and have no anti-smog devices. East European buses belch a thick, black diesel smoke that would get them banned in most Western countries. Depending on the terrain and winds, smog often extends far into the countryside that surrounds large East European cities. Many East European forests are dying from air pollution and acid rain.

In the 1980s, word began to leak out of serious health problems from environmental pollution in East Europe. Deaths from lung cancer in certain areas of Poland, Czechoslovakia, and Romania were extremely high. Chemical factories and power plants had no stack scrubbers, and they dumped their waste products into the ground, contaminating the water. Some areas are known to be dangerous for children and expectant mothers. In one particularly bad area, in Katowice in the south of Poland, people retreat to deep salt mines to give their lungs respite from the poisonous surface air. Environmental degradation by itself would have eventually forced major changes in the Communist systems of East Europe.

European thinkers to speak of developing their own paths to socialism. By the 1960s, criticism of the Stalinist system was widespread among economists and other intellectuals. Poland's Oskar Lange and Czechoslovakia's Ota Sik articulated ideas on economic liberalization and decentralization. Some East Europeans studied abroad, including in the United States and Yugoslavia, and brought back ideas for an economy that could combine socialism with free markets. The ruling conservative party elites rejected such notions, and the struggle between party conservatives and party liberals forms much of the history of East Europe from the 1960s to the ouster of communism in 1989.

Party conservatives feared—correctly, as it turned out—that anything but minor reforms could make the entire system fall apart and cost them their comfortable jobs and perquisites. Many party elites in East Europe lived quite well, some at a standard of living comparable to that of Western millionaires. The ideological argument offered by conservative ruling Communists (few of whom really cared about ideology) was that the form of socialism had already been determined and tested by time. New forms did not need to be developed because the system—essentially a somewhat modified Stalin model—works and is moving us along to an ever-improving socialism. Experiments can only wreck a working system. Increasingly, of course, such arguments looked ridiculous in the face of stagnant growth, declining living standards, growing mass discontent, and a poisoned environment.

The interesting thing about the liberal or reform Communists is that they shared many of the perspectives of non-Communist intellectuals. Both knew the system had to change in a major way. Both saw that the economy was defective, that public morale was declining, and that that environmental damage could soon become irreversible. Neither could accept the Soviet Union as a model for anything. The difference between the two groups was that the liberal Communists wanted to work within the system for major reform; most non-Communists wanted to chuck out the system. The liberal Communists were willing to grant autonomy to new political movements—for such causes as worker rights, protection of the environment, civil liberties, and so on—and to open a dialogue with them. Some liberal Communists could envision a mixed or hybrid system with the Communist party taking the leading role but sharing some power with non-Communists.

For as long as they could, conservative Communists rejected such notions and refused to budge, either politically or personally. Most of them became quite elderly in office, as Communist systems have no mechanism for the regular and orderly replacement of persons in power. The longer they stayed, the more they delayed. Their systems cried out for reform. Many younger party members along with non-party intellectuals simmered in frustration. All the ingredients for major upheaval were present, but to move the systems of East Europe it took Soviet party chief Mikhail Gorbachev's conclusion that the Soviet Union could no longer afford its East European empire.

There were many and strong underlying factors that preceded Gorbachev's decisions: no regime legitimacy, mass discontent, lagging economies, a split party, and growing foreign indebtedness. But these factors had been present for years, in some cases for decades. What suddenly made them operative in 1989? Why weren't Communist regimes thrown out in 1979? In 1969? Only one explanation fits: The regimes of East Europe liberalized and threw out the old conservative Communists because Gorbachev told them to. Specifically, during 1989 Gorbachev had personal meetings with nearly every Communist chief of East Europe, either in their capital or in Moscow. His public statements indicated support for change with no Soviet interference in the process. He bluntly repudiated the Brezhnev Doctrine.

The Debt Factor

Starting in the 1970s, most of the Communist regimes of East Europe played one last desperate card to try to keep from having to introduce market systems and political democratization: They plunged their countries deeply into debt, borrowing from the West in the vain hope that Western loans and technology would lift their slowing economies. By the end of 1988, the external indebtedness of East European countries, overall and per capita, was as follows:

	Overall (in billions)	Per Capita
Poland	$38.9	$1,000
East Germany	20.4	1,250
Yugoslavia	22.7	960
Hungary	17.7	1,800
Bulgaria	6.1	820
Romania	4.9	90
Czechoslovakia	2.5	400

Soon enough, East Germany didn't have to worry. Its big brother, rich West Germany, amply covered the GDR's external debt—most of it owed to West Germany—when they united in 1990. In fact, getting East Germany into debt with West Germany had long been, since the 1960s, Bonn's unstated strategy. The more dependent the GDR became upon the Federal Republic of Germany (FRG), the easier it would be for West Germany to eventually swallow East Germany. It worked.

Romania's external debt had been cut to almost nothing by the end of the 1980s but at a terrible price. Ceausescu decreed that everything must go for export to pay off Romania's substantial debt, leaving nothing for consumption. Romanians were so materially starved that eventually they erupted in violence and murdered Ceausescu. Czechoslovakia never got deeply into debt and didn't have to worry.

The other nations of East Europe, especially Hungary, had to worry. They had purchased a temporary pause in their economic decline and made life a little more comfortable for their citizens. Regimes had used foreign debt to paper over their deep economic problems. Then the loans came due, and many East European lands could not repay them. Their leaders stood unmasked as frightened fools. External debt was another reason the conservative Communist regimes of East Europe were pushed out of power.

GORBACHEV'S NEW THINKING

Between 1986 and 1989, Soviet president and party leader Mikhail Gorbachev changed his mind about East Europe, turning from adherence to the Brezhnev Doctrine to benign indifference about East Europe's fate. By 1989, whatever East Europe wanted to do—even ousting Communist regimes—was acceptable to him. The "New Thinking," a phrase Gorbachev used to describe his foreign policy, in the case of East Europe was actually forced on him and probably went farther than he wished. Did Gorbachev know what he was doing when he urged the conservative Communist leaders of East Europe to carry out major reforms? His chief interest had never been East Europe itself. He was preoccupied with saving the Soviet Union. East Europe mattered to him only insofar as it made that goal easier or harder to achieve. He was applying a double standard—firmness for the Soviet Union and flexibility for East Europe—when he told the Communist regimes of East Europe in 1989 that the Soviet Union would no longer support them.

It is likely that Gorbachev initially foresaw nothing more than the partial transformation of East European lands into some kind of liberal Communist or "middle way" systems that brought in certain features of pluralism, democracy, and a market economy but which held their overall structures under Communist party control. And he was willing to tolerate less change for the Soviet Union than for East Europe. Once liberalization got under way, however, it kept going farther and faster than Gorbachev had envisioned. It is likely that Gorbachev had little or no overall plan but merely improvised as events hit.

Early in his tenure—he came to power in 1985—Gorbachev did not sound at all flexible on East Europe. Addressing the 1986 Polish party congress, Gorbachev warned that "socialist gains are irreversible" and that the Soviet Union would make sure no one "undermined" the "socialist community." It sounded pretty much like the straight Brezhnev Doctrine. But during the next three years, Gorbachev changed his tune. His situation worsened considerably. With his marginal and ineffective economic tinkering, the Soviet economy declined. Food shortages appeared, and citizens complained bitterly. Non-Russian nationalities took advantage of his *glasnost* ("openness") program to publicize their demands for autonomy or even independence from the Soviet Union. Violence broke out in several areas.

Afghanistan, which the Soviets invaded in 1979, looked like a never-ending war. In 1986, the *mujahedin*, the Afghani anti-Soviet guerrillas, received U.S. Stinger missiles and started downing Soviet helicopter gunships; the tide of battle turned against the Soviets. In 1988, the Kremlin announced that Soviet troops would be withdrawn from Afghanistan; they were out by early 1989. Altogether, the Soviets had lost some 15,000 troops in Afghanistan (a number low compared to the 60,000 U.S. troops killed in Vietnam). Some observers suggest that the impossibility of victory in Afghanistan forced Gorbachev to change his mind about using Soviet military power to prop up Communist regimes in East Europe. There

The 1989 Pattern

With many variations, the events of 1989 and 1990 in East Europe unrolled more or less like this in each country:

1. A group of liberal Communist officials, who were the seconds in command in the party structure, formed to quietly discuss ways to get rid of the conservatives who were still first in command.
2. This group of liberals was emboldened by Gorbachev's urgings to reform.
3. Anticommunist moral heroes stepped forward to lead strikes or protests, the regime would crack down, and this provoked more unrest.
4. The liberal Communists took this as their signal; they would step out of the closet and call for major reforms and democracy.
5. A phone call from the Kremlin would put Gorbachev on the side of the liberals; power then tilted to them.
6. The old Stalinist leaders would then resign or retire, and they were soon stripped of all their offices and even kicked out of the party.
7. The coalition of liberal Communists would then change the party's name from "Communist" to "Socialist" and promise free elections for early 1990.
8. In most of East Europe, new centrist parties would win the free elections; the Socialists (ex-Communists) would become small parties.
9. Gorbachev would then congratulate the new non-Communist government.

is no firm evidence for this, only an interesting coincidence in time.

The only bright spot on Gorbachev's international horizon was, curiously, the United States. President Reagan, who operated on the basis of gut instinct, met Gorbachev and decided he could be trusted. Reagan's harsh rhetoric about the "evil empire" of the Soviet Union ceased. Moscow made some important concessions leading to a treaty banning all intermediate-range nuclear forces (the INF treaty), which was signed in the White House in December 1987 and ratified by the Senate by the time Reagan visited Moscow in May 1988. Clearly, Gorbachev was calling off the Cold War. To really end it, however, he knew the Soviet Union could not retain firm control over East Europe.

Kremlin signals that East Europe could go its own way started in 1988. In his visit to Yugoslavia in March 1988, Gorbachev foreswore any "interference in the internal affairs of other states under any pretext whatsoever," and he further stated that all nations have the right to "their own roads of social development." It sounded like a replay of Khrushchev's 1955 visit to Belgrade. Later that same year Gorbachev told the UN General Assembly that "freedom of choice" for all nations to decide their own path "is a universal principle which allows no exceptions."

Imperial Overstretch

The incredible changes in Gorbachev's policies are illuminated by Paul Kennedy's "imperial overstretch" thesis. Kennedy's massive and controversial 1987 book, *The Rise and Decline of the Great Powers*, argued that powerful nations are driven to expand until they overexpand, until their economy can no longer maintain their extravagant imperial costs, especially military commitments. The empires then slowly contract, sometimes collapse, from economic causes. Especially important to Kennedy's thesis is the imperial power's *relative* economic performance. Devoting so much of its economy to imperial and defense needs drains its economy so that after some decades smaller but more efficient economies start outperforming it. The imperial power's economy may still be growing, but not as fast as those of the upstart powers. Gradually, the empire it has built over many decades and at great expense becomes a drain and hindrance, pulling the imperial power down.

A storm of controversy erupted around Kennedy's suggestion that the United States might fit the pattern of imperial overstretch. But hardly anyone disputed Kennedy's contention that the Soviet Union fit the pattern very well. The collapse of communism in East Europe could have been scripted by Paul Kennedy.

In 1989 Gorbachev got stronger and more explicit about East Europe. The final communique of the annual Warsaw Pact meeting said "there are no universal models of socialism." Gorbachev urged the ministers to get in touch with their own peoples and traditions and make their economies work. He didn't specifically say to throw out socialism, but he publicly and repeatedly told the Communist regimes of the region to liberalize and democratize. He warned them that if they refused to move or went too slowly, they would be overthrown. And later, when they were overthrown, that was fine with him. He cabled congratulations to the non-Communist successor regimes and has so far gotten along well with them.

In short, sometime between 1986 and 1989—probably during 1988—Gorbachev decided to lift the Soviet hold on East Europe and let it go its own way, even if that meant the ouster of Communist regimes. He sacrificed the Soviet Eastern empire in order to join the West.

Domestically, Gorbachev avoided mention of the upheaval in East Europe. Perhaps he was embarrassed; perhaps he simply didn't care. One of his few references to East Europe came at the July 1990 party congress, when some hard-line Soviet generals complained about the loss of East Europe. Gorbachev sharply rebuked them: "Do you want the tanks again? Shall we teach them again how to live?"

Gorbachev gave a green light to sweeping changes in East Europe but only a cautious yellow light to modest changes in the Soviet Union. At home, Gorbachev wished to keep things under party and personal control. But the changes he had unleashed turned on him. What Gorbachev welcomed in East Europe, he tried to hold back in the Soviet Union.

Particularly revealing is Gorbachev's adamant refusal to consider, in November 1989, parliamentary debate over deleting Article 6 of the Soviet Constitution, the clause that gave the Communist party a monopoly on political power. Harshly, almost brutally, Gorbachev squelched discussion on the matter. He even told Andrei Sakharov, the "conscience of Russia," then a member of the Congress of People's Deputies, to shut up and sit down. There was nothing moderate or liberal about Gorbachev at this time. The way Gorbachev saw it, a cohesive Communist party under his control was the indispensable tool for economic restructuring. To fragment political power and allow competing parties would dilute, distract, and ultimately block his design for a market socialist economy.

Ultimately and grudgingly, Gorbachev did relent, and Article 6 was repealed in early 1990. But Gorbachev continued to try to preserve the Communist party's monopoly on power. The repeal of Article 6 did not have the same rapid and decisive impact on the Soviet political system that similar repeals had had on East European regimes. What Gorbachev gladly granted East Europe he fought against and delayed in the Soviet Union.

By the time Brezhnev died in 1982, after eighteen years at the Soviet helm, the ship of state was dead in the water. By the time Gorbachev took over in 1985, all thinking Soviets knew the economy was bad and fast getting worse. Moscow's imperial commitments were costing a bundle. East Europe, figuring the expenses of stationing Soviet armed forces in those countries and economic subsidies, cost the Soviet Union an estimated $17 billion a year in 1970, which then grew to $40 billion a year in 1980. Subsidies to East Europe included selling petroleum and natural gas at below world-market prices and purchasing East European manufactured goods that could not compete on the world market. Soviet economic and military support for Third World client states such as Cuba, South Yemen, Syria, Angola, and Vietnam cost many billions more. The Soviet empire, with an inefficient, backward economic base, was severely overstretched.

As we considered earlier, precise figures on the size and condition of the Soviet economy do not exist; all are estimates, some foreign, some Soviet. The Soviets themselves issue no Gross National Product figures, and the numbers they do issue on other measures are dubious. Moscow gets its GNP estimates from the CIA, which has a large section devoted entirely to measuring the Soviet economy. (In a sense, we are subsidizing the Soviet economy by making their GNP calculations for them.)

The measure the CIA is looking for is the percentage of Soviet GNP devoted to defense. This figure measures the strain on the Soviet economy. For many years the CIA estimated that the Soviets spent roughly twice as much (about 12 percent) of their GNP on defense as did the United States (about 6 percent). In the mid-1970s, when George Bush headed the CIA, he cast a skeptical eye on CIA estimates. A "Team B" of outside academics, with fierce anti-Soviet reputations, was appointed to review and criticize the CIA's methods of estimating both the Soviet GNP and the portion of it devoted to defense. Team B argued that the CIA had overestimated the size of the Soviet GNP and underestimated Soviet defense spending. They thought Soviet defense spending was around 20 percent of the Soviet GNP. The CIA, bending with the political winds, adjusted its number upward to 16 percent, and for much of the 1980s this was the standard estimate.

At a 1990 Washington conference, however, two maverick Soviet economists said that everyone was wrong, that the Soviet GNP was smaller and the defense expenditures greater: some 25 to 28 percent of the GNP! This, of course, would be a crushing burden on any economy. Whatever figure you pick, 16 or 28 percent, the drain on the Soviet economy was enormous, stunting growth, depriving citizens of consumer goods—even necessities—and robbing them of any incentive to work. Later in 1990, Soviet foreign minister Shevardnadze used 25 percent as the portion devoted to defense. With costs like that, the Soviet empire was economically unsustainable. Brezhnev had been able to pretend that it was sustainable; Gorbachev, after four years in office to ponder the facts, could not. Trying to continue the imperial game could cost the Soviet Union everything.

Gorbachev actually worsened the Soviet economy. He announced early in his tenure a series of modest economic reforms under the grandiose title of *perestroika* (restructuring). These reforms did not go nearly as far as the earlier efforts of Hungary and China. Perhaps Gorbachev wished to go faster on economic reform, but he faced powerful conservative forces whose jobs and perquisites would be threatened by any major makeover of the economy in a market direction. Hesitation, improvisation, and outright mistakes characterized Gorbachev's economic program. By 1989, amidst glaring food shortages, Gorbachev knew that changes would have to go much farther and the Soviet budget drastically trimmed. Moscow had been operating at a mammoth budget deficit for many years and was printing money far in excess of the amount of goods people could buy, producing a monumental "ruble overhang" ready to erupt into wild inflation.

East Europe appears to have little concerned Gorbachev at this desperate stage. Said one Hungarian economist: "We were the last thing he was thinking about." Still, letting East Europe go its own way would help Gorbachev in several areas:

1. Soviet forces stationed in East Europe could be reduced and demobilized, saving on defense expenditures.

2. The pullback of Soviet forces in East Europe would assure the West that the Soviet Union posed no military threat and was therefore a fit partner for arms-control agreements. Arms cuts would further trim the Soviet defense budget.

3. By the same token, the Soviet Union would demonstrate its suitability for badly needed Western trade and investment, naturally on credit.

Hard Currency

Money that is freely traded and widely used and respected in world trade and tourism is called "hard" currency. Dollars, deutsche marks, and Swiss francs are instantly recognized and welcomed everywhere. Currencies that are either not convertible or are inflating so rapidly that few want them, are called "soft." In world trade and tourism, no one uses Soviet rubles, Polish zloty, or Brazilian cruzeiros. Sometimes the terms "dollars" and "hard currency" are used interchangeably, for the dollar is the most recognized hard currency.

---

4.   Moscow could also end its supply of subsidized raw materials to East Europe. If the East Europeans wished to purchase Soviet oil and natural gas, they could pay for it in hard currency at world prices.

Now, some policies logically flow from the preceding points. The Brezhnev Doctrine had to be declared legally dead. Repeatedly in 1989 Gorbachev declared to East European Communist leaders, who came to him with fear in their faces, that he would not prop them up. To avoid mass anger and shore up their legitimacy, he advised them to undertake major reforms of a sort that went much further than anything he had in mind for the Soviet Union. In many East European lands, the visiting Gorbachev was greeted by enthusiastic chants of "Gorby! Gorby!" He was seen as the liberalizing hero who was ordering the ossified local party gerontocracy to open up the system. And when East European liberalization led to the ouster of Communist regimes, Gorbachev said not a word against it, and scarcely anything about it.

This does not mean that Gorbachev was necessarily delighted with the nearly clean sweep from power of party comrades from the Baltic to the Black Sea. More likely, he simply didn't have time or patience to care. Economic considerations far outweighed ideological considerations. Indeed, by this time probably no one east of the Elbe had any Marxist ideological considerations. And Gorbachev had warned the old East European leaders to liberalize before it was too late.

THE DOMINOES FALL

President Eisenhower first used the image of a row of falling dominoes in describing the Communist threat to Southeast Asia in the 1950s. The image fits East Europe better. In 1989, one domino after another toppled into the next. Once the toppling of the regimes started, it could not stop until communism was effectively finished in East Europe.

Poland

During the 1980s, things grew worse in Poland. Solidarity was decimated and went underground, but it stayed very much alive in the hearts and minds of Poles.

The Popieluszko Factor

In October 1984, a pro-Solidarity Catholic priest, Father Jerzy Popieluszko was abducted. Eight days later, amidst a massive popular outcry, Poland's interior minister, General Czeslaw Kiszczak, announced with shame and regret that Popieluszko had been taken by some of Kiszczak's own security police, beaten to death, and dumped in a reservoir. The three policemen involved said they acted under orders "from the top." Kiszczak and Jaruzelski denied issuing such orders, and they were probably telling the truth. Still, it was their regime that set the police against the church. The hated security police, who had been arresting and beating Solidarity activists for years, were repeatedly denounced from the pulpit.

The Popieluszko incident shook the Jaruzelski government and deepened mass hatred toward it. Morally, the government did not have a leg to stand on. Five years later, when Gorbachev withdrew its Soviet prop, the Communist government collapsed. In the end, Father Popieluszko triumphed.

The economy got worse, with annual growth rates near zero. General Jaruzelski, never popular to begin with, gained no followers. Approximately one-fourth of Polish Communist party members had quit the party in disgust. The Roman Catholic Church stood as a bastion of traditional and humane values; masses were full to overflowing and sermons were frequently pro-Solidarity and antiregime. Lashing out at the anti-Communist clergy, security police beat to death a leading priest.

In 1987, the Jaruzelski government released the last of the Solidarity activists it had held in prison, some since 1981. It was intended as a goodwill gesture but earned the regime nothing. In 1988, new strikes broke out, again under the familiar banners of Solidarity, which was technically still illegal. Now the Jaruzelski regime was at the end of its tether. Economists worried that if the economy slipped much further, Poland would become, in effect, a Third World country. Environmental poisoning was so bad that some biologists worried about the genetic degradation of the Polish people.

In February 1988 General Kiszczak, the interior minister, called some of the very Solidarity people he had earlier imprisoned to meet with him for what became known as the "roundtable talks" to save Poland. The roundtable connoted meeting as equals. This was a major breakthrough, for it signaled the beginning of shared power. The Solidarity side was headed by Lech Walesa. The talks ended in April with the legalization of Solidarity and an agreement to hold semifree elections in 1989.

Kiszczak and prime minister Mieczyslaw Rakowski were playing a relatively liberal role—although their earlier actions in suppressing Solidarity gave few Poles

---

The Contagion Factor

Related to the word "contagious," contagion in political science means the spread of ideas by copying. Economists call this the "international demonstration effect." Something happening in one country suggests to people of another to try the same thing. Contagion does not happen universally or automatically. If conditions are unalike, there will be no copying. But if conditions and attitudes are similar—as in East Europe in the late 1980s—what transpires in one land immediately inspires people in other lands.

---

much confidence in them at the time. In meeting with Solidarity leaders at the 1988 roundtable, they were treating them as equals and asking for their cooperation. They proposed a power-sharing arrangement: In new elections, Solidarity would get 35 percent of the seats of the legislature, the Sejm (pronounced "same"), with the larger part still reserved for the Communist and some small puppet parties. A new upper house, the Senate, would be wide open for free elections. The Senate would have the power to veto bills passed by the Sejm. In effect, Kiszczak and Rakowski offered Solidarity a partnership with right of veto.

Could this have been a long-term, stable solution? No. The reasons are explained in the box on "Fried Snowballs" on page 138. It was an inherently temporary arrangement, although the Communist side may not have realized it at the time. Solidarity swept the Senate races so thoroughly that it clearly indicated the popular wave was with Solidarity. In *unopposed* contests for the lower house, many Communist candidates still lost, for voters could strike off their names in a negative vote. Some of the small parties previously controlled by the Communists in the Sejm—the Peasants party and Christian Democrats—cut their ties to the Communists and drifted over to Solidarity. When the Polish parliament convened after the elections in July 1989, Solidarity, occupying the opposition benches, was morally if not numerically stronger than the Communist party occupying the government benches.

In August 1989, the Sejm voted General Kiszczak as the new prime minister, but everyone understood that he could not really govern without a popular mandate. To solve the impasse, General Jaruzelski, still president and still with the power to nominate the prime minister, named a Solidarity activist and Walesa aide, Tadeusz Mazowiecki (pronounced "mah-zov-yet-ski"), as prime minister. There was one more hurdle, as Communist leaders balked at supporting and participating in a Mazowiecki cabinet. But on August 22, Gorbachev held a 40-minute telephone conversation with Rakowski, after which the Communists announced "partnerlike cooperation" with Solidarity. At a key moment, Gorbachev had talked the Polish Communists into giving up power. On August 24, 1989, the Sejm confirmed Mazowiecki as prime minister by a vote of 378 to 4, with 41 abstentions. The

Sejm was no longer the same; even most of the Communists voted for Poland's first non-Communist government.

Hungary

Poland was first, but Hungary was not far behind. Furthermore, Hungary did something extremely important for the unraveling of communism in all of East Europe. In the summer of 1989, the liberal Communist government in Budapest decided to stop enforcing an East-bloc agreement to keep visitors from other East European countries from fleeing to the West through Hungary's borders. Thousands of East German "tourists" fled across the Hungarian border to Austria, starting a sequence of events that forced the East Berlin regime to change its personnel and policies. This led to the November 1989 opening of the Berlin Wall and in short order to the end of East Germany. Without East Germany to lock in Poland, the East bloc geographically does not hold together.

A change in Hungarian policy—to no longer be a good player in the Warsaw Pact—marked the beginning of the end for the Warsaw Pact. How did this change come about? We cannot exclude the possibility that West Germany—Hungary's biggest creditor—offered financially strapped Budapest some favors (new loans, a delay in repaying the old loans?) in return for opening its western border. Bonn's diplomacy long included economic carrots. In December 1989, West German Chancellor Helmut Kohl addressed the Hungarian parliament with his thanks for the "unforgettable days"—from May to November—that led from the Hungarian border opening to the Berlin Wall's opening.

For this sequence to have taken place, however, considerable change had been required in the Hungarian Communist leadership. In 1988, the now doddering Janos Kadar was dropped as party chief in favor of Karoly Grosz. Kadar was blamed for Hungary's economic woes, but the considerably hard-line Grosz did no better. In 1988, for example, Grosz had police with sticks and tear gas break up a Budapest rally in favor of honoring Imre Nagy. Said Grosz of the idea: "Never." By 1989, however, Grosz had come under tremendous pressure to ease up. In February, amidst growing discontent, Hungary's parliament on the banks of the Danube legalized non-Communist political parties. Groups that had existed as "forums" turned themselves into parties. In March, 75,000 marched in Budapest to demand free elections and the withdrawal of Soviet forces from Hungary. The authorities did not stop them, and Gorbachev pledged not to interfere in East Europe.

In June 1989, a ceremoney of great symbolic importance took place: the reburial, with full honors, of the 1956 hero Imre Nagy and four of his aides. A quarter of a million Hungarians attended, including government ministers. It was as if the Communist regime were admitting error and regret.

Hungarian relations with West Germany changed dramatically, almost as if Hungary were trying to please the FRG. In May 1989, Hungarian troops started tearing down the barbed-wire fence on their Austrian border, making it easier for

"Fried Snowballs": Is Reform Communism Possible?

Decades ago the Polish philosopher Leszek Kolakowski—at that time a sort of Marxist humanist—concluded that it was not possible to reform, liberalize, or seriously modify a Communist system. Reformed communism, wrote Kolakowski, was a contradiction in terms, about as likely as "fried snowballs." If you attempt to fry a snowball, it melts and disappears. Kolakowski subsequently despaired of Marxism and of change in Poland, and he moved to England and later to the United States, where he now teaches at the University of Chicago.

Events in 1989 and 1990 prove Kolakowski right. Throughout East Europe, reform Communists took power with the announced intention of liberalizing and democratizing. Within a few months, all had been replaced by non-Communist regimes. Did this have to happen? Yes, because "communism" and "liberal" do not mix. The crux of communism is control; the crux of liberalism is freedom. The minute you start liberalizing a Communist regime, you start dissolving it; you start frying snowballs.

A regime that attempts to impose near-total control over the economy, politics, society, culture, and even personal relations must fail. Leaders are simply not that smart, nor are the followers that obedient, so as to make society run like a well-oiled machine. Humans, Thomas Hobbes noted centuries ago, are not biologically programmed like bees and cannot form perfect societies like hives, where all know their place and do their jobs without question.

In attempting to impose an impossible and undesirable system, the regime must apply a great deal of coercion and injustice. Humans, again as Hobbes noted, have long memories of the injustices that have been dealt them; their resentments do not fade with time. Accordingly, when the unjust regime, in this case Communist, seeks to mend its ways by liberalizing, many citizens greet it not with a sigh of relief but with a cry of anger.

Permitted to express their views in newly uncensored and accessible mass media, people do so. The regime would like them to criticize the status quo moderately and nicely. Instead, long-smoldering resentments burst out, and then they criticize the regime for everything from economic calamity and political corruption to police repression and environmental degradation. They do not thank the liberal Communist regime for easing up; they want the whole Communist package out. Give them a free-speech inch and they take a democratic mile.

The irony is that the liberal Communist regimes that held power only briefly were composed of relatively nice guys, people (usually younger) within the party who had come to much the same conclusions as anti-Communist critics: that the decaying system had to change. As Alexis de Tocqueville wrote in his classic study of the French Revolution, "The social order overthrown by a revolution is almost always better than the one immediately preceding it." By admitting that things are wrong, the reform regime is also revealing its weakness and fear. The old, pre-reform regime could keep people cowed and silent; the new regime has let them speak. As Tocqueville observed: "The most perilous moment for a bad government is when it seeks to mend its ways."

In a nutshell, reform communism is not possible. If attempted, its life is brief. Both the writings of the classical philosophers and recent empirical evidence illuminate this point. When attempted in East Europe, liberal communism lasted about as long as a snowball in a frying pan.

East German "tourists" to flee. (Hungarian entrepreneurs attached small pieces of barbed wire to plaques to sell as "your piece of the Iron Curtain." People like that will surely succeed at capitalism.) In September, despite angry protest from East Berlin, very liberal Communist foreign minister Gyula Horn opened the Hungarian-Austrian border so that East Germans could simply drive across. Next spring, Horn was awarded West Germany's Grand Cross of the Federal Order of Merit, the highest honor Germany can bestow on foreigners. After the Hungarian elections in the spring of 1990, the very able Horn was out. He had served as foreign minister less than a year, but it was Horn who in large measure had unplugged the Iron Curtain.

While this was happening, reform Communists elbowed aside conservatives. In May 1989, liberal Communists such as Imre Pozsgay and Reszo Nyers, both Hungarian Politburo members, called for meetings with opposition groups and major economic liberalization. In June, they became part of a three-man collective party leadership, pushing Grosz aside.

In September 1989, the now liberal Communist government met with opposition groups to agree on holding multiparty election in 1990. In October, the Communist party met to renounce Marxism and embrace democratic socialism. They changed their name to Socialist and made Reszo Nyers their new leader. He also became prime minister. In the spring of 1990, the Hungarian people elected a moderate anti-Communist coalition. Hungary's liberal Communists exercised power for only a few months, but they moved the system from Communist to free. Did they know what they were doing? Did they understand that they were ending the old system and putting themselves out of jobs? Probably not, but what difference does it make?

East Germany

During the first eight months of 1989 the neo-Stalinist regime of Erich Honecker was not about to put up with the kind of liberal and reformist nonsense that was ruining communism in Poland and Hungary. But by the end of 1989, Honecker was under arrest for stashing public money (obtained from trade with the West) in private Swiss bank accounts.

Like most East Europeans, East Germans were hungry for travel. The regime rarely let them travel to the West, fearing (correctly) that they wouldn't come back. By way of compensation, they generally let them visit other countries within the East bloc. Bloc governments agreed among themselves to impose the same border controls on East European visitors to their countries as they imposed on their own citizens. An East German vacationing in Hungary, for example, was not permitted to cross the border into Austria. That way the East German regime could be sure their citizens would return from vacation.

When Budapest decided that it no longer wished to act as enforcer of East German border regulations, word soon got out among East Germans that a vacation in Hungary could be an escape ticket to West Germany. Hungarian vacations became extremely popular. East Germans would go "camping" near the Austrian border, abandon their flimsy little Trabant cars, and walk across to freedom. Hungarian border guards didn't stop them. Thousands of others took refuge in the West German embassy in Budapest. By September 1989, over 13,000 East Germans had left via the Hungarian route. The East Berlin regime protested; Budapest shrugged. What started in Hungary spread to Czechoslovakia, which borders both East and West Germany. More than 17,000 fled via Czechoslovakia. As before the Berlin Wall went up in 1961, East Germany was again hemorrhaging. To staunch the flow, East Germany closed its border with Czechoslovakia. East Germans became madder than ever.

In September 1989 massive demonstrations broke out, centered in Leipzig. In October Gorbachev visited to urge reform. He told Honecker: "Life punishes those who delay." East Germans greeted the Soviet president with the happy chant, "Gorby, Gorby!" By now 100,000 protesters were marching in Leipzig. Honecker ordered security police to get ready to fire on the Leipzig protesters—to copy the "Chinese solution" carried out the previous June in Beijing. But Egon Krenz, 52, and a much more flexible Communist, sensed catastrophe. As the Politburo member in charge of security, Krenz countermanded Honecker's order. (In another action that proved to be a calming factor: world-famous conductor Kurt Masur opened the Leipzig Gewandthaus concert hall for talks between the protesters and the party and police.) On October 18, Krenz became the new party chief and president. Krenz and his moderate assistants, trying to appease the population, in November allowed travel once again across the Czech border, and thousands crossed a corner of Czechoslovakia on the way to West Germany. By this time a million East Germans, led by a group of intellectuals calling themselves the New Forum, were in the streets demanding far-reaching democratization. The entire East German Politburo and cabinet, including the prime minister, then resigned.

In one last desperate act to restore some order and legitimacy, East Berlin opened the Wall to show citizens that there was no urgent need to flee, that they could go any time they wished to and come back when they wanted to. Thousands poured into the West, and many did not intend to come back. At that moment, on November 9, 1989, East Germany effectively collapsed into the waiting arms of West Germany. The rest was an endgame until East Germany disappeared on

October 2, 1990. Liberal Communist Hans Modrow became prime minister and named many non-Communists to his cabinet. In December, the country's parliament, the Volkskammer, voted to end the Communists' monopoly on power. The regime agreed to free elections in the spring of 1990. Honecker and five Politburo cronies were arrested for corruption. Their posh homes, country estates, and Swiss bank accounts (containing money skimmed from foreign-trade deals) were revealed on television. The public seethed with resentment. A very liberal Communist lawyer, Gregor Gysi, 41, became party chairman; he abandoned communism and changed the party name to Socialist. A few days earlier, amidst revelations of the elite's opulent lifestyle, Egon Krenz resigned in embarrassment as president and as party chairman. He had been in power only 46 days, but much happened because he gave the order to not fire on protesters.

Czechoslovakia

Like East Germany, the Stalinist regime of Czechoslovakia was not going to give in to the tide of change. Prague held out the longest, but the new leaders of December 1989 were non-Communists, some of whom had just been released from prison. In a parallel with Hungary, the old party chief Gustav Husak, who had been in power since the 1968 Soviet invasion, was replaced in late 1987 with the younger—but not necessarily better—Milos Jakes (prounounced "yah-kesh"). As late as November 12, 1989, Jakes was telling a Communist youth conference that the government would neither relinquish control nor stand for protests. Twelve days later, Jakes was out.

The year 1989 began with thousands marking the twentieth anniversary of the death of Jan Palach, who had burned himself alive to protest the 1968 Soviet invasion. Protesters used the occasion to voice demands for human rights. The regime arrested some 800, including playwright Vaclav Havel, whom they sentenced to nine months in prison. He was paroled six months early, in May. As a founding member of Charter 77, a group formed in 1977 by intellectuals protesting civil-rights abuses, Havel spent more than five years in jail. In August, on the anniversary of the Soviet invasion, a Prague rally of 3,000 in favor of reform was broken up by the police, who arrested 370. In October, a protest by 10,000 was broken up.

Things really got rolling in November 1989. Early in the month, Moscow warned the Prague regime not to make the same mistakes as other East European regimes but to carry out major reforms before things worsened and got out of hand. It was another example of Gorbachev telling the old guard to give way. Jakes, the obdurate fool, thought he could stand firm. Baton-wielding police broke up a student rally in Prague, injuring many. The brutality galvanized many Czechs into joining the new Civic Forum opposition group. In Slovakia, its counterpart, Public against Violence, also mushroomed in size. On November 19, some 20,000 protesters marched in Prague. The next day, a quarter-million gathered to demand the government's ouster. On November 24, Jakes quit, and was replaced by Karel

Urbanek, a relative liberal. Alexander Dubcek returned to Prague to the cheers of 300,000. A day later, half a million rallied in Prague and workers staged a two-hour general strike that brought Czechoslovakia to a standstill. By now, students and intellectuals had come together with the workers, a combination that made the regime tremble. At the end of November, parliament voted to end the Communists' monopoly on power.

In December 1989, the new, flexible prime minister, Ladislav Adamec (the c is pronounced "ts") named a cabinet of sixteen Communists and five non-Communists. This was not nearly enough for the citizens, and 150,000 marched in Prague to protest the cabinet. Three days later, Adamec quit, and was replaced by a young (43) and very liberal Communist, Marian Calfa, who soon quit the party. On December 10, a sourpuss Husak, still the country's president, swore in a non-Communist cabinet and then resigned. At the end of the month, Dubcek was elected speaker of parliament, which in turn elected Havel president of Czechoslovakia. Havel mused that nothing prepared him for the job as well as prison. In a month and a half, beginning with the student protest of November 17, communism in Czechoslovakia collapsed in what Havel called the "velvet revolution."

Bulgaria

In the Balkans, Bulgarians have long been known as followers of the Russians, the Slavic big brothers who liberated them from the Turks in 1878. Under the Communists, Bulgaria closely aped Soviet ways, including the reforms wrought by Gorbachev. The word *glasnost*—the same in Russian and Bulgarian—was widely used. When Gorbachev said to reform, the Bulgarian Communists reformed. In so doing, the Communists of Sofia were more clever than those of Prague. Seeing change coming, they jumped with it in late 1989. Perhaps for this reason, a liberal Communist party—now calling itself Socialist—was able to retain power, even after the elections in 1990. Todor Zhivkov, a classic Stalinist, had ruled with an iron hand for an incredible 35 years.

Inspired by what was happening elsewhere in the bloc, agitation began to boil up in 1989. Some of the Bulgarian protests, though, were of a bizarre note: anti-civil rights. Bulgaria's Turkish minority, estimated to number from 900,000 to 1.5 million (at least a tenth of the population), had been long hated as a dangerous foreign element, and had been under great pressure to assimilate or leave. In the early 1980s, they were forced to take Bulgarian names and to stop speaking Turkish. In 1989, over 300,000 Bulgarian Turks were brutally expelled or fled to Turkey to live in squalor. This policy was just fine with most Bulgars, and it was one of the areas where the regime and people saw eye-to-eye. Trouble came when the regime indicated it would, under international pressure, *stop* mistreating its Turks. Some Bulgarians, using primitive fear images of a Turkish takeover, then rallied against the regime.

It was under these circumstances that younger and more flexible Communists, in telephone communication with Moscow, on November 10, 1989 (the day after the Berlin Wall was opened), replaced Zhivkov as party chief with the foreign minister, reformist Petar Mladenov, who also then became president. Mladenov named a reformist cabinet, gave up party leadership, changed the party name to Socialist, and led the party to a narrow victory in 1990. This election, as we shall explore in the next chapter, may not have been completely fair, but it must be said that many Bulgarians supported the party as the only force that could hold the country together.

Romania

Romania was the last overthrow of a Communist regime in 1989, and by far it was the bloodiest. Several hundred people were killed by the Securitate, the security police, in December before the tyrant Nicolae Ceausescu, in power 24 years, was overthrown and executed by his own military. Why was Romania bloody and the other East European overthrows of communism not? The clue here is that Romania was not closely tied to the Soviet Union; its leaders and party did not follow the Kremlin line. Accordingly, Gorbachev had no input or leverage with the Romanian Communist party.

Ceausescu, who came to power in 1965, soon took Romania on an independent course. He resented Romania's economy being subjected to Comecon. In 1968, Romania (along with China) denounced the Soviet invasion of Czechoslovakia; after all, they might be next. Internally, though, Ceausescu was a complete Stalinist. He kept Romanians oppressed and poor in order to wring out every bit of industrial production. He ordered the historic heart of Bucharest torn down to make way for monstrously distasteful architecture, including the immense House of the Republic, his personal palace. He ordered ancient villages razed and forced their inhabitants to relocate to prefab apartments elsewhere. To pay off Romania's foreign debt, he sweated workers and lowered living standards. Food was hard to find. Heat and electricity were often off. Demanding a high birthrate, Ceausescu outlawed abortion. Unwanted children, though, were housed in unheated zoolike conditions until they died. Romania's backward medical system gave unnecessary blood transfusions to newborns; hundreds of babies got AIDS from unscreened donors and slowly died.

The Hungarians of Transylvania triggered the Romanian uprising. Ceausescu was especially intent on razing Hungarian villages. In early 1988, ethnic Hungarians fled from Romania across the border into Hungary, which for them was relatively free and prosperous. A Hungarian Calvinist pastor, Reverend Laszlo Tokes, in Timisoara began to denounce the repression of Hungarians in Romania. The Securitate tried to arrest Tokes on December 15, but demonstrators—of all ethnic groups and religions—encircled his church to protect Tokes. The next day, the Securitate opened fire on the Timosoara demonstrators, killing hundreds, who were buried in mass graves. Ceausescu gave orders to shoot any protester anywhere and then flew off to visit Iran. But the protests spread. Ceausescu returned quickly and called the protesters "fascist, reactionary groups." On December 21, Ceausescu staged a rally but was shouted down by protesters in Bucharest. Romanian television broadcasted nationwide the look of shock on his face. At that moment, the "hero of the Carpathians" was finished. The next day the regular army, which always resented the Securitate, joined in to protect the revolution; they battled Securitate snipers. Altogether, several hundred Romanians were gunned down by the Securitate. Ceausescu and his wife Elena were captured, given a quick, secret military trial, and executed by firing squad on Christmas Day 1989.

Relatively liberal Communists, some of whom had been under house arrest for criticizing Ceausescu, formed a Council of National Salvation and pledged democracy. The Council named Ion Iliescu president and Petre Roman prime minister. Critically minded Romanians, especially students and Bucharest intellectuals, quickly noticed that the new regime was staffed by holdovers from the old. They demanded total ouster of ex-Communists from power, but Iliescu stood firm and was confirmed in power in the spring 1990 elections. The clean sweep of Communists from power that took place in Central Europe, from Hungary north, has not occurred in the Balkan lands of Romania, Bulgaria, Yugoslavia, or Albania—at least not yet.

SUGGESTED READINGS

ABEL, ELIE. *The Shattered Bloc: Behind the Upheaval in Eastern Europe.* Boston: Houghton Mifflin, 1990.

BRUMBERG, ABRAHAM. "Poland: The Demise of Communism," *Foreign Affairs: America and the World, 1989/90.* 69 (Winger 1990) 1.

DAWISHA, KAREN. *Eastern Europe, Gorbachev, and Reform: The Great Challenge,* 2nd ed. New York: Cambridge University Press, 1990.

ECHIKSON, WILLIAM. *Lighting the Night: Revolution in Eastern Europe.* New York: William Morrow, 1990.

GARTON ASH, TIMOTHY. *The Magic Lantern: The Revolution of '89 Witnessed in Warsaw,* *Budapest, Berlin, and Prague.* New York: Random House, 1990.

_____. *The Uses of Adversity: Essays on the Fate of Central Europe.* New York: Vintage Books, 1990.

GILBERG, TROND. *Nationalism and Communism in Romania: The Rise and Fall of Ceausescu's Personal Dictatorship.* Boulder, CO: Westview, 1990.

GRIFFITH, WILLIAM E., ed. *Central and Eastern Europe: The Opening Curtain?* Boulder, CO: Westview, 1989.

GWERTZMAN, BERNARD, AND MICHAEL T. KAUFMAN, eds. *The Collapse of*

Communism. New York: Times Books, 1990.

HAVEL, VACLAV. *Disturbing the Peace: A Conversation with Karel Hvizdala.* New York: Knopf, 1990.

HOARE, QUINTIN, ed. *The Street and the Castle.* New York: Verso Press, 1990.

LUERS, WILLIAM H. "Czechoslovakia: Road to Revolution," *Foreign Affairs* 69 (Spring 1990) 2.

CHAPTER EIGHT _____

"Now You Can Choose": The Elections of 1989 and 1990

In 1989 and 1990, elections ousted every Communist regime in East Europe from Hungary north. In the Balkans, Communists or ex-Communists retained power, at least for a while. Why this difference? In examining the differences between these areas, we learn about both East Europe and elections. East Europe can (and probably should) be divided into Central Europe, a reasonably advanced area, and the Balkans, a backward area.

Democratic elections, to be really free and fair, generally require an educated population. Elections thrust on an uneducated population are easy to manipulate. Poor and ignorant people, especially in the countryside, are under the thumb of local political bosses who tell them how to vote; they usually obey. Bulgaria and Romania are among the poorest countries in Europe and considerably behind the Central European countries of Hungary, Czechoslovakia, East Germany, and Poland in terms of per-capita income and education. In the Balkans, much of the population is rural and much of the work force is still in agriculture. Local Communist party bosses were still quite powerful in 1990.

The beginning phases of democracy are rarely democratic. Suddenly handing people a ballot does not mean they will use it intelligently. In the late nineteenth century, for example, Spain and Brazil held regular elections, but the results were rigged by local—especially rural—political bosses who were coordinated by the central government. The leading parties in these countries simply alternated in power by prearrangement. Local bosses could do favors for those who voted as they suggested. Even with secret ballots, the bosses told the voters, they can figure out who voted for whom. Unsophisticated rural voters, who didn't see much worth in the ballot anyhow, viewed it as a way to get a favor. Much the same has happened in the Balkans. Industrialization, urbanization, and education lifted Spain and Brazil out of this very typical pattern.

Elections can come too suddenly to be democratic. People have to be able to think about things, to examine alternatives, and to hear from several parties. Where education and communication are good, word may spread quickly and people may be able to orient themselves politically in a few months, especially if they have a political identification that has been passed down from their parents. Where these are lacking, as in the Balkans, political orientation may take much longer.

The role of organization is extremely important in this process. Poland had two organizations, the Roman Catholic Church and Solidarity. Even though Solidarity was underground for most of the 1980s, it helped orient Poles. They knew what Solidarity stood for and overwhelmingly voted for its candidates in 1989. Czechoslovakia had a core of intellectual critics in Charter 77, plus many citizens who fondly remembered the Prague Spring of 1968. This allowed Civic Forum to mushroom overnight into a major organization. East Germany had a looser group of oppositionist intellectuals, many of whom were connected to the peace movement sponsored by the large Lutheran Church. They provided a core for the sudden growth of New Forum in 1989. In Hungary, intellectuals had formed proto-parties called "associations" or "forums" months in advance of the 1990 elections. Only one of these, Poland's Solidarity, started as a broad-based movement. The others were small movements of urban intellectuals in the country's capital, but they were capable of quickly linking up with the working class and with the countryside.

The Balkan lands lacked such movements. (Yugoslavia had opposition movements, but they were at the republic level or lower, and they aimed at breaking up the country.) Albania, of course, was a Stalinist straitjacket that permitted not even the faintest opposition. Bulgaria and Romania were not much better; police controls prevented the formation of any organized opposition. In Bulgaria's case, change came largely within the party, because Gorbachev told it to change to save itself. In Romania, hatred of the Ceausescu regime was widespread, but, lacking any organized opposition, it was Communists in the Council of National Salvation who grabbed the reins of power. In Bulgaria and Romania, change hit so fast and unexpectedly that no opposition movement had time to organize before liberal Communists consolidated their hold. The key question, then, is whether or not non-Communists were able to organize before the ouster of hard-line Communist regimes. If they were allowed to organize only after their ouster (by relatively liberal Communists), then the liberal Communists retained the upper hand and guided things their way in elections, which were held too soon.

In sum, the Balkans are economically, educationally, organizationally, and politically more backward than Central Europe. Whether in the Balkans or in the Third World (and the Balkans are a lot like the Third World), backward countries do not do well at electoral, democratic politics. Power tends to be manipulated by those who already wield it. We can no more expect Bulgaria to jump immediately into free and fair democratic elections than we can expect it of Mexico.

The Trouble with Complex Voting Systems

Some political scientists sense something wrong with a very complicated electoral system. Complex ballots are confusing; many citizens don't know how to vote with them. After all, they don't vote every week. Such ballots are especially confusing to people who have previously "voted" by simply depositing a ballot with no choices on it in the box, the standard voting style of Communist "elections," which are the only ones most East Europeans had ever known.

The simplest ballots are generally the clearest and fairest for individual voters. Casting a ballot for one candidate (as in Britain) or one party (as in Italy) is understood by nearly all. Make the ballot complicated by adding numerous offices and questions (as in the United States), and voter confusion mounts while turnout falls. Make your elections in two stages, with a runoff election a week after the first election (as in France), and you increase the complexity and get a lower turnout on the second round. Split the ballot, with one vote for a candidate and another for a party (as in Germany), and you get some Germans unable to understand the ballot even after four decades. For balloting, the acronym KISS should rule: Keep It Simple, Stupid.

Many East Europeans had in 1989 and 1990 ballots of incredible complexity thrust on them. Hungary's system, for example, featured a *combination* of the already complex French and German systems mentioned previously, plus a Swedish twist. One suspects two culprits: Communist officeholders who wanted to confuse voters and keep themselves in power and purists so intent on theoretical fairness that they neglect human and political factors. The Communists—or ex-Communists recently renamed Socialists—hoped the complexity would favor them, not necessarily the case. The "perfect fairness" types are the more enduring problems. Some of them are mathematicians who live in a world of ideal forms. They point out how virtually all electoral systems penalize someone. The Anglo-American system of single-member districts, with a simple plurality needed to win, severely underrepresents third parties. The purists' ideal is to reproduce in the parliament a close approximation of the views present in the population as a whole. This can lead to voter confusion and cynicism, to too many parties (some of them extremist), and to difficulty in forming and holding together coalition governments. Balloting complexity adds to the burdens on East Europe's fragile new democracies.

POLAND

Poland was the first with elections, held in June 1989, but they were only partially free. As mentioned in Chapter 7, the roundtable of early 1989 held between the Communist government and Solidarity had reached a compromise. The Polish parliament, the Sejm, consists of 460 seats; 161 of these seats (35 percent) were reserved for Solidarity and other non-Communist candidates. The other 299 seats were reserved for the Communist party and its puppet parties. Each voter could thus vote for both Communist and Solidarity candidates. In addition, a new upper house, the Senate, was created, and all 100 of its seats were open on a competitive basis. Polish voters got several ballots—up to seven, with as many as 35 candidates on each. For the Sejm there might be three Communist ballots, two ballots for Solidarity and the other non-Communists, and one for Communist-affiliated puppets, plus one for the Senate.

Borrowing from the French system, a candidate had to get more than 50 percent of the vote in the first round to be elected. Lacking that, a runoff between the two leading candidates was held two weeks later. Adding to the complication and confusion, voters were asked to *cross out* the names of all the candidates they opposed. Such a monstrosity of a voting system could work only thanks to Solidarity's teaching and their leaflets, which explained the election system to voters and instructed them on which names to cross out. Solidarity urged voters to cross out the names of non-Solidarity candidates on the non-Communist ballots, and to cross out *all* the names on the Communist ballots. Imagine teaching this system to first-time voters, many of them politically unsophisticated. Nonetheless, Solidarity's instructional outreach got through to enough Poles so that Solidarity handily won practically all its contests, and a number of top Polish Communists lost their incumbent seats on the first round, even though they were essentially running unopposed. Frankly, it served the Communists right for inventing such a complex voting system, which Solidarity then turned against them.

When the official results of the first round were announced in June 1989, General Czeslaw Kiszczak, the same interior minister who had ordered Solidarity leader Lech Walesa arrested in 1981, shook Walesa's hand and congratulated him. (Kiszczak was among the Communists who lost on the first ballot.) Solidarity took 92 of the 100 Senate seats in the first round with an outright majority; in the runoff two weeks later they took another seven seats. Only one Communist, an oddball, wealthy private businessman, made it to the Senate. This gave Solidarity the power to veto new laws coming from the Sejm, which could override the Solidarity majority in the Senate only with a two-thirds vote (306 seats), which the Communists might not have. Two of the original brains of KOR, Jacek Kuron and Adam Michnik, were now in the Senate.

For the lower house, with its assigned percentages, all but one Solidarity candidate topped 50 percent on the first round. The remaining Solidarity candidate won on the second round, giving Solidarity all the 161 seats reserved for non-Communists. For the Communist candidates, the first-round results were an embarrassment: Most obtained between 5 and 25 percent of the vote, and only three topped the 50 percent mark to win outright. Solidarity's campaign to cross out Communist candidates on the ballot had worked. In the runoff, of course, Communists "won" their assigned seats, but by then all of Poland knew they had actually lost.

Psychologically then, the Polish parliament that convened in July 1989 was dominated by Solidarity, even though the Communists had a majority. Soon the Communists lost their contrived majority, for their puppet parties began to desert them. The puppet parties—the Peasants with 76 seats, the Democrats with 27 seats, and the Christians with 23 seats—cut their strings to the Communist party. When Kiszczak, the interior minister, became prime minister after the elections, many deputies from these small parties indicated they would not support him. Kiszczak, sensing he did not have a parliamentary majority, resigned. General Jaruzelski, the president, then had little choice but to name a Solidarity deputy as prime minister. Tadeusz Mazowiecki—a lean and greying 62-year-old, a quiet intellectual, a devout Catholic, and an aide to Walesa in Solidarity—had a majority of the Sejm behind him, thanks to support from the newly independent small parties. Communists kept control of the defense and interior ministries, a chilling reminder of postwar salami tactics of the Communists. (In 1990, Mazowiecki picked his own, non-Communist, defense and interior ministers.) But Communists in the Sejm balked at having to share responsibility with a Solidarity-led government. Then Mikhail Gorbachev held a 40-minute telephone conversation with new Polish Communist chief Mieczyslaw Rakowski (Jaruzeski had stepped down as party chief but stayed on as president). Gorbachev persuaded the Polish comrades to support Mazowiecki, who was inaugurated as prime minister with a nearly unanimous vote in the Sejm.

What was happening here? "Normal" politics was happening: the making of deals and the lining up of support in order to get half or more of a parliament to sustain a cabinet. What West Europe had been practicing for decades, Poland was just limbering up for. After fully free elections, which will probably reduce the Communists—who in early 1990 dissolved the party and renamed themselves the Social Democracy party—to just a few percent of the electorate, Polish politics will likely become more West European but not necessarily calm or workable.

EAST GERMANY

Once the Wall was opened, it was curtains for the East German Communist regime, although they may not have realized it at the time. They hoped that opening the Wall in late 1989 would calm the population and buy them some time to put a reform Communist system into place that would allow East Germany to survive as a separate state. Krenz also promised free elections. But the exodus continued. In late 1989, some 350,000 East Germans moved to West Germany to take advantage of the Federal Republic's generous arrival and welfare benefits. In the first quarter of 1990, another 150,000 poured across the border. East Germans still could not be sure that their regime was really going to change. The government was still Communist, and the security police, the Stasi, still operated. In January, an angry mob ransacked Stasi headquarters in East Berlin and flung out the voluminous files the Stasi had been keeping on thousands of citizens. Graffiti daubed on the building's walls read "Stasis = Nazis." (It is most interesting that neither the Stasi nor the regular police forcibly resisted the raid.) East Germans were not going to settle for half measures. East Germans in doubt about the future moved west. Why take a chance on what the Communists might do? The only thing that could assure them was a new, freely elected government pledged to German reunification.

Furthermore, West Germany's welfare system was quickly overburdened. Apartments had long been in short supply and expensive. West Germans began to resent the flood of cousins who were helping themselves to the benefits funded by West German tax revenues. Several West German states, then the federal government, began to limit benefits to newcomers. It was Bonn, more than East Berlin, that urged East Germans to stay home. For East Germany, of course, the outflow was its lifeblood—the young, skilled, and productive.

East Germany thus held the bloc's first fully free elections. It would be hard to describe these as a model for the rest of East Europe, because West German influence was so heavy in these elections that it quickly turned them into a branch of FRG politics. Some leftist critics complain that this was unfair, that a distinctive East German politics was snuffed out before it got a chance. These critics imply that, if left to themselves, the East German electorate might have produced a new and viable blend of freedom and socialism. This elusive combination appeared nowhere else in East Europe, and we may doubt that it would have appeared in East Germany. The one hope here was the indigenous New Forum that played a major role in toppling the Honecker regime. The leaders of the informally structured and ideologically vague New Forum, unfortunately, either were not able or did not wish to transform it into a party. Perhaps, given time, it would have become an interesting new party, but already in November 1989 West German politicians were crisscrossing the GDR; setting up branches; delivering funds, computers, copiers, and faxes; and supplying abundant personal advice. By March 1990, it was an essentially West German election that happened to be taking place on East German soil.

The Social Democrats (SPD) were off to an early lead. SPD chairman Willy Brandt, who as chancellor in the early 1970s developed an *Ostpolitik* (eastern policy) of building bridges to the east, was much admired in East Germany. He was the hero who had begun the process of opening up the GDR to the West. When Brandt visited Erfurt, East Germany, in 1970, the crowds were so delirious he could have instigated an uprising on the spot. Further, historically much of East Germany had voted SPD in pre-Hitler days. With West German SPD help and visits from Brandt, the East German branch of the SPD quickly grew to 100,000 members, the biggest democratic party of East Germany. (The Communist spinoff party, the Party of Democratic Socialism, claimed a dubious 700,000 members, way down from the 2.3 million who were once in the Communist party.)

But the SPD's early lead melted away. After more than four decades of "socialism," many East German voters didn't like any party with "social" in its title. The SPD, worrying about a recrudescence of German nationalism—not a trivial concern—wanted to go a little slower on unification. This played into the hands of West Germany's ruling party, the moderately conservative Christian Democratic Union (CDU), which stepped up its efforts in East Germany. Quickly, CDU chancellor Helmut Kohl seized the initiative. In late November 1989, he issued a ten-point plan for German reunification. He did not bother consulting his Western allies. East Germans loved the idea of speedy unification, not so much out of idealism but out of a desire to quickly attain West German living standards. Kohl understood that the only way to get East Germans to stay home and not flood into the West was to show them fast progress toward unification. Kohl offered East Germans the extremely favorable one-to-one exchange of hard currency West German marks for the nearly worthless East German marks. On July 1, 1990, the exchange took place, and at that point West Germany absorbed East Germany, economically if not yet politically.

Kohl also advocated the fast path to unification via Article 23 of the FRG's constitution, allowing West Germany to simply swallow East Germany. The excellent FRG constitution would simply become the constitution of all Germany. The SPD wanted to go the slow path via Article 146, which would mean having the two German states meet as equals to draw up and ratify a new constitution.

The East German electoral system was the classic and relatively straightforward proportional-representation system. The 400-seat Volkskammer (people's chamber), which had been filled through fake elections by a Communist-dominated National Front, was now wide open for competing parties. East Germans voted for a party, and the percentage of the total vote that the party received was the percentage of Volkskammer seats it got. The seats were filled from party lists with the leaders' names higher up on the list, insuring their chance of entering the Volkskammer. (In the all-Germany elections held later this system was scrapped in favor of West Germany's hybrid of proportional representation plus single-member districts.)

Voter turnout in March 1990 was an amazing 93.2 percent, one of the highest ever in a free election in postwar Europe, perhaps a measure of how much East Germans appreciated the right to cast a free ballot. (U.S. voter turnout in 1988 was only 50 percent.) The main parties and their voting strengths are shown in the following table:

	Percentage of popular vote	Volkskammer seats
Alliance for Germany (led by the CDU)	48.1	193
Social Democrats	21.8	87
Party of Democratic Socialism (the renamed Communist party)	16.3	65
Free Democrats	5.3	21
Minor parties	8.3	34

The results of the March 1990 East German elections looked somewhat like West German election results. Of the four major parties, all but the renamed Communist party were closely linked to their West German counterparts. Three-quarters of East German voters, then, cast their ballots for a party supported by West Germany. Nearly half the votes went to the Alliance for Germany. In this alliance, the Christian Democrats won 41 percent, the German Social Union 6 percent, and the Democratic Awakening 1 percent. In effect, this was a Christian Democratic party, and it became such after unification. Its leader was musician Lothar de Maizière (the French name came from the Huguenots who fled to Germany from France in the late seventeenth century), who became prime minister of the short-lived non-Communist East German government until it merged into the Federal Republic on October 2, 1990.

The 1987 West German election results were not too different: The CDU took 45 percent, the SPD 37 percent, and the Free Democrats 9.3 percent. The main difference in East Germany was that in early 1990 the left vote was split between the SPD and the PDS; together they totaled 38 percent. Another difference is that West Germany has a small Green party which took 5.6 percent of the vote.

One interesting—and probably temporary—phenomenon of the 1990 East German elections was the reasonably good showing of the renamed Communist party, the Party of Democratic Socialism. Elsewhere in free East European elections—and this does not include Romania or Bulgaria—the Socialists (i.e., the ex-Communists) won less than 14 percent of the vote. Why the relatively good showing of the East German PDS? Part of the explanation may be that they really were the liberal wing of the old Communist party, which went by the name Socialist Unity party (SED), a forced merger of the Communists and SPD. In 1990, in effect, the latent Socialist wing of the old SED took over from the Communists and proclaimed a West European-style Socialist party, democratic but more left than the FRG's Social Democrats, who have become a center-left party. The PDS, then, was not perceived by some voters as a Communist party.

Further, the PDS was led by rather popular figures, prime minister Hans Modrow, who calmly led the way to elections and unification, and party chairman Gregor Gysi, who recast the party in democratic terms. They were not seen as ogres and were, in fact, the only East German candidates with name recognition. The candidates of the parties with West German connections were very little known. And there was a certain resentment factor. The West German parties had just moved in and taken over, brushing aside anything East German as worthless. Some people felt the PDS was the only *East* German party running. The minor PDS success is likely to be short-lived, however. Under West German electoral law, which became the law of unified Germany, a party must either top 5 percent nationwide or win three seats in the single-member contests to get any seats in the Bundestag. A one-time exception allowed East Germany's parties to meet the 5 percent standard in East Germany alone in the December 1990 elections. The PDS will likely fall below this threshold in subsequent elections; many of its March 1990 voters will drift over to the SPD.

The outcome of the East German elections could have set the pattern for other Central European elections: a large center-right party, a smaller center-left party, and an even smaller ex-Communist party. This pattern was particularly clear in Hungary, where elections were held just a week after the East German vote.

HUNGARY

The second fully free elections were held in Hungary on March 25, 1990, with runoffs two weeks later, for the single-chambered 386-seat parliament. The electoral system was complex and eclectic, operating on three different levels: district, county, and national.

1. For 176 members of the new parliament, Hungary used essentially a French system: single-member district elections with runoff elections. This is like the Anglo-American system—one person elected per district—but with a catch: The winner needs a majority (more than half) rather than just a plurality (the biggest number) as in Britain and the United States. In Hungarian contests where no one got more than 50 percent (and only five candidates did), a runoff was held two weeks later between those who got at least 15 percent on the first round. Single-member districts provide for much closer representation; citizens have someone they have elected that they can complain to.

2. For another 152 members, Hungary used a classic proportional-representation system, such as found in Italy or East Germany (described previously). Each of Hungary's 19 counties got several seats depending on population. In each county parties put up lists of their candidates; seats were awarded based on the percentages won.

3. For yet an additional 58 seats, the biggest parties could put up lists at the national level. These seats were apportioned on the basis of "scrap" votes, votes left over from the local-level and county-level contests. For example, if a Hungarian county had ten seats and party X won 43 percent of the vote, it would be entitled to four seats, and it would have 3 percent left over as a "scrap" vote. Likewise the votes of the losing parties in the individual constituencies went into a nationwide pool, and the larger parties got seats in proportion to their share of the scrap-vote pool. This idea of reserving some seats to be apportioned at the national level resembles the Swedish electoral system, in which 39 Riksdag seats are held out of the county contests and used to even up the mathematical discrepancies that come with the inability to send a fraction of a person to parliament.

What kind of lunatics designed the Hungarian electoral system? There must be mathematicians somewhere in the mix. Few Hungarians had the slightest idea how this system worked; that may help explain why voter turnout on the first round was an anemic 68 percent, and even lower on the second. The idea of combining single-member districts with proportional representation is a good one, perhaps

"Liberal" and "Conservative" in East Europe

Until now, we have been using the terms "liberal" and "conservative" in relation to the Communist parties of East Europe. A conservative Communist wanted to essentially preserve Stalin's centrally controlled single-party system; a liberal wanted to bring in elements of a market economy and political pluralism. Now, in post-Communist East Europe, we must make clear that we are using liberal and conservative in relation to non-Communist parties.

East Europe borrows its concepts of liberal and conservative from West Europe, and these terms do not mean the same thing in American usage. *Liberal* in Europe means the original liberalism of Adam Smith, the concept of *laissez-faire*, of government leaving the economy alone to run on the basis of supply and demand. (In the United States, this concept has become known as "conservatism." American "liberalism" resembles European welfarism as espoused by German and Scandinavian Social Democrats.) Some Europeans call praise of the free market "neo-liberalism" to connote the revival of this concept in recent years. In European terms, Reagan (and Thatcher) practiced neo-liberal, not conservative, economic policies. European liberals also have non-economic beliefs. In religion, they want the separation of the church and state in order to keep religion personal and private. European liberals tend to be internationalists rather than nationalists and to favor the integration of their countries into the European Community.

European conservatism also differs from U.S. conservatism. In most of Europe, the state has long played a major role in supervising the economy. Many European conservatives wish to preserve this role, or at least phase it out cautiously. They are a bit suspicious of the free market, fearing chaos and national weakness. They also wish to preserve noneconomic conservative values such as religion and nationalism. Charles de Gaulle of France, for example, was this kind of conservative: He nourished France's large state sector in the economy while building a nationalistic France with Catholic values.

borrowed from West Germany. The French-style runoff election and Swedish-style national contest may be unnecessary complications. The German system, using two votes on the same ballot, one for an individual candidate and another for a party, is less confusing to voters and easier to implement, as there is no runoff election or national-level pool. Hungary's two leading parties agreed to try to come up with a simpler electoral system. This is not surprising, as simpler electoral systems tend to benefit larger parties.

Quick off the mark, as soon as parties were allowed to organize in 1989, was a grouping of Budapest intellectuals long opposed to the Communists who took the name Alliance of Free Democrats. Headed by the casually dressed Janos Kis (pronounced "kish"), they advocated a free society and economy as soon as possible. Soon overtaking them, however, was the Hungarian Democratic Forum, under medical historian Jozsef Antall, which was also for freedom but with a Christian and nationalistic flavor. They wished to proceed more slowly toward private enterprise, as they worried about how painful such a transition could be for the masses of Hungarian working people. These two parties, the liberal Alliance and the conservative Forum, were the main contenders in 1990 for political power.

Two smaller parties were a trifle more conservative than the Forum. The old Smallholders party, quite important in the interwar period, was revived. It pledged to return state-controlled socialized land to the people who owned the land in 1947. As such, the Smallholders attracted small-town votes from the older generation. The Christian Democratic People's party was also rural and conservative and was sometimes supported by village priests. These two small parties formed a coalition under the wing of the Alliance; in time they could merge.

Hungary also added an interesting party, one missing from other new democracies: a youth party. The Federation of Young Democrats (known by its Hungarian initials as "Fidesz"), ideologically close to the Alliance, limited its membership to those under 35. (Persons over 35 could vote for it; Hungary's oldest citizen, a 106-year-old woman, proudly did.) Some saw Fidesz as the Alliance's youth wing, but its clever leaders ran a cheeky campaign stressing their independence and fresh, new ideas. One Fidesz poster (featured on the cover of this book) had two photos. One showed Soviet party chief Brezhnev bestowing a gooey kiss on an East European Communist chief. The other showed two young people necking on a bench. The caption: "Now you can choose."

The old Communist party split. Liberal Communists around Rezso Nyers and Imre Pozsgay renamed themselves the Socialist party and advocated a West European democratic type of socialism. Some bureaucrats and workers supported them. A small rump of old-style Communists around ousted party boss Karoly Grosz called themselves the Socialist Workers party. They won only 3.7 percent of the vote.

The real contest was between the front-running Democratic Forum and the Free Democrats. Their struggle echoed some of the political splits of interwar Hungary and got a bit nasty. As mentioned in Chapter 2, Hungarian politics tends to divide between rural "populists" and Budapest "urbanists." Antall's new Democratic Forum inherited the old populist mantle, with its conservative, nationalistic, Catholic, and peasant orientation. His father, in fact, had helped lead the old Smallholders' party to a 58 percent win in 1945, Hungary's last free election. The Free Democrats inherited the old urbanist mantle, with its intellectual sophistication and stress on individual and civil liberties.

The nasty part of the campaign came from some Democratic Forum people dropping anti-Jewish hints aimed at the Free Democrats. As elsewhere in East Europe, some Jews served Stalin—as Rakosi did in Hungary—and in the mass mind all Jews were stereotyped as pro-Communist. A few Forum candidates played this stereotype, hinting that Free Democrats were essentially Budapest Jews who had recently quit the Communists. The Free Democrats—among whom there were some Jews—shot back that the Democratic Forum was anti-Semitic and slightly fascistic. Antall, head of the Forum, was pained and angered by the charge, for he was personally spotless, and his father had been honored in Israel for saving Jews from the Nazis at the end of the war. Still, anti-Semitic undertones were present among some of his followers. Spray-can graffiti showed the initials of the Free Democrats, an equal sign, and a Star of David. It should be noted, however, that there was far less anti-Semitism in Hungary, where there are some Jews, than in Poland, where there are practically none.

A bigger vote-getter was the Transylvania problem. Most Hungarians are convinced that Transylvania belongs to them. The Democratic Forum played the nationalist card by stressing its urgent concern for the plight of ethnic Hungarians in Romania. It is not clear what can be done about this situation, but the very same issue was important in Hungarian politics in the interwar years: Save our brothers in Transylvania. Thousands of ethnic Hungarians had recently fled from Romania into Hungary and were a constant reminder of the Transylvania issue as they tried to eke out a living by selling carvings and embroidery in public places.

The Democratic Forum sounded another nationalistic theme, one that most Hungarians heartily shared. The most controversial poster of the campaign showed the back of a beefy Soviet soldier with the Russian words, "Comrade, finished," and the Forum name. Some critics felt this was potentially dangerous, as it might seem to be advocating the murder of Soviet troops still garrisoned in Hungary. The more benign interpretation was that it was simply time for the Soviet forces to go home.

The results of the first-round county-level proportional-representation vote (shown in the first column of the following table) gives us a snapshot of Hungarian political views in 1990. The parliamentary seats finally awarded after the second round (shown in the table's second column) is not proportional to this vote, as these seats include single-member and national-level winners.

	Percentage of votes	Number of seats
Democratic Forum	24.7	165
Free Democrats	21.4	92
Smallholders	11.8	43
Socialists (ex-Communists)	10.9	33
Young Democrats (Fidesz)	8.9	21
Christian Democrats	6.5	21
Others	15.8	11

The Hungarian political spectrum is thus not too different from those of West Europe, with one glaring exception. The Democratic Forum, which formed a coalition cabinet with the Smallholders and Christian Democrats under prime minister Antall, is basically a Christian Democrat party like the large German CDU or Italian *Democristi*. The Free Democrats, along with Fidesz, are basically a European liberal party (in the European, not American, sense) favoring a free economy and society, like the small German Free Democrats or the Swedish and Italian Liberals.

Obviously, what is missing is a significant party on the left, a major socialist or social democratic party. The Hungarian Socialists are still suspect as ex-Communists. A tiny Social Democratic party barely got off the ground with 3.6 percent of the first-round county votes, a trifle lower percentage than the hard-line Socialist Workers received. Added together, the total left vote was only 18.2 percent. This is understandable but probably temporary. People just emerging from communism are entitled to distrust any party with "socialist" in its name. Ex-Communists regrouped as Socialists have yet to prove their democratic *bona fides*. In West Europe, the total left vote (Socialists, Social Democrats, Communists, and Greens) is rarely less than a third of the total vote and is sometimes as much as a half. Perhaps Hungary, like Ireland, will simply lack the left end of the political spectrum. More likely, however, is that a Hungarian left will slowly be reconstructed on a democratic basis. The Hungarian working class has plenty of grievances, but none of the major 1990 parties really spoke to its needs; this may help explain the low voter turnout. My hunch is that the Free Democrats will merge with the small party of the Social Democrats and pitch their appeal to the Hungarian working class. Then Hungary will have a "normal" political spectrum.

ROMANIA

The next elections in East Europe came on May 20, 1990, in Romania, but they were tainted. First, they came too quickly for opposition parties to organize. In Hungary and Poland, proto-parties had been organizing for years before they were legalized. East Germany imported a working party structure from West Germany. But in Romania, there was no decompression period, no time for discussion groups to coalesce into proto-parties. Suddenly, in late December 1989 a coalition of relatively liberal Communists, who dubbed themselves the National Salvation Front, took power and had Ceausescu shot. In Central Europe, these liberal Communists would have played an important but temporary role; they would have been voted out in free elections.

Second, and because of this, indigenous non-Communist parties were very weak. Some 80 "parties" put forward candidates, but they were local, in some cases individual, efforts, which did not amount to serious opposition. Romania's main opposition came from its past, the Liberal and Peasants parties, which had been totally banned since the Communist takeover and lacked local roots. Their leaders quickly flew in from long exiles abroad. Liberal leader (and presidential candidate) Radu Campeanu, 66, had been in Paris for 17 years. Peasant leader (and another presidential candidate) Ion Ratiu, 72, had spent four decades in London. They urged postponement of the elections to give their parties more time to organize, but the Salvation Front refused, for they knew the early date favored them.

Third, balloting was complex. It consisted of simultaneously voting for president; for the lower house, the 387-seat National Assembly; and for the upper house, the 119-seat Senate. Romanian voters had 37 pages of ballots: one for the presidency, 24 for the National Assembly, and 12 for the Senate. Unless carefully schooled in how to use such a complicated electoral system, people tend to vote for the most known and visible party, the National Salvation Front.

Fourth, there was some outright crookedness; no one knows how much. In most of the country Communist structures were still intact and still capable of intimidating voters and vote counters. Some candidates were not allowed to campaign in certain towns by Communist thugs; some were beaten. There were scattered reports of multiple voting (using the names of the deceased) and of the running out of the rubber stamps used to mark ballots. Some small towns had suspiciously large turnouts. Even a little rigging of the elections discredits both the results and the regime's commitment to democracy.

To be sure, Ion Iliescu and his National Salvation Front were rather popular and would likely have won a totally fair contest. The Front had gotten rid of Ceausescu and, given the shortage of alternatives, seemed to many Romanians the best chance of keeping things reasonably stable. Iliescu had further insured Front popularity by releasing stored foodstuffs, raising many wages, and starting to redistribute land to peasants. He swore the Front was committed to a democratic form of socialism, to pluralism, and to gradual marketization of the economy. Some of his actions, however, made one wonder about his commitment to democracy.

The results gave Iliescu the presidency with 85 percent of the vote. Liberal Campeanu obtained only 11 percent. The Salvation Front also swept both houses. The vote shown here is for the lower house, the National Assembly:

	Percentage of vote	Number of seats
National Salvation Front	66	233
Democratic Hungarian Union	7	29
Liberals	6	29
Greens	3	12
Peasant party	3	12
Others	15	81

There were two small surprises that will bear watching. The Democratic Hungarian Union speaks for over 2 million ethnic Magyars living in Transylvania.

The fact that it emerged as Romania's second largest party (although far behind the National Salvation Front) indicates strong solidarity among Hungarians and demonstrates how much they dislike being part of Romania. Future unrest among them is likely. Another interesting feature was the first appearance of Greens in an East European parliament. Romania, and indeed most of East Europe, has terrible environmental pollution, but Green parties have generally appeared only in the most advanced nations of West Europe. Perhaps Romania is ahead of the other East Europeans in this respect.

Students and intellectuals loudly denounced the election results; they claimed the election had been rigged and the revolution stolen by renamed Communists. Their protests were broken up in the best Communist tradition, as we shall consider in the next chapter. We are entitled to treat the 1990 Romanian elections with suspicion. The key test will come after a new constitution is completed, which is supposed to be by the end of 1991. New elections are to be held a year later. If the previously mentioned unfair aspects are still present in the 1992 elections, we will know that the members of the National Salvation Front are still essentially Communists.

CZECHOSLOVAKIA

In contrast to Romania, the Czechoslovak elections of June 8 and 9, 1990, were clean and reaffirmed the leading role of Civic Forum, the loose grouping of anti-Communists who brought down the Jakes regime in 1989. Czechoslovakia used the classic proportional-representation system discussed previously, with a 5 percent threshold vote required in either republic to eliminate very small parties. Czechoslovakia (like Yugoslavia) is a federation, so voting was for both a federal parliament and for Czech and Slovak National Councils. The federal parliament is bicameral, consisting of a lower house, the 150-seat House of the People (with 101 seats from the Czech lands and 49 from Slovakia), and an upper house, the 150-seat House of the Nations (with 75 seats each for the two component republics).

Although 22 parties competed, only three were important. Civic Forum (in the Czech lands of Bohemia and Moravia) and its Slovak sister, the Public Against Violence party, were, like Poland's Solidarity, a very broad catchall of the center that included most political viewpoints except communism. One could find in Civic Forum everything from neo-Marxists to Catholics. Civic Forum's leadership consisted largely of dissident intellectuals—mostly secular, some Catholic—who had earlier been associated with Charter 77. Most of them had served time in prison. This gave them a certain charisma as having the guts to do what many only thought about: saying no to communism.

The Communists kept their original name, one of the few Communist parties to do so in East Europe. On the conservative side of the spectrum, the Christian Democrats stressed Catholic values while the Slovak branch also emphasized

Slovak national rights. A Slovak National party talked about Slovak national determination, but stopped short of demands for independence. One Czech party was for laughs: the Friends of Beer party.

Voter turnout was an amazing 96 percent, even higher than in East Germany. Results were not surprising. For the House of the People, the most representative body, the results looked like the following:

	National percentage	Czech	Slovak	Seats
Civic Forum and	46.6	53.2		87
Public against Violence			32.5	
Communists	13.6	13.5	13.8	24
Christian Democrats	12.0	8.7	19.0	20
Moravian and Silesian autonomists	5.4	7.9		9
Slovak Nationalists	3.5		11.0	6
Coalition of minorities	2.8		8.6	4
Other	16.1	16.7	15.1	

The good news was that Civic Forum could comfortably form a cabinet and govern alone with no help from the other parties. Like most proportional-representation systems, the Czechoslovak system deliberately overrepresents the big parties, so Civic Forum got 58 percent of the seats with only 47 percent of the vote. Vaclav Havel was elected president (he had been acting president) and Marian Calfa, a Slovak, was reappointed prime minister. Calfa had been a very liberal Communist; he soon quit the party and joined Public Against Violence. One of Havel's main points is to refrain from carrying grudges against anyone, including former Communists.

The bad news was not the moderate Communist showing but the potentially dangerous tendency to ethnic splintering. Notice that Civic Forum won over half the vote in the Czech lands but less than a third in Slovakia. Thirty percent of the Slovak vote went to their Nationalist party and to the Christian Democrats, who are Slovak Catholics with a nationalist bent. Slovaks have long resented being ruled from Prague, and if the new Czechoslovak democracy does not deliver both prosperity and genuine home rule in Slovakia, there could be growing breakaway sentiment. The coalition of minorities in Slovakia is another disquieting sign. It consists mostly of Hungarians, who have lived for centuries in the southern part of Slovakia. Just as Slovaks resent domination by Czechs, so do these Hungarians resent having their language and culture discriminated against by Slovaks. The problem here parallels that of the Hungarians of Transylvania, who also voted heavily for a Hungarian party. The Slovak problem, of course, is much smaller and less dangerous.

Even the Czech lands were not untroubled by ethnic splintering. Moravia has long been considered as Czech as Bohemia—there is no language difference—but the strongly Catholic Moravians resent being ruled from Prague and want local autonomy, much like the Slovaks already have. The Silesians are a small minority in the north of the country, akin to the people of Polish Silesia. In sum, the Civic Forum sweep is not nearly as broad or deep as some think. Further, Civic Forum, like Poland's Solidarity, is not a party but a temporary grouping of anti-Communist forces that will surely fall apart. What will take the place of Civic Forum? The best thing to happen would be to develop a "normal" party system of two large parties, one center-right and one center-left, plus a sprinkling of smaller parties. The danger in Czechoslovakia is that ethnic and regional parties will grow, making cabinet formation difficult, thus fostering political instability. We are reminded again that Czechoslovakia, like Yugoslavia, was an artificial country set up only after World War I, and that the stresses of the interwar era are still present.

BULGARIA

In Bulgaria, as in its northern neighbor, Romania, relatively liberal Communists deposed a hard-line regime and kept control during elections the following spring. The difference in Bulgaria is that aging Todor Zhivkov was ousted bloodlessly, upon advice from Moscow, and the regime stayed "socialist" although it was redirected to a market economy. One suspects that the Bulgarian course of events is the one Gorbachev would have preferred in other East European countries, rather than the total removal from power of Communists as happened in Central Europe.

Like Hungary, Bulgaria's electoral system blended elements of the French and German systems but was not as complex. The 400 seats of Bulgaria's unicameral Grand National Assembly were filled in a split fashion. Half of the seats were filled by individual contests in single-member districts with runoff elections a week later in case no one got a majority. The other 200 seats were filled by proportional representation in 28 multimember districts. This is actually cleaner and simpler than the German system, which uses proportional representation to set the total house membership.

In April 1990, the Bulgarian Communists changed their name to Socialist and set elections for June. The Communist structure in the countryside was still intact, however, and this gave the Socialists a considerable advantage, as they could intimidate voters with tales of unemployment and hunger if the opposition won. Four opposition supporters were killed during the campaign. Newsprint for opposition newspapers was in curiously short supply. Although not as brutal as in Romania, the Bulgarian ex-Communists took steps to keep themselves in power.

A unique factor also helped the Socialists. In practically all of East Europe, communism represented Russia, and Russia was seen as the barbaric occupier. Thus anti-communism and local nationalism merged. Not so in Bulgaria, for Russia had liberated Bulgaria from the Turks in 1878, and Bulgarians have long been pro-Russian. Further, Bulgarian Communists could point out that their party has old indigenous roots—it was founded in 1891—and that communism in Bulgaria was not imposed by Soviet bayonets. No Soviet troops were stationed in Bulgaria. Bulgarians, therefore, did not harbor quite the same anti-Communist and anti-Soviet hatred found elsewhere in East Europe.

The leaders of the Socialists were rather popular characters, although all had served the Zhivkov regime in high places. They had, after all, deposed the brute and without bloodshed. New president Petar Mladenov had been foreign minister and was seen in Moscow just prior to Zhivkov's ouster. One presumes that Mladenov carried back to Sofia advice from Gorbachev. Prime minister Andrei Lukanov, who had been foreign-trade minister, was born and educated in Moscow. A very bright and witty technocrat, who speaks five languages, Lukanov swore he and other party reformers were just waiting for the chance to introduce a market economy and democracy.

The fragmented and poorly organized opposition also helped the Socialists. Sixteen small parties and other political organizations hastily grouped themselves into the Union of Democratic Forces (UDF), led by Zhelyu Zhelev, a quiet dissident philosopher who later became Bulgaria's president, with Socialist support. Among the UDF's constituent parties was the free labor union, Podkrepa, the environmentalist Ecoglasnost party, and a peasant party named after Nikola Petkov, the agrarian leader executed by the Communists in 1947. Given more time, the UDF might have spread more fully from Sofia out into the countryside. Toward the end, UDF was gaining quite fast. There was also an Agrarian Union that had been linked to the Communists and the Movement for Rights and Freedom, essentially a party for Bulgaria's ethnic Turks, with some support from Bulgarian Muslims and gypsies. An openly Turkish party was not permitted.

The first round took place June 10, 1990, and produced the results seen in the following table. The number of parliamentary seats is not proportional because half of them are from single-member contests.

	Percentage of vote	Number of seats
Socialists (ex-Communists)	47	211
Union of Democratic Forces	36	144
Agrarian Union	8	16
Rights and Freedom (Turks)	6	23
Others	3	6

Unlike Romania, the Socialists in Bulgaria did not win a majority, but they still controlled the National Assembly. Protests by Sofia intellectuals were smaller than Romanian protests; neither were they brutally crushed. As in Romania, the real test will come with Bulgaria's next elections. If campaign irregularities continue and if the Socialists seem to have locked themselves into power, we will know that the Bulgarian revolution has been a managed or fake revolution.

YUGOSLAVIA

With Tito's death in 1980, Yugoslavia began unraveling. There was no one with a fraction of his stature to hold the country together. Economic growth slumped so badly that by 1990 Yugoslav living standards were back where they had been in 1965. Inflation turned astronomical. For many, emigration was the only hope. Resentment between republics, long present, came into the open. Slovenia and Croatia, the westernmost republics who are also the most economically developed, earned by far the most foreign currency, both from exports and from tourism on the Dalmatian coast. They bitterly resented having to share their foreign-currency earnings with the other, less-developed republics. Even the Communist leaderships in Slovenia and Croatia entertained thoughts ranging from confederation to outright independence.

In April 1990, free multiparty elections put non-Communist governments in power in both Slovenia and Croatia. The new Slovenian parliament immediately declared the republic sovereign, and it said that federal legislation would be binding only if also passed by the Slovenian legislature. The leaders of both Slovenia and Croatia were at one time highly placed Communists who got fed up with Yugoslavia's domination by Serbia, exactly the same complaint that pulled the country apart between the two wars.

Croat leader Franjo Tudjman (pronounced "toodg-man") fought as a Partisan officer against the Ustasha Nazi puppets and then stayed in the Yugoslav army until his retirement with the rank of general. Taking a doctorate in history at the University of Zagreb, he became outspoken in his views that Croatia was being unfairly treated and joined the Croatian nationalists. For this he was jailed in 1972 and again in 1981. In the late 1980s, when it became legal, Tudjman formed the nationalistic Croatian Democratic Association, which swept into power in the free elections of 1990. Tudjman called for a confederal Yugoslavia, but many suspected that he really aimed for Croatian independence. He also uttered some of the same themes as his old Ustasha enemy, for example, that Bosnia historically belongs to Croatia. Hints of anti-Semitism surfaced, even though there are very few Jews in Yugoslavia.

In December 1990, Serbia held multiparty elections, but they were not completely fair. Opposition parties were permitted to register only at the end of August, and this gave the recently renamed local Communists, the Serbian Socialist party, the same sort of lead enjoyed by its Romanian and Bulgarian counterparts. As expected, the new "Socialist" party won. It was still headed by the republic's president, Slobodan Milosevic (pronounced Miloshevich). There was nothing very communist or socialist about this party; it was straight Serbian nationalist.

Milosevic, wildly popular among Serbs, swore to retain every piece of territory that had ever belonged to Serbia, from the Voivodina in the north to Kosovo in the south. The Voivodina is the home of many Croats, and Kosovo is mostly ethnic Albanian. Accordingly, Yugoslavia's two largest republics, with a long history of hostility, were now headed by militant nationalists.

Free, multiparty elections, far from calming things in Yugoslavia, sharpened nationalistic rivalries. Conceivably, nationwide elections might help calm things, but Yugoslavia is already so fragmented into its republics that national authorities—if there are any left—lack either the will or the power to call them.

In sum, free elections played a major role in moving Central Europe into democracy. The Balkan elections of 1990, rigged or fragmented, played no such role. We may hope that in the near future they will. Harvard political scientist Samuel P. Huntington proposed a "two-turnover test" for the establishment of democracy: Two changes of the government by free and fair elections demonstrate that democracy has been consolidated. Most of East Europe has completed one turnover, but not yet the Balkan lands.

SUGGESTED READINGS

FURTAK, ROBERT K., ed. *Elections in Socialist States.* New York: St. Martin's, 1990.

CHAPTER NINE

The Odds for Democracy

ECHOES OF THE PAST

East Europe is reborn. Unfortunately, it is reborn with some of the same deformities that damaged its earlier, pre-World War II, incarnation. Some East Europeans, like the Bourbons returning to France after Napoleon, learned nothing and forgot nothing. Many are nationalistic, intolerant, and frightened of a free society and economy. Many have populist notions of democracy as a system that solves problems quickly and grants few rights to minorities. East Europe between the wars was weak and divided, a pushover, first for the Nazis and then for the Communists. It was weak because it had just emerged from imperial rule that had not allowed proper institutions, loyalties, and borders to develop.

Reborn East Europe is still weak. Now emerging from the wreckage of the Soviet empire, its new governments face gigantic problems, and they have little experience. Most of the leaders of the new governments were until recently dissident intellectuals who had only their moral purity with which to stand up to brutal state power. Some swore they would never accept political office, for that would sully their lofty, humanistic aims. Czechoslovakia's Havel, among others, spoke of "antipolitics," a moral and literary condemnation of Communist regimes that did not have to offer anything concrete to put in the place of those regimes when they collapsed.

East Europeans are also quick to blame others for their troubles. First, and justifiably, they blame the Soviets for inflicting hated regimes upon them. Some blame President Roosevelt for letting Stalin arrange this at Yalta. In multiethnic countries, East Europeans of one ethnic group blame the other ethnic groups (e.g., Slovaks blame Czechs, Romanians blame Hungarians, Croats blame Serbs). Some

---

Side-Effect: Crime Increase

One of the side-effects of the collapse of dictatorial power is a jump in the number of crimes. It seems to be a natural if unfortunate concomitant of a transition to democracy. Under a dictatorship, the police have plenty of manpower and few legal restraints. Many would-be criminals are deterred. When a dictatorship ends and democratic controls are placed on police, criminals quickly lose fear. Spain under Franco was swarming with police, and there was little crime. After Franco, Spain became democratic, and the crime rate soared. Precisely the same thing is happening in East Europe. The police have been discredited for enforcing Communist rules; many have quit. New, democratic police forces have not yet been established. A flood of tourists from the West has increased the targets for street crime. If you tour East Europe, be especially aware of pickpockets in railroad and bus stations and city promenades. Don't carry a wallet; certainly don't carry one in your hip pocket. If you get currency on a black market, beware of short-change artists; know exactly what the banknotes look like and what the exchange rate is.

---

blame Jews, an old East European reflex. Few blame themselves.

One of the best things going for the rebirth of Spanish democracy after Franco was the willingness of most Spaniards to blame themselves for what had gone wrong. The "Two Spains," the society badly split for centuries between the Catholics and the anticlericalists, between the urban and the rural, and between the rich and the poor led to the terrible Spanish Civil War of 1936 to 1939. Thoughtful Spaniards in building a new democracy pondered repeatedly: "We did it to ourselves. If we don't watch it, we'll do it to ourselves again." In a spirit of restraint, Spaniards crafted a democratic party system, a new constitution, and free elections. Then Spain joined Europe as a fit member of the democracies that make up the European Community.

East Europeans tend to lack this sort of introspection and humility. Granted, their histories are very different from that of Spaniards; they were the subjugated peoples of empires while Spaniards were not. But East Europeans often fail to notice that their internal hatreds and their inability to form alliances with their neighbors doomed them to takeovers by Hitler. West Europeans have had a lot of practice in living with neighboring nations; they have all but abolished the borders between themselves. East Europeans have had no practice at living with their neighbors on a voluntary basis; they still dislike each other. And they have no practice at democratic stability. Can they become good European democrats?

I'm an optimist. I think the lands of Central Europe (from Hungary north) can, with much trial and error, become stable European democracies. The Balkan lands will have a longer and rougher time of it. All will have to overcome some truly horrendous problems. Mercifully, one problem of earlier times has been largely settled: the problem of borders. Some of East Europe's borders arouse concern and dissatisfaction, but no government puts forward any claim to change them, nor is likely to. The territorially dissatisfied countries between the wars—Germany, Hungary, and Bulgaria—have abandoned hopes of regaining lost lands. In the 1975 Helsinki Final Act, all the countries of Europe (except Albania) agreed to regard all European frontiers as inviolable. Although it is not a treaty, all participants have stood by the agreement. The biggest question—the Oder-Neisse line as Germany's border with Poland—has been confirmed several times.

STABLE DEMOCRACY

Modern democracy is a permanent tug of war between two large, nonextremist parties (or coalitions) that compete for and alternate in power but do so without hatred. Typically, these parties are center-left and center-right. Politics is not seen as a game of total and permanent victory. Alternation of parties in power is the norm. Today's "ins" are next year's "outs." Each party regards the other major party as considerably less than the devil incarnate. Ideologies are moderate; all recognize that no party has a monopoly on truth or wisdom. There are not too many parties, as this means that some of them will be extremist or breakaway. But neither can there be one big party that dominates the system. Democracy requires a lively and critical interaction between the "ins" and the "outs."

Poland's Solidarity has broken up, and Czechoslovakia's Civic Forum probably should break up. Both were rather artificial groupings of elements that logically should be in disagreement. They were united temporarily in their hatred of the Communist regime. With the Communists defeated, they have turned on themselves. This is normal and to be expected. By splitting apart the right way, however, they can render great service to Polish and Czechoslovak democracy: They can create a moderate two party or two-plus party system.

Poland

Solidarity consisted of a large body of workers with a small leadership of intellectuals. The two joined together when intellectuals set up KOR (the Workers Defense Committee) in 1976. It was a magnificent and effective combination. During the summer of 1990, the two components split apart, because they are quite different. Lech Walesa is and always has been a trade-union leader. He looks out, quite properly, for the rights of the working man and woman. He worries that Poland's plunge into a market economy is inflicting terrible pain and unfairness on working people. He wants all the old Communist officials—the *nomenklatura,* the persons on the list of reserved positions—fired immediately. Walesa is also a gruff, uneducated personality who bears some of the old prejudices of Poles. He wants

Is the West European Model Applicable to East Europe?

Some readers of this chapter may object that the author shows a bias toward the politics and party systems of West Europe, and that he would like to see them paralleled in East Europe. True enough. East Europe should follow the West European pattern because, empirically, it seems to produce democratic stability.

First, we'd better define what we mean by West European politics. It is a tendency toward the following:

1. A two-plus party system seems to be standard; that is, there are two big parties and one or more smaller ones. The two big parties seem to get at least 70 percent of the vote. Some systems, such as Sweden, due to historical factors and electoral laws, may retain several medium-sized parties.

2. Ideology is severely attenuated. Ideology, defined here narrowly as a plan to improve society, is reduced to a vague mood in West Europe. Party leaders rather fear ideology among the militants; it will likely get the party stuck with the causes and issues of the past, leaving the opponent free to claim his party is the party of modernization, of a fresh uncluttered future that sweeps out the rubbish of yesteryear's futile political quarrels.

3. The two big parties stick close to the political center, for that is where the votes are. Socialist, Social-Democratic, and Labor parties become center-left, supportive of both free enterprise and the welfare state. Christian Democratic and conservative parties become center-right; they want to curb the growth of the welfare state and emphasize the free market a bit more than their opponents. Alternation in power between the center-left and center-right produces mostly minor policy differences. Thatcherism in Britain is an exception here and probably a temporary aberration. More representative are the Socialists, such as France's Mitterrand, calling off his socialist experiment, and Spain's González, improving the market system. And notice how West Germany's Kohl, a conservative, used the lavish benefits of his welfare state to buy East Germany.

4. The performance of the economy is the chief factor by which incumbent parties are judged. Voters punish poor economic performance (such as too high inflation or unemployment). Elected leaders know that their plans and promises are laughable if the economy falters. Accordingly, the main selling point of each campaign is the incumbents' claim that they've done a good job and the opposition's claim that the incumbents haven't. Elections become referendums on the economy. If the economy gives no major grounds for complaint, they become referendums on the personality of the politicians.

5. Personality is emphasized, often to the exclusion of party ideology and even party label. This seems to be equally true in parliamentary and presidential systems. Photos and film clips of the top candidates are the main form of electoral propaganda. Some ads don't even contain a party

name or logo. The big parties learn, usually by losing repeatedly, that running an election is not an intellectual excercise but the application of good marketing techniques.

The West European pattern is not a particularly stirring or inspiring kind of politics. Compared with the great clashes of ideologies and the rigid convictions of yesteryear, it is a rather boring type of politics. But it does work and has brought West Europe to new heights of democracy, stability, and prosperity. You don't like this model? Got a better one?

Plainly, East Europe has a long way to go to approximate this pattern. It needs, first and foremost, an economic basis. In comparison with West Europe, the nascent party systems of Central Europe are strange, irrational. Instead of a moderate tug of war between center-left and center-right, the East European parties simmer with ill-defined resentments. If East Europe doesn't move in the West European direction, however, the chances of instability are high. If the system becomes sufficiently unstable, its democracy will end in authoritarianism. The way I see it, East European politics will either resemble modern West European politics or it will resemble the instability and authoritarian tendencies of the interwar years. Accordingly, I feel it within my scope as a political scientist to give East Europeans warnings and advice—free, and worth every penny of it—along these lines. The message: East Europe, get modern.

strong leadership, in the manner of Marshal Pilsudski, and offered himself as a candidate for presidency. Some fear Walesa harbors dictatorial tendencies. Some of his supporters used anti-Semitic code words ("cosmopolitan intellectuals") and denounced Jews (Bronislaw Geremek and Adam Michnik) who had worked for Solidarity and served time in prison for their opposition to communism.

Walesa soon scorned the intellectual wing of Solidarity, and this is not surprising. Within months he was denouncing the very man he made prime minister, his longtime advisor Tadeusz Mazowiecki. The reason? Mazowiecki, a Catholic intellectual, applied economic "shock therapy" that did indeed inflict terrible (if temporary) hardship on average working-class Poles. Mazowiecki, looking out for what is good for Poland in the long run, understood that there was no painless way to fix the economic mess. Mazowiecki's government also patiently debated how to privatize Poland's industry; Walesa impatiently charged Mazowiecki with stalling on privatization. (We will consider the difficult question of how to privatize in the box, "Who Will Own the Factories?" later in this chapter.) The Mazowiecki government also went slow in firing Communist holdovers; some of them were the only competent people around. Walesa, appealing to the working class, offered populistic simplifications.

The Walesa wing denounced the Mazowiecki cabinet as an "elite," removed from the daily hardships and concerns of average Poles. It was only right and

---

The Return of "Civil Society"

One of the terms most often used in post-Communist East Europe has been "civil society," a vague but important concept having to do with the people's ability to govern themselves democratically. *Civil society* means the customary standards of politeness, pluralism, and tolerance that have grown over time. It means citizens instinctively able to "do the right thing" without being told to do so by an authoritarian regime. Few East Europeans know of Edmund Burke, but this is essentially what Burke was talking about in positing the "moral, civil, and social habitudes of the people" as the basis of the English constitution. East European intellectuals are worried that the decades of Communist rule have eroded the habits of civil society by attempting to supplant them with a contrived socialist ethic under party supervision. With the party now gone, society has been left without rules. People will have to learn civil behavior from scratch, and they don't have much time. Without the unstated rules of the civil society, authoritarianism is likely.

---

natural that Solidarity split into a Walesa wing that turned itself into the Center party and a Mazowiecki wing calling itself the Democratic Alliance, known by its Polish acronym, ROAD. With Jaruzelski's resignation as president, Walesa and Mazowiecki ran against each other for Poland's presidency in late 1990. Walesa, with a larger base of support and a populistic program, won. Governing Poland, however, proved to be harder than Walesa had portrayed it.

It would have been better if Solidarity had split into something akin to the Labour and Conservative parties, as in Britain, or Social Democratic and Christian Democratic parties, as in Germany. Poland, alas, is more complicated and did not fall neatly into West European patterns. The Center Alliance was conservative in its anti-communism—it wanted all Communists and ex-Communists speedily out of positions of influence in both government and industry—and it is nationalistic. But it was also a workers' party, complaining that a too-rapid transition to a market economy would hurt workers. It wanted a private, market economy, but without pain. ROAD, on the other hand, was conservative (i.e., taking a classic liberal stand) on economic matters, although many of its top people ultimately wished to see a Swedish-style welfare state in Poland. Some call it a center-left party. Said Jacek Kuron, one of the founders of KOR and labor minister under Mazowiecki: "I have always said I would like to be a man of the moderate left in a decent capitalist country. Unfortunately, we don't have capitalism, so I have to take part in a program of creating capitalism."

A fine mess: In Poland we find a Catholic workers' party espousing the nationalism associated with conservatives and an intellectuals' free-market party with social-democratic ideals. It will take some time for Polish parties to sort out just what they stand for and which segments of the population they represent.

Conspicuously missing from Poland was a major Christian Democratic party. The Catholic Church had long stood up to the Communist regime and had sheltered both Solidarity and intellectual discussion groups. Hungary is now ruled by a sort of Christian Democratic coalition. Why isn't Poland? It would seem to be natural for the most strongly Catholic country in the world. Here we return to the problem we touched on in the previous chapter: Why have Bulgaria and Romania lagged behind Central Europe in ousting the Communists? To a considerable degree, it is a question of who organizes first. Solidarity was so early and so big that it preempted other organizations. There is only so much political space, and Solidarity occupied most of it. Strongly Catholic Poles were, of course, politically active, but they were active as Solidarity members, not as Christian Democrats.

Poland also lacks important peasant and socialist parties, although this may change. The weakness of any socialist party, no matter how democratic and anti-Communist, is understandable in a country where the Communists for decades corrupted the term. A small Socialist party was started in Poland, but its political space was blanketed by the Walesa wing of Solidarity, the Center Alliance. A peasant party could have a better chance. Poland's last free government before the Communists was led by Mikolajczyk's Peasant party. Solidarity, based on the urban working class, cannot speak for Poland's farmers. Solidarity wants food prices low; farmers want them high. In 1980, something called Rural Solidarity appeared briefly; it shared Solidarity's anti-communism but not its economic interests. In 1990, a new and still small Peasant party demanded state protection for farmers against price fluctuations.

If Polish parties were to arrange themselves like West European parties, Polish political life might be more rational and stable. My free advice to Poland's parties would be for the group around Mazowiecki to declare itself a middle-of-the-road liberal party in the European sense, that is, for a free market and a free society. It very nearly is this already. My next bit of free advice would be for Walesa's Center Alliance to declare itself a Christian Democratic party, conservative in its Catholic values but solicitous of workers' rights. In time, I would expect the Socialists to grow and draw off some of Walesa's worker support and to win over most of Mazowiecki's social-democratic intellectuals. The objective here would be to set up the stable tug of war between center-right and center-left forces that has characterized democratic stability in West Europe. The confused jumble of Polish party life as it is now could end up resembling Poland's short-lived attempt at democracy between the wars.

Czechoslovakia

Civic Forum is also breaking apart, and this, too, need not be mourned. In 1990, one group, the Democratic Initiative, departed. Like Solidarity, Civic Forum and Public Against Violence were somewhat unnatural groupings of those who oppose communism. Civic Forum, like Poland's Solidarity, was also divided over how far and fast to go with economic privatization. Complicating matters in

Czechoslovakia was the traditional Czech tension between secularists and Protestants on the one hand and Catholics on the other. Czechs tend to be secular humanists in outlook. Some Czechs have disliked Catholicism and have viewed it as a reactionary force that was imposed on them centuries ago by the Habsburgs. In opposition to the Communists, of course, secularists, Protestants, and Catholics pursued a common cause and even learned to like each other. Vaclav Havel is Catholic but secular in outlook. Foreign minister Jiri Dienstbier is strongly Catholic. In 1990, shortly after the Czechoslovak elections, secular-Catholic differences started to show within Civic Forum. Furthermore, Slovak nationalism, itself strongly Catholic, grew and showed a nasty side. In 1990, a nationalist mob besieged the Slovak parliament in Bratislava, demanding (and getting) a law making Slovak the only official language, to the detriment of Slovakia's 600,000 ethnic Hungarians.

My free advice here, as in Poland, would be for serious Catholics to break away from the generally secular Civic Forum and set up a Christian Democratic party in which both Czech and Slovak Catholics could unite. The purpose here would be to establish what political scientists call a "cross-cutting cleavage," a line of fracture that pulls together elements of groups previously at odds with each other. In this case, the object is to get Slovak Catholics feeling that they have much in common with Czech Catholics in order to dampen a potentially dangerous Slovak nationalism that is also strongly Catholic in character. The secularists in Civic Forum and Public Against Violence could then turn into a European sort of liberal party that unites Czech and Slovak liberals in opposition to the Christian Democrats. If Czechoslovakia develops no cross-cutting cleavages, Slovakia will depart from the federation.

Hungary

Hungary initially appeared to have a more stable and modern party system. The Hungarian Democratic Forum, in coalition with the Christian Democrats and Smallholders, form, in effect, a Christian Democratic party, moderate and Catholic in outlook. If the three groups merged, Hungary could follow in the footsteps of the early postwar West German CDU, which swallowed its coalition partners to become the FRG's dominant party and pillar of stability. The key ingredient here was Konrad Adenauer, the CDU's chairman and first chancellor of the FRG. His strength of character, steadiness of purpose, smart economics minister (Ludwig Erhard, father of the *Sozialmarkt*), and sheer longevity forged the CDU into the bulwark of FRG stability.

The West German model of party development may not match Hungary, however. The Democratic Forum was hesitant and indecisive in office. Jozsef Antall was no Adenauer. Instead of its smaller coalition partners moving toward merger with the Democratic Forum, things went the other way. Factions within the Forum became restless, threatening breakup. It may be that the Democratic Forum was cobbled together too quickly to become a cohesive party. If the Forum falls apart, though, we need not despair. Spain shows an alternate path to a stable party system. The first post-Franco elections brought to power a large Union of the Democratic Center, but it lacked cohesion and fell apart in a few years. The Spanish Socialists in the meantime dropped their socialism to become a center-left party that won three elections in a row. If the Hungarian center-right doesn't get its act together and take center stage, the Hungarian center-left might.

Hungary at present has no left. The Socialists, still known as ex-Communists, cannot expect much growth. The small Social Democratic party had such erratic leadership that it wrecked itself. Does every country need a left? Not necessarily, but moderate tension between center-left and center-right seems to characterize stable democracy. Such tension, over the size of the welfare state and the degree of government intervention, is far less dangerous than tensions over religious and nationalist values. The 1990 Hungarian election was fought along the latter lines, between the Catholic nationalists of the Democratic Forum and the secular liberals of the Free Democrats. If the contest keeps going along these lines, Hungary could see a large, shrill, and intolerant Catholic right that dreams of recovering Transylvania. A left party helps structure the political debate around the relatively benign welfare question and not around the deadlier questions of religion and nationalism.

If Hungary has no left, is there something to serve in its place? Janos Kis, leader of the Free Democrats, the main opposition to the Democratic Forum, thinks his party can. After the 1990 elections, Kis started defining the Free Democrats as liberal in the American sense, that is, akin to European social democrats, who want a market economy plus a welfare state. Kis was cleverly repositioning his Free Democrats to the left in order to try to attract center-left voters who otherwise had no political home. If Kis can consolidate his forces as a large center-left party and Antall his forces as a large center-right party, then Hungary will achieve stable democracy.

Encouraging party amalgamation would be simplification of Hungary's monstrously complex electoral law, perhaps in the German or Bulgarian direction, in order to give a premium of extra seats in parliament to larger parties. The Young Democrats, for example, would be encouraged to merge with the Free Democrats. A youth party is a clever way to arouse youthful interest in politics, but almost by definition it is a self-liquidating enterprise, for everyone ages, even politicians.

AUTHORITARIAN INSTABILITY

Central Europe has a decent chance to develop democratic stability. The odds for this to happen in the Balkans are much worse. As we discussed in the previous chapter, backwardness is not conducive to democracy. Authoritarians—Communist or otherwise—argue that they are preserving stability in a dangerous situation.

"Give these people free rein and they'll murder each other. Only our firm rule keeps reasonable order." There is much truth to this claim. Authoritarian rule grows out of disorder. Unfortunately, it also contributes to disorder by systematically stunting the growth of social forces, especially political parties, that build order.

Massive disorder is erupting in the Balkans. Communist rule kept a lid on problems that are now boiling out of the pot. Multiparty democracy in such circumstances might be the opening round of civil war, for there are few cross-cutting cleavages to hold together these badly divided societies. The Balkans are likely to stay Europe's backward corner for a long time.

Romania

Many observers, both Romanian and foreign, doubt that there was a genuine revolution in Romania at the end of 1989. The revolution was hijacked en route by a coup that saved the Communists from total ouster. Intellectuals and students chanted at Bucharest rallies: "Thieves, thieves!" and "Down with communism!" The regime of President Iliescu and Prime Minister Roman responded in the best Communist tradition. Against students the regime sent riot police with electric prods. Protesters stormed police headquarters and a television station. Iliescu then trucked in miners (who had recently had their pay doubled), who bashed with metal pipes anyone suspicious. Unidentified officials in plainclothes directed the miners, who then destroyed the offices of Romania's two main opposition parties. Several people were killed. Iliescu personally thanked the assembled miners as "democratic forces" who had crushed "fascist rebels." Some democracy.

It appeared increasingly that the dread Securitate was not dismantled but merely renamed. According to some reports, as Ceausescu fell in December, several top Securitate officers made a deal with Iliescu: They would pledge their support to Iliescu in return for keeping their jobs. Iliescu seemed to be making decisions with a small clique of advisers, none of them elected and most of them unknown.

Bucharest sought to assure the West that everything was on the up and up, that a pluralist democracy was moving to a free market economy amidst ample human rights, but the West didn't buy it. Romania was isolated and received practically no financial help from West Europe. Its most-favored-nation trading status with the United States—which let Romanian goods into the U.S. at low tariffs—was not renewed.

Can Romania stay frozen in mid-leap between communism and democracy? No, it must complete the jump. Unrest in Romania is rising. Especially discontent are the large Hungarian minority (some 2.3 million) and the students. Hungarians have been killed in Romania. The old fascist Iron Guard has reappeared, focusing its hatred on Hungarians and gypsies. (There are few Jews left.) Many ordinary Romanians are starting to see the National Salvation Front for what it is, a front for the salvation of the power and privilege of the recently ex-Communist elite. The economic pressures by themselves are strong. Romania, the second poorest country in Europe (after Albania), is shut out of the recovery process that much of the rest of East Europe is engaged in. The newly created European Bank for Reconstruction and Development, aimed at building capitalism in East Europe, is not interested in helping the present Bucharest regime. The same factors that brought down communism elsewhere—the fear of falling behind, miserable living standards, and jealousy of the progress in other countries—will be very much in play in Romania. By the time you read this, Iliescu could be out.

Bulgaria

Bulgaria is in better shape democratically than Romania, but not by much. Its 1990 elections were flawed, but not as badly as Romania's. The ex-Communists, running as the Socialists, won only 47 percent of the vote (but a majority of the seats). If the election had been seriously rigged, they would have won a substantial majority. Protesters in Sofia were fewer than in Bucharest and neither were they roughly handled by the authorities. The Bulgarian Socialists put former dictator Todor Zhivkov under arrest for corruption and the misuse of power, and they ousted his cronies from office. The body of Georgi Dimitrov, long idolized, was removed from his Lenin-style mausoleum in Sofia and cremated. When an amateur videotape revealed that President Petar Mladenov in December 1989 had ordered tanks against anti-Communist protesters, Mladenov resigned in July 1990, "in order not to be a reason to increase political tension." Romania should be so lucky.

The presidency was vacant for nearly a month until it was filled by opposition leader Zhelyu Zhelev, head of the Union of Democratic Forces, a 16-group coalition that had won 36 percent of the vote in the elections. In a gesture of goodwill, Socialist deputies voted for Zhelev. In return, Zhelev nominated a Socialist, who had earlier been interior minister, as vice president. The nominee won in an overwhelming show of hands. Socialist Andrei Lukanov agreed to stay on as prime minister. Some Bulgarians weren't buying the spirit of reconciliation, though; they wanted the Communists out. A mob ransacked and burned the Socialist party headquarters, claiming the Socialists were the same old Communists. As angry crowds protested in Sofia, the Lukanov cabinet resigned in late 1990.

Bulgarian food shelves were nearly bare and patience wore thin. As elsewhere in East Europe, Bulgarians lashed out at a minority ethnic group, the million or so Turks. Bulgarian nationalists protested against seating deputies from the largely Turkish Movement for Rights and Freedoms, arguing that it was not a party but a fifth column preparing the way for Turkish reconquest. Some Bulgarians have reawakened the old Macedonian question, urging its return from Yugoslavia to Bulgaria. In light of what is happening in Yugoslavia, that possibility cannot be totally dismissed.

Yugoslavia

By the time you read this, there may not be a Yugoslavia. The impending breakup of this rather artificial country may provide a chilling foretaste of what the Soviet Union could go through. Yugoslav and Soviet problems regarding nationalities resemble each other. Each has a dominant Slavic core (respectively, Serbia and Russia), an advanced and European northwest (Slovenia and the Baltic republics), and a backward south where Muslims and Christians fight (Kosovo and Azerbaijan). There is also massive economic and political discontent throughout each country. The differences, of course, are that Yugoslavia already has a partially free market system and its republics already have a great deal of autonomy.

Notice that republic autonomy does not calm and soothe the nationalities question in Yugoslavia; it may make it worse. Local control of politics but federal control of taxes and investment policy, including the control of foreign currencies earned by exports, is an explosive mixture. Gorbachev should take note. Croatia and Slovenia produce at European levels, but the federal government in Belgrade treats their profits and foreign earnings on a national basis, redistributing much of these profits to Serbia and the poorer republics. Croatia and Slovenia cry they are being drained of their wealth. If cut free, they could turn their backs on the Balkan part of their country and join Europe. They also complain that the federal government is dominated by Serbs—Belgrade is the capital of both Serbia and Yugoslavia—who stack the deck in favor of Serbia. This is virtually the same argument that ripped Yugoslavia apart between the world wars. The conflict was held in check by Tito, himself of mixed Slovene-Croat origin, who appointed many non-Serbian helpers and kept the party and army under close personal control.

But Tito died in 1980, and with him died the dream of a united Yugoslavia. The old Tito slogan, "Brotherhood and Unity," rang hollow. As economic conditions worsened, many Yugoslavs realized that Tito's prosperity was false, based on foreign credits. When these foreign debts had to be repaid, Yugoslav living standards declined. By 1990, few Yugoslavs honored Tito any longer, and a few cursed him.

Massive rioting erupted in Kosovo, the ancient heart of Serbia that has become 90 percent Albanian. Kosovo is under virtual military rule. Ethnic Albanians, who have an enormous birthrate, say they want nothing more than democracy and the status of a full republic. Until now, Kosovo has been an "autonomous province" of Serbia, still under Belgrade's ultimate control. Serbs suspect that Albanians want to take Kosovo out of the federation and possibly join it with Albania. During World War II, the Italian puppet state of Albania seized part of Kosovo. In 1990 the Kosovo legislature voted Kosovo republic status, removing it from Serbian control. In retaliation, the Serbian parliament suspended Kosovo's local government and took over direct rule. Virtually all Serbs approved, while all ethnic Albanians seethed.

The paladin of Serbian nationalism is Slobodan Milosevic, the president of the republic of Serbia, a powerful orator and gifted demagogue, who is worshiped by many Serbs as their savior. He is fiery about Serbia retaining Kosovo. Some suspect him of dictatorial tendencies and of harboring visions of a "Greater Serbia." Milosevic worked his way up through the Communist party as a banker. He is still nominally socialist—the Communists of Serbia renamed themselves the Socialist Party of Serbia in 1990. In economics, he favors a free market, but that's what practically everybody in East Europe says these days.

Facing Milosevic is his Croatian counterpart, Franjo Tudjman, former Partisan fighter and Communist turned Croat nationalist. His conservative, nationalist Croatian Democratic Union won the 1990 republic elections and propelled him to the presidency of Croatia. Tudjman claims that only in 1987 did he learn that his parents, whom he had long believed were killed by the Ustasha during World War II, had actually been killed by Communists. Whether true or not, the story is an awfully good vote-getter among the Croats, many of whom lost relatives to the Communists during and after the war. Tudjman harkens back to an older Croatia, one that includes much of Bosnia and the Voivodina, now part of Serbia.

Thus, in 1990, two of the strongest and angriest nationalists in Yugoslavia faced each other as heads of the largest republics. Each draw their respective boundaries grandly, including parts of the other's territory. During World War II, the Croatian fascist state staked out an eastern border that was just across the Sava River from Belgrade. Serbs cannot forget how the Ustasha massacred Serbs. One can easily envision a breakdown into civil war: Slovenia and Croatia declare their independence; the Yugoslav army, largely officered by Serbs, moves to stop them; Kosovo Albanians rise in revolt; and Bulgaria presses its old claim to Macedonia. The outcome is likely to be either the breakup of Yugoslavia or a repressive military takeover. Either could be accompanied by bloodshed. Because of conflicting boundary claims, there is no way Yugoslavia could break up peacefully.

The tragedy of Yugoslavia is that the League of Communists of Yugoslavia, as the party liked to call itself, was the only national institution that cut across republic lines. For many decades, all the top figures in each republic were Partisan veterans. This gave them a bonding that overshadowed ethnic differences. As they retired and a younger generation took over (Milosevic was 49 in 1991), this bond disappeared. By the 1980s it was effectively gone. Now, not even the army cuts across ethnic lines; its officers are mostly Serbs and Montenegrins. Croatian and Slovenian officers might not obey orders to crush independence movements in their republics; they would be more likely to side with them. Tudjman, for example, was a general who retired in the late 1960s and by 1972 was jailed for his Croatian nationalist activities. One presumes his sentiments were not unique among Croatian officers. Yugoslavia also has territorial defense units (like the U.S. National Guard) in each republic with weapons of their own. A military takeover attempt might lead to civil war.

Could the domineering presence of the Communist party in the decades after

The Albanian Museum

Lenin, who spent 17 years in Zurich, once wisecracked that after communism had triumphed worldwide, they would preserve Switzerland as a museum of capitalism. We might consider preserving Albania as a museum of communism. In a few years, there might not be any other Communist countries left. How then will we explain communism to our children and students?

The long-suffering Albanian people, however, might object. We learned in 1990 that massive discontent was just beneath the surface of the last Stalinist paradise. Actually, Albania shows rather neatly the impossibility of easing up a little, for when you do, the people demand more, much more.

Enver Hoxha (pronounced "hod-ja") took over Albania in 1945 and held it in a tight Stalinist isolation. Few persons were allowed in or out. With the Sino-Soviet split, Tirana sided with Beijing and left the Soviet orbit in 1961. When Mao and Nixon got together in the 1970s, Tirana distanced itself from China and had absolutely no friends in the world. Albania stayed agricultural and backward, the poorest land in Europe.

Hoxha died in 1985 and left Ramiz Alia as his heir and as president. For four years Alia seemed little different from Hoxha, but the events of 1989 penetrated even into Albania. Many Albanians picked up news of the East European upheaval from Italian and Yugoslavian television, and public discontent stirred. Alia announced some cautious reforms and admitted Western journalists for the first time. It turns out that Alia was, relatively speaking, a liberal and in conflict with an old guard of Hoxha holdovers.

Alia's slight changes triggered an outpouring of the anger that had been there all along. On the spur of the moment, some 4,500 Albanians leaped the walls into foreign embassy compounds, chiefly the Italian, German, and French. There they stayed, packed like sardines, for two weeks until Tirana relented and let them depart in July 1990. Many Albanians told the visiting journalists that they hate the system and want the Communists out. It is unlikely that Albania will be preserved as a museum of communism.

World War II have choked off the growth of other organizations that might have knit Yugoslavia together? One strains to see such unifying ties. Religion, economic levels, and historical feelings all reinforce the split nature of Yugoslavia, which is half Central European (the former Austro-Hungarian areas of Slovenia and Croatia) and half Balkan (the former Turkish areas of Serbia, Bosnia, and Macedonia). The Communists were the only organization holding the country together, and they too fractured along ethnic lines. Perhaps Yugoslavia as a country was simply not meant to be. I say this in genuine sorrow, for I have studied in and traveled the length and breadth of Yugoslavia; I like it. The problem is the Yugoslavs don't like it.

If there is one ray of hope it is in the economic policies of federal Prime Minister Ante Markovic. Starting in December 1989, he applied drastic antiinflationary measures such as freezing wages, making the dinar fully convertible, and turning off the printing presses at the federal mint. (His advisor: Harvard's Jeffrey Sachs, who gave the same advice to Poland.) In 1989, inflation had reached 2,400 percent a year; in a few months under Markovic it was below 10 percent. The moves were painful, and unemployment, already high, climbed as previously subsidized money-losing enterprises were forced into bankruptcy. Overall, though, Markovic was popular for ending the hyperinflation. Markovic, a Croat, also sought multiparty electoral democracy. This, of course, would mean the end of communism. A Yugoslavia with a free economy and free political system might be eligible to join the European Community. Over a million Yugoslavs already work in the EC countries; they have already joined Europe.

WHICH WAY TO A FREE MARKET?

The make or break for democracy in East Europe is a market economy that can deliver rising living standards equitably. Bear in mind that only a part of the upheaval in East Europe can be attributed to intellectuals thirsting for freedom and democracy. There were indeed such people, and they were the sparkplugs of the upheaval. Some then became the leaders of post-Communist systems. The masses they led, however, were largely motivated by anger at poor living conditions. If the new governments cannot improve the standard of living fairly quickly and visibly, East Europe may become something less than democratic. The Argentina model sometimes comes to mind: snarling masses, their living standards depressed by inflation, recurrently falling under the sway of authoritarian strongmen who promise them salvation.

Almost everyone agreed that the solution was a market economy. Even the Albanian regime talked about markets. But many had no clear idea what "market" meant. Did it mean getting rid of all state-owned enterprises, or most, or some? How fast should this process take place? Should the fragile new democracies be willing to tolerate very high rates of inflation and unemployment in the transition period? Suppose the transition is not so short. Who would own the formerly state-owned enterprises?

There seems to be no durable middle way between the controlled economy of socialism and the endlessly changing and adjusting nature of market systems. Many have talked about a middle ground between capitalism and socialism. Gorbachev's supporters often mention a market socialism or regulated market economy as their goal. Some countries tried "middle ways"—Yugoslavia, Hungary, China—and experienced initial rapid growth, especially in the area of consumer goods and services. They find, however, after some years that the economy will not stay in the middle; it veers more and more toward the free market. When this is impeded

More "Fried Snowballs"?
Is Market Socialism Possible?

No, at least not in a stable, long-term manner. Introducing elements of a market economy into a centrally run economy quickly bring new difficulties and bottlenecks that can be solved only by introducing more market elements. After a while, you have only a market economy left.

The question is an important one that has enticed thinkers for decades. The idea of a system that combines the theoretical best of socialism—its emphasis on equality and fairness—with the consumer plenty of the market has long been intriguing. Some socialists still think that such a combination is possible and desirable.

The evidence seems to be against it. Where tried, market socialist economies veer more and more toward the free market. The regime, worried that it is putting itself out of business, curbs and restricts the market elements and returns partway to the centrally run economy. The experiment of market-plus-socialism becomes a zigzag of looser and tighter state controls that never find a stable balance and often contribute to economic decline.

To be sure, one can, on paper, chart out which portions of an economy should be state-controlled and which should be left to the marketplace's law of supply and demand. Typically, planners specify that major industries, such as steel manufacturing, stay state-owned and run according to a central plan. Consumer-oriented industries, such as the making of refrigerators, on the other hand, should become private and competitive. It looks, on paper, like the best of both worlds: big industries for the state and small industries for private entrepreneurs who are better attuned to consumer needs.

Quickly problems appear, what economists call "distortions." The refrigerator manufacturers, operating competitively, try to make the best product in large numbers to obtain the lowest price. But they need steel, and the state-run steel mill will have no incentive to make the best steel in large quantities at the lowest price. Under the government plan, the mill produces only so much steel at a set price. What if not enough steel were produced to satisfy the consumer demand for refrigerators? What if the quality of the steel were wrong or the price too high? "Tough," says the state-owned steel mill, "take it or leave it." State ownership of the steel mill, therefore, produces distortions in the output of refrigerators. A market socialist economy would still have some of the rigidities of straight-out socialism, namely, an inability to respond to markets.

The cure in this case is to make the steel mill part of the market sector by selling it to private investors or its own workers. Competition would quickly appear. The steel mills, now seeking a profit and responding solely to market forces, make more steel at the right quality and price for refrigerator manufacturers. The economy is now a little less distorted. But the steel mills still depend on state-owned industries for their raw materials, namely, iron ore and coal. These industries, operating under a government plan, have little reason to boost their output to suit the now-private steel mills. The solution: Do to the iron and coal mines what you have earlier done to the steel mills. Privatize them into profit-seeking, competetive entities and thereby eliminate another market distortion.

As you can see, by the time you eliminate all the distortions of a market socialist economy, you have no socialist elements left. Like a little Pac-Man, the market sector tends to eat up the socialist sector.

This is what happened to the two biggest experiments in market socialism, Yugoslavia and China. Communist authorities, trying to add the vigor of the market to the control and planning of socialism, permitted the market sector to expand in both these countries. But they choked because they saw that it would keep expanding until it subverted the entire socialist structure. So, when the process started picking up speed, they clamped down with new restrictions on the market sector, such as limits on profits and firm size. They subsidized money-losing state industries because they feared bankruptcy and unemployment. Massive distortions appeared. Inflation, inequality, and unemployment—long portrayed as evils of capitalism—shot up. Corruption grew worse than ever because there were now more ways to use public office for private gain.

The Yugoslav solution, after decades of not wanting to admit that their highly touted market socialist economy was in decline, was to go almost all the way to a free market economy and to end the ruinous subsidies for state-owned industries and the limits on private capital. It means, in effect, the end of socialism. The Chinese solution, alas, was to go partway back to a controlled economy. Farming stayed private—the "responsibility system," whereby families farmed leased acreage—but much free industrial activity was snuffed out. Sooner or later, it seems, a market socialist economy must choose one system or the other.

by state controls, the controls create terrible distortions. Ultimately, the middle way countries had to go one way or the other. Gorbachev, too, is finding this out the hard way.

Once a country has decided to marketize, it must decide whether to do it rapidly or gradually. We might call the first the Polish model, the second the Czech or Hungarian model. Poland, in dire economic straits, felt it had little choice but to marketize quickly. Hungary, having already moved part way to a market economy during the 1980s, did not feel under such pressure to move fast, and it feared the suffering induced by the Polish approach. Economists found themselves flabbergasted and speechless when confronted by the problem of how to transform a state-owned and centrally controlled economy into a free market and capitalist economy. It had never been done before. There was no theory or models. Economists could tell you how they wished the economy would end up—perhaps like Austria or Finland—but they couldn't tell you how to get there.

Some economists argued that a gradual transition was like pulling a tooth slowly. Another analogy: If a country drives on the left (like Britain) and decides to switch to driving on the right, it cannot make the switch gradually. This was the reasoning that finally prevailed in Poland. A group of bright, young Polish economists, some of whom had studied in the United States, decided to apply "shock therapy" to Poland's rapid inflation and growing economic chaos. They were advised by Harvard economist Jeffrey Sachs, who had earlier given advice to the Bolivian government (with good results). Finance minister Leszek Balcerowicz (pronounced "bal-tsur-ov-itch"), who has both a Polish doctorate and an American MBA, at the beginning of 1990 set prices free to find their proper market levels, devalued the Polish zloty and made it freely convertible, cut the budget deficit, and limited increases in wages, credit, and monetary growth.

It was like a sudden dunk in icewater. Inflation initially skyrocketed as prices, especially food prices, increased severalfold to world levels. Then inflation calmed. Empty store shelves began filling up, although many people could not afford to buy much. With real money to work for and real things to buy, Polish workers began to work harder and Polish farmers began to produce more. Subsidies were withdrawn and firms were allowed to go bankrupt. With this, unemployment also shot up. Most Poles suffered declining living standards. By mid-1990, food prices were 15 times higher than they were a year earlier while Polish earnings had declined 40 percent. Under these circumstances, one can understand why Solidarity remembered its worker origins. Solidarity was particularly mad at Balcerowicz.

The hoped-for turnaround was slow in coming. Foreign investment did not pour in. In 1989, Poles counted on massive West German investment, but by 1990 that was absorbed by East Germany. Poland had to compete for scarce investments with Hungary and Czechoslovakia. The Polish infrastructure was horrible: a primitive banking system, no office space, and an antique telephone network. Much bureaucratic red tape remained, partly inherited from the old regime, which required permits for everything.

There were some bright signs. The zloty held steady against the dollar. There was no more currency black market; visitors got the same rate of exchange in a bank or on the street. By 1990, Poland was running a trade surplus. Foreign investors were interested but cautious. The Sejm passed a privatization law that gives all citizens vouchers to buy shares of formerly state-owned firms. Then they could trade those shares on a stock market.

Many other East Europeans were frightened by the Polish model. They heard news reports about the economic distress and in some cases saw desperate Poles arrive like gypsies to sell cheap goods in flea markets. If that is what the Polish shock therapy produces, figured many Czechs and Hungarians, we don't want it. During 1990, Prague seesawed back and forth between speeding up marketization or going slow. The new Prague government debated for months on how to marketize, how to cut prices free, and how to withdraw subsidies in such a way that prices would not skyrocket. Finance minister Vaclav Klaus, a more

Who Will Own the Factories?

Decontrol of prices is the logical first step to a market economy and, painful as it may be, a relatively easy one. The next step is harder: How to privatize? One of the most difficult questions each East European country faces is who will own and manage the previously state-owned industrial plants. It is both a political and an economic issue. Virtually all East European lands are going to privatize, that is, they are going to make state factories private. But who then will own them? Who will be the bosses? Whatever you do will be unfair.

The simplest way to go is to declare that the factories belong to those who work in them. But this has a lot of problems. Should a worker who has been there one year have the same share as a worker who has been there 30 years? More basic, some enterprises are efficient or capable of adapting to the new competitive age. Others are chronic money-losers that will fold the day their state subsidies are withdrawn. Giving a worker a share of an efficient factory is a nice benefit. Giving a worker a share of a white elephant is no benefit. Quickly, you would have rich workers at prosperous factories and poor workers laid off from closed factories whose shares are worthless. The obvious unfairness would turn into an explosive political issue.

The Polish approach is to distribute certificates to everyone that could be exchanged for shares in any enterprise they prefer. The desirable shares would, under market conditions, soon cost more certificates, but every Pole could own a small piece of a productive enterprise, solving the problem of some workers getting good shares and others getting poor ones. This would also be the beginning of a Polish stock market.

Another way to privatize is simply to sell enterprises for the highest price. Governments badly need revenues, and some East Europeans either have savings or can get loans. The trouble here is that those likely to be in a position to buy enterprises are the previous bosses under the Communists. They know what the factory is worth, how to run it, and where to get the loans. Often, the old bosses are the only ones who know the factory is for sale. Throughout East Europe, workers noticed that their new boss under capitalism was the same as their old boss under communism, only now he was making more money than ever. In many cases, the director had been a Communist party member with a comfortable life. Anger erupted at the fat cats of communism turning themselves into the fat cats of capitalism.

There may be no way around this unfairness. The Communist managers were often bright and educated. They had no ideological allegiance to communism; they were just opportunists who turned happily from communism to capitalism. Most knew the socialist economy worked badly and welcomed a market economy. Many of them, with a little training, make excellent capitalist managers. With greatly increased material rewards, they work harder than ever. It may be vexatious to see such blatant opportunists rewarded, but isn't opportunism the nature of

> capitalism? If ex-Communist managers are capable, there is no reason to throw them out. And if they aren't any good, the competition of the free market will soon consign them to bankruptcy and unemployment. Besides, who can replace them? East Europe has few business or management schools; almost all trained managers until recently worked in state enterprises.

enthusiastic free-marketer than President Vaclav Havel, had to fight with the go-slow ministers in the Prague cabinet. The hesitation was not good for the Czech economy.

Budapest, too, hesitated. Although Hungary had begun marketizing in 1988, the new leaders were afraid to totally decontrol prices and quickly sell off factories. Cautiously, Budapest moved to sell over 100 of Hungary's large state enterprises by 1992. By 1995, private enterprise was supposed to encompass more than half of the Hungarian enconomy; in 1990, only a fifth was private. Hungary had much lower unemployment than Poland, but very sluggish growth. Ultimately, every East European country will have to do approximately what Poland has done. Middle ways of mixed socialist and market economies are not viable. To enter the world market, East European products must be able to compete in quality and in price not only with West European products but with those from the Pacific rim as well.

"WHO WILL BUY OUR [LOUSY] PRODUCTS?"

The actual word used here, by a Hungarian economist, was somewhat stronger than "lousy." The question, though, sums up pithily what the East European economies face. For decades, they have been locked in the Comecon bloc, producing mediocre goods to be bartered among themselves or sold in exchange for Soviet raw materials. In 1989, a quarter of Poland's, East Germany's, Hungary's, and Romania's exports went to the Soviet Union. A third of Czechoslovakia's exports went there, and more than half of Bulgaria's. In return, they imported similar values of Soviet raw materials, chiefly oil. Soviet prices lagged behind world levels. These prices, in so-called transferable rubles, were based on five-year rolling averages of world prices. For example, when world oil prices shot up in 1979, the Soviet price to their East European partners initially went up only a little, because it was based on an average of world prices from 1975 through 1979. It was a sweetheart deal for the East Europeans: cheap raw materials and unfussy Soviet customers. Products didn't have to be good; the Russians would accept anything.

At the start of 1991 this "paradise" came to an end. Moscow put its East European trade deals on a hard-currency basis. Soviet oil flowed, but it had to be paid for in dollars or other Western currency. And Soviet prices no longer lagged behind world levels. The message from Moscow was: "No more economic giveaways. We can get higher prices for oil from the West, and they pay in dollars. You will do the same." East Europe's energy bill about doubled, costing them another $6 billion in hard currency that they didn't have. The Soviets still purchased a great deal from East Europe—many of their factories are stuck with unmodern East European equipment and need spare parts—but they paid in hard currency.

This immediately caught East European between the blades of a scissors. Their costs went up as their sales went down. Why, for example, should the Soviets buy inferior Hungarian buses for dollars when, for those same dollars, they could buy better French, Japanese, and Korean buses? Comecon was an inefficient and ultimately retarding trade mechanism, but it did give East Europeans a security blanket that they had gotten used to. Suddenly, the blanket was snatched away, and many East European factories saw their sales decline sharply.

Thinking East Europeans were justifiably frightened. Who indeed would buy their [lousy] products? The answer, of course, is to get unlousy fast. East Europeans are not used to producing for the world market, but they can do it. They are unaccustomed to rapid design innovation, high quality, marketing, and competitive pricing. They will learn fast, for they have no choice.

SUGGESTED READINGS

DAHRENDORF, RALF. *Reflections on the Revolution in Europe.* New York: Random House, 1990.

KORNAI, JÁNOS. *The Road to a Free Economy: Shifting from a Socialist System; The Example of Hungary.* New York: Verso Press, 1990.

MAGAS, BRANCA. *The Widening Gyre: Class and Nation in Yugoslavia.* New York: Verso Press, 1990.

SACHS, JEFFREY. "Eastern Europe's Economies: What Is to Be Done?" *The Economist,* 13 Jan. 1990.

_____ and DAVID LIPTON. "Poland's Economic Reform," *Foreign Affairs,* 69 (Summer 1990) 3.

SIMONS, THOMAS W., JR. *The End of the Cold War?* New York: St. Martin's, 1990.

Lessons, Hopes, Fears

SOME LESSONS

1. Socialist Economies Work Poorly

They don't collapse overnight; they simply slow down and fall behind capitalist economies. Let's get straight what is here meant by socialism: state ownership and control of the means of production. What is not meant by socialism is the welfare state, which is actually just a variation on capitalism. The welfare state, which is promoted under a variety of labels (social democracy, democratic socialism, social market, and American-style liberalism), taxes the better-off to pay for a welfare floor or social safety net for those lower down the economic ladder. It also supervises the macroeconomy by guiding interest rates, the money supply, and foreign trade.

All industrial societies are welfare states, some more than others. We can get a rough idea of the magnitude of a welfare state from the percent of gross national product that is absorbed by taxes each year. This figure ranges from 30 percent in the United States to around 50 percent in Scandinavia. (Much of this money of course, does not go for "welfare" expenditures but for ordinary government expenses such as defense, police and fire departments, and administration.) In other words, there is only about a 20 percentage point difference between the expenditures of the highly developed cradle-to-grave welfare states of Sweden, Norway, and Denmark and the relatively parsimonious expenditures of the United States. The expenditures of the rest of West Europe falls between these two extremes. The amount of welfare a country has is largely a matter of taste and political culture. Swedes want and like a big welfare state; Americans do not.

The economies of advanced industrialized countries are pretty much the same:

Is Marxism Dead?

For most applied purposes, yes; but an honest thinker can still be a Marxist. One might at first suppose that the colossal failure of communism and its ouster in East Europe "proves" that Marx was wrong. It certainly demonstrates that trying to apply a system based on Marx's ideas can easily lead to catastrophe. Clearly Lenin's concentration of power led directly to Stalin's abuse of that power. But remember, Marx concentrated on criticizing capitalism and predicting its downfall; he had practically nothing to say about socialism except that it would be better than capitalism.

Various interesting and valid criticisms of capitalism are still around. Some of them might fit under the label of Marxist or Marxian. Just asking certain questions shows the continuing relevance of Marx. For example, does capitalism, unless regulated, increasingly concentrate wealth in the hands of a few? Does capitalism require massive amounts of debt—consumer, business, government—in order to keep running? Does big money influence elections in democracies?

Where Marxism is simply a mode of inquiry, it is quite useful. It trains us to look below the surface, to ask who really benefits, and to view conflict as the norm. Where Marxist political systems are put into practice, Marxism becomes an excuse for tyranny. Marxist regimes resist probes below their bland surface lest they reveal sharp class differences and smoldering conflicts. If Marx returned to life, he'd get in trouble in Communist countries. One can and should split the theoretical from the applied. Unfortunately, politically committed Marxists emphasize the connection between theory and practice. (They often use the German word *Praxis* to make it sound more scientific.) But if they persist in arguing that practice determines theory, they in effect are refuting the whole Marxist package. One of the great challenges for modern Marxists will be to explain what went wrong in East Europe. After they find a valid explanation, many will no longer be Marxists.

They all have capitalism, markets, and competition. Swedish capitalists, for example, are among the world's fiercest. The "social market" model of West Germany is frequently discussed in East Europe. The *Sozialmarkt* of Ludwig Erhard in the 1950s certainly promoted economic growth, and the term has a nice ring to it, a combination of a market system with social concern. Examined more closely, West Germany's social market is just plain capitalism with a little state prodding to direct investment into recovering from war damage, such as encouraging apartment building construction.

In only a few West European countries does the government own much of the means of production. France, Austria, and Italy have considerable state ownership (Sweden does not), but these firms are run largely like capitalist enterprises. They compete on a world market, are expected to make money, and are not run by

Is There an Alternative to Capitalism?

Do you mean to say that there is no alternative to capitalism, the reader may ask. You mean this is it? The capitalist rat race: work hard, consume a lot, and never know quiet contentment. No, I think there is an alternative to capitalism, only it's not socialism. If you don't like the sometimes brutal forces of the market and of materialism, you can opt out by joining bohemia. Bohemianism is a rejection of the prevailing bourgeois culture of hard work and high consumption in favor of a laid-back ethic of beards, battered clothes, and individualism. Bohemia (mistakenly named after the Czech lands in earlier centuries that were the supposed homeland of the gypsies) has taken many forms over the years, but it always features a rejection of conventionality. Artists in garrets (as in the opera *La Bohème*), angry writers in blue jeans, or hippies with guitars, all show their contempt for the conventional or "square" life. They do not live to work and would rather have leisure time than material possessions. Bohemians and leftists overlap; both reject the bourgeoisie, the former culturally and the latter politically. Most bohemians have leftist political values, and leftists tend to bohemian lifestyles.

Individuals can opt into bohemia; society as a whole cannot. This was the great mistake of socialist thinkers, such as Marx, Engels, and Lenin, who themselves were bohemians in lifestyle. They supposed that their contempt for bourgeois culture could become dominant and serve to build a humane, just society where material output would be so high that people would cease being materialistic. It didn't work; the socialist economy never delivered the high material output. Nor did socialist teaching create a New Socialist Man, who would work for the sake of society. People generally need the motivation of material rewards to persuade them to work hard and produce a lot. And if one could devise a society composed entirely of bohemians, no one would do much work. Actually, bohemians need a square society to live off and make fun of. Bohemians define themselves in their opposition to a conventional lifestyle.

When I say, "Socialism works poorly," I am not urging everyone to become an eager capitalist or a conformist bourgeois. I am suggesting that the opposite of capitalism is not socialism but bohemianism. If you don't like capitalist society—and there are several good reasons why you might dislike it—you can make an individual choice to drop out, all the way or part way. But, please, do not try to inflict your individual choice on the rest of society.

government. They may be able to get government loans and subsidies more easily than private industry, hence they may be less efficient than privately owned companies. These state sectors grew haphazardly and piecemeal for a variety of reasons—to boost industry, develop poor regions, prevent bankruptcies and unemployment, and punish wartime collaborators—but not to usher in a socialist utopia. There is little element of socialist planning about these industries; they operate on the basis of supply and demand. Accordingly, please do not confuse the welfare states of West Europe—even if they have some state-owned factories—with the socialist states of East Europe. Neither are welfare states "middle ways" between capitalism and socialism. They are capitalist economies with some of the rough edges smoothed by government programs.

For the socialist systems, where the state owns and runs virtually all the industry, the verdict is now in: They work poorly. In absolute terms, they show some growth. In relative terms, they are weak performers and fall behind the market economies. Their technologies, designs, workmanship, and quality control render their products uncompetitive on world markets. Has anyone bought a Romanian stereo lately? Missing from their economies are the crucial ingredients of innovation, risk taking, and customer service, items Marx and the Marxists have ignored. Without them, socialist economies fall behind.

This is not such a tragedy, some people say. So what if socialist economies underperform capitalist economies? Socialism, by promoting greater equality, is inherently fairer than capitalism. Incomes probably were more equally distributed in East Europe than in Western countries, but highly placed Communist party people gave themselves generous extra helpings. Some had lavish estates and secret Swiss bank accounts. But more basically, is equality of income and of the standard of living a good thing? Should lazy workers be paid as much as energetic ones? If they are, motivation collapses and productivity declines.

Well, some defenders of socialism say, material goods are not the be-all and end-all of human existence. Capitalism has brainwashed people to want more and more, they argue (and it may well be true). Socialism teaches people to move away from material pursuits and toward cultural and leisure activities. Perhaps such a shift would be a good idea, but it certainly hasn't happened in socialist countries, where people are often more obsessed than Westerners with acquiring a bit of material comfort. One of the great lessons of East Europe is that people really are materialistic, and little but material incentives motivates them to work. As someone once said, this is a material world.

2. Political Culture Is Not Very Malleable

The Communists had over 40 years to remold East European political culture, and they failed miserably. The basic Stalinist premise that attitudes can be molded is simply wrong. The Communists may control the overt means of socialization, the mass media and school system, but these are vastly outweighed by the informal means of socialization found in family, friends, and the church. The biggest factor working against popular acceptance of communism is probably the direct and personal perceptions by people of the system's pervasive inequality, inefficiency, and corruption. The Communist media's constant spouting of propaganda in the

Anti-Ifonlyism

As noted previously, I think honest Marxists can contribute to our understanding of the debacle of communism in East Europe. Dishonest Marxists (and other shallow thinkers) will try to dodge intellectual responsiblity by advancing "if only" claims. They will pick out one or more specific problems and announce that things would have gone differently and better "if only" such and such a factor had been corrected. You may encounter such speculative arguments as the following:

1. If only Lenin had lived a few years longer, he would have been able to establish real socialism.
2. If only Lenin had been firmer and prevented Stalin from rising to power, the Soviet system and subsequently the East European systems would have been much better.
3. If only Stalin had had a nicer personality...
4. If only Poland had stuck to the Curzon Line as its eastern border...
5. If only Stalin hadn't signed the 1939 pact with Hitler...
6. If only Roosevelt hadn't signed the Yalta agreement...
7. If only Stalin hadn't selected such repulsive little puppets to set up the first Communist regimes in East Europe...
8. If only Truman hadn't overreacted and started the Cold War...
9. If only Moscow had permitted East European lands to take their own paths to socialism, as in Yugoslavia...
10. If only Communist officials had been more honest and energetic and had set a better example...
11. If only East Europeans had worked harder and been more enthusiastic about socialism...
12. If only Communist regimes had eased up a bit and offered major reforms much earlier...

You can go on and on with such philosophical junk food. The basic line is a tautology: If only things had been different, then they would not have been the same. A person who makes an "if only" claim doesn't want to come to grips with the fact that things happen for good and sufficient reason, not by accident. Indeed, the non-accidental nature of history is a basic point of Marxism, one Marx picked up from Hegel.

The structure of the Soviet system let the most ruthless power manipulator take it over. Stalin and his system were no accidents. The Stalinist straitjacket imposed on East Europe was required to make sure these lands stayed absolutely obedient. When the Stalinist controls were eased, a tidal wave of criticism and even hatred poured out. When the controls were abandoned, the regimes collapsed. There was nothing accidental or gratuitous about the East European police states. Their draconic controls flowed directly from the Soviet effort to establish alien, unpopular regimes. When the Soviets abandoned that effort, the police controls eased and then the regimes folded. An "if only" claim can be fun as a game of speculation, but nothing more.

face of a deficient reality simply turns people off. They become anti-Communist or cynical or both.

3. Empires Are Expensive

Retaining East Europe cost the Soviets a bundle and economically netted them very little. Their imperial costs, plus the slow deterioration of the socialist economies, left them broke and behind the West. It is for reasons such as these that no empire lasts forever.

4. There Is No Middle Ground between a Communist and a Democratic System

The two cannot be blended. Communist regimes are so unpopular that permitting even a little criticism unleashes a torrent of protest. Then the regime must either crack down with repression or go all the way to democracy, thus putting itself out of business. Happily, the Communist regimes of Central Europe consented to going out of business; we may hope that those of the Balkans will soon do so.

5. Likewise, There Is No Middle Ground between a Centrally Controlled and a Market Economy

Elements of the market, introduced experimentally into centrally controlled economies, subvert them. In Yugoslavia, Hungary, and China, such experiments produced initial growth but soon developed bottlenecks that could be relieved only by further marketizing the economy. After a while in such mixed systems, the state sector will be minor and the hold of Communist officials weak. Again the regime must decide whether to put itself out of business or revert to the controlled economy. China partially pulled back. The Soviets face the same choice.

SOME HOPES

1. East Europe Will Eventually Join the European Community

It will take some time and much adjustment, but East Europeans hardly have a choice in the matter. At first, only six West European countries (France, West Germany, Italy, Belgium, the Netherlands, and Luxembourg—Charlemagne's original Holy Roman Empire) signed the Treaty of Rome that founded the Common Market in 1957. Britain and Scandinavia turned up their noses at the Six and joined a looser grouping, the European Free Trade Association, dubbed the Outer Seven. The Common Market, though, produced such prosperity that by 1963 Britain too had applied to join. Although rebuffed by de Gaulle's "Non," Britain, along with Denmark and Ireland, did join the European Community, the EC (as

A Revival of Central Europe?

An echo of old Central Europe reverberated at the 1990 Venice summit meeting of prime ministers and foreign ministers of Italy, Yugoslavia, Austria, Hungary, and Czechoslovakia. What Italians call the *pentagonale* (five-sided) summit sought to lay the groundwork for extensive cooperation in the Danube-Adriatic area. At one time, all or portions of the five nations had been part of the Habsburg Empire. Could they form a kind of natural unit for commerce? Perhaps, but getting into the EC is far more important than a new regional trade grouping.

Behind the *pentagonale* meeting was Italy's interest in giving itself room to maneuver in the shadow of mighty Germany. Italy, said Italian foreign minister Gianni de Michelis diplomatically, wanted the "restoration of part of Central Europe" as a "region of small and medium-sized nations between Germany and Russia." The results of the summit were minor—a pledge to improve road and rail links—but psychologically many of the participants seemed to share de Michelis's concern.

the Common Market now calls itself), in 1973. Later Greece (1981) and Spain and Portugal (1986) felt compelled to join. EC membership means a gigantic market, efficiency, modernity, and prosperity. Goods, services, labor, and capital freely flow across members' borders.

A few countries with peculiar situations may decide to stay outside the EC. Norway with its oil and Switzerland with its neutrality and banking secrecy have so far not joined (but look for them to change their minds). Austria and Finland would love to join but, until recently, were prevented by a Soviet veto over their foreign policies; they will likely join soon. For most countries, belonging to the EC is the ticket to economic growth. Membership has its privileges.

Can East Europe decide differently? No East European country has the luxury of saying, "No, we won't join the EC. We'll become another Switzerland—rich and aloof. Or maybe we'll discover lots of oil and become another Norway." East Europeans look at the EC and ache to join a paradise of 330 million well-fed West Europeans with a combined GNP of around $5 trillion. East Europeans see in the EC their only major market, investor, and employer of surplus labor. They simply have no choice about joining the EC, and several have already applied for associate status. Full membership will take some years.

It won't be easy. The EC headquarters in Brussels does not confer membership casually. Applicants must demonstrate that they have a market economy, political democracy, and a will to become Europeans. Brussels made Spain and Portugal wait several years and participate in difficult negotiations. Some West Europeans are cautious or even afraid of expanding the EC; they fear too much competition from low-cost producers. Already many German workers complain that their factories have been shipped to Spain and Portugal. How will they like seeing them shipped to Poland and Czechoslovakia, where labor costs are a fraction of German labor costs? French farmers already protest over cheaper Spanish and Portuguese vegetables. How will they like competing with the beautiful vegetables of Bulgaria? How will Danish pork producers like competing with their Polish counterparts?

The good news here is that stringent membership requirements will force the East European countries to shape up. They will not be considered for membership if they still have a state-run economy; it must be a free market economy. They will not be considered if they do not have a thorough and proven democracy; the Balkan lands flunk on this ground. Regimes that govern with riot police, abuse ethnic minorities, and mouth anti-Semitism will likely not be admitted. For example, when Slovakia passed a Slovak-only language law in 1990, a Prague spokesman worried that "this violates human rights" and "would keep us from taking our place in Europe." Remember, the EC is not eager to admit everyone. Furthermore, East Europe will have to clean up its pollution catastrophe and meet fairly demanding EC environmental standards. East European air may become breathable again.

2. The Soviets Will Withdraw Their Forces from East Europe

Some have already left. One reason they have not been withdrawn more quickly is that there is no housing for them in Russia. West Germany is actually subsidizing Soviet troops in East Germany and building barracks for them back in Russia to facilitate their exit. With the departure of Soviet troops from Central Europe, the Cold War definitively ends. The Warsaw Pact becomes a dead letter (as does NATO), a paper alliance with no national interests behind it. Most European armies will be small; many countries will end conscription in favor of all-volunteer armies, as Britain had done for many years.

The happiest point about the rebirth of East Europe is that the Soviets will demonstrate to themselves that the retention of East Europe is not vital to their security. At long last Moscow has shaken off the argument posed by Stalin, Khrushchev, and Brezhnev, that East Europe is the Soviet Union's defensive shield that must never be given up. It was simply not true. In fact, Soviet control of East Europe made the Cold War happen and created the massive insecurity that has plagued the Soviet Union and the world. Giving up East Europe increases Soviet security. The Finlandization of East Europe—its becoming neutral, lightly armed, and with an implied Soviet veto over major foreign-policy shifts—gives the Soviets all the security of the Warsaw Pact with none of its costs.

Moscow requires only two things of East Europe:

1. Don't join NATO.
2. Pay in dollars.

These are the gut national interests that Moscow has in East Europe. In terms of their economies and the move toward democracy, East Europe can do what it

Is Germany a Menace?

No. Some people fear that a reunited Germany will become a Fourth Reich, an expansionist military power. This is improbable. German democracy is as firm as any in Europe. Only a fringe of Germans talk about the recovery of lost lands to the east. The Oder-Neise border with Poland has been confirmed and reconfirmed. Germany has accomplished so much more with peace than with war that it is unlikely to return to militarism.

But let's imagine a worst-case scenario. Suppose an economic depression once again puts a right-wing extremist party in control of Germany. Berlin talks about altering the treaties that gave up the eastern territories and builds a large military machine. Does the rest of Europe worry? No, because three European powers have nuclear weapons, and Germany does not. Germany is bound by treaty to acquire no ABC (atomic, bacteriological, or chemical) weapons. The Soviet Union, Britain, and France, either alone or in concert, would be able to block German expansionism.

Let's take an even worse scenario. This rearmed Germany breaks its treaty commitment, acquires some nuclear weapons, and threatens to use them. Such a threat would not be credible. Even if Germany could fling a few dozen warheads at its neighbors, Germany would simply disappear into radioactive rubble under a rain of nuclear weapons from the other European nuclear powers. Crowded Germany—where, as the peace movement noted, the towns are only "two or three kilotons apart"—is extremely vulnerable to nuclear strikes.

Those who hate all nuclear weapons and would ban them worldwide might consider that they are the ultimate guarantee that Germany stays peaceful. Europe and the world simply do not have to worry about a militarily aggressive Germany. German dominance in trade, as we shall consider, is another matter.

pleases. As for NATO, Moscow need not worry. NATO is also becoming a dead letter and has no interest in adding new members. As for paying in hard currency, that became the norm in Soviet-East European trade at the beginning of 1991. The Soviets can get world prices for their oil and natural gas, and they no longer have any interest in selling these commodities to East Europe at bargain prices in funny-money currency. Why sell oil to the Poles for "transferable rubles" when you can get D-marks from the Germans? The "pay in dollars" requirement is thus self-enforcing.

3. East Europe Turns Capitalist and Prosperous

This is not an unreasonable hope, but it will take some time and much pain. East Europeans have little choice: Get efficient fast or starve. Most East Europeans are frightened of the tremendous economic restructuring they must undergo in order to compete on world markets. As noted in a previous section, "Who will buy our [lousy] products?" is a question that can be heard throughout the region. But East European economies have a few things going for them.

First, their wage rates are lower, in some cases much lower, than West European wages. Only Portugal and Greece can compete with East Europe in terms of low wages. And much of the East European workforce is educated (at least through high school) and skilled, although they lack the high-tech knowledge of the advanced countries' labor forces. Most East Europeans want to work. They have glimpsed the good life in the West and want it. In contrast, some of the more prosperous West European lands are showing signs of taking things easy after several decades of hard work. East European productivity is weak, but the introduction of modern machines and methods should produce some spectacular percentage gains in productivity. The U.S. firm of Schwinn, for example, bought a majority share of a Hungarian enterprise that built clunky, unfashionable bicycles. With expensive new high-temperature welding and electrostatic painting systems, with a carefully selected workforce (pared by 40 percent), and with incentive wages of about $210 a month (some 30 percent higher than the Hungarian average wage), Schwinn is profitably turning out bikes for the European market. The arrangement is good for Schwinn and good for Hungary.

At first it may seem that all the good products are made elsewhere in unbeatable quality and price. But no one knows what tomorrow's fast-growth areas will be. If you had predicted a quarter century ago that people would be wearing fancy, mostly leather athletic shoes, selling for $50 and up, and made in South Korea, you would have been dismissed as a nut. Who would pay that much for sneakers? If you had predicted even ten years ago that people would be sending mail by fax, you would be asked, "What's a fax?" (All faxes are made in Japan.) Who knows what East Europe will make? They will probably start out by imitating the West, but soon they will develop their own designs and innovations.

West European, American, and Japanese investors will set up shop in East Europe to take advantage of the low wages plus the presumed access to the EC. Without such access, foreign investors will quickly lose interest. You're not going to manufacture light bulbs, cars, or cosmetics for the Czech market; you're going to manufacture them for the European market. Westinghouse didn't go into Spain in the 1970s just because the Spanish economy was growing and wages were low. It went in because Spain was likely to enter the Common Market, which it did. This is the great motivator for East Europe to join the EC. No EC membership, no major foreign investment.

Some critics on the left may object that foreign investment means exploitation. The foreigners are not investing out of the goodness of their hearts but to take advantage of the low wages and the fear of unemployment. They plan to sweat the maximum profit from helpless East Europeans. East Europe will become the poorly paid proletariat of the First World. The answer to this silly argument is that if you don't want the exploitation, keep out the foreign investment and stay poor. Virtually all foreign investment flows into situations where investors think they can get the best returns. American industry was in large part founded in the nineteenth century by massive inflows of British and French capital seeking to "exploit" American workers. After World War II, U.S. capital flowed to West Europe for the same reason. Such workers do not stay exploited for long, however. After a while their productivity and wages catch up with those of the higher-cost nation. Playing on a famous quip of Oscar Wilde's, a 1990 British report noted: "There is only one thing worse than being exploited, and that is not being exploited."

The foreign investors will provide badly needed management skills, technical know-how, and competitive designs. They will show East Europeans how to market for export. Just as important, they will get East European competitive juices flowing after four decades of socialist sloth. New service industries and subcontractors will spring up around the foreign investments. Soon the East Europeans will be showing the foreign capitalists a thing or two. Capitalism is contagious.

SOME FEARS

1. A United Europe Locks Out Foreign Goods

The hopeful notion that East Europe will join West Europe in an enlarged European Community has a dark side to it. The EC of twelve West European states is already protectionist. They especially protect and subsidize their farmers, and this keeps out much U.S. agricultural production. We get mad. They severely limit the number of Japanese autos that can be imported. The Japanese get mad. The Europeans couldn't care less. Their attitude: "Our first and foremost responsibility is to European farmers and workers. The massive influx of foreign products will put them out of work, and this we will not do."

This attitude could get worse. As East Europe moves to join the West, we could hear statements such as: "We Europeans have taken on extraordinary burdens to lift up our brothers in the east. We are transferring much capital eastward and opening our markets to them, thereby placing at risk our farmers and workers. Do not expect us to become the dumping ground for every low-cost producer in the world, especially during this delicate time of uniting East and West Europe."

The danger here is a series of retaliatory trade barriers. American farmers, who historically have always exported grain, are already getting angry at being excluded from free competition in Europe. The feeling grows that we buy European products freely while they buy few of ours. The mood to retaliate by tariffs or quotas on European goods grows. Any U.S. retaliation, of course, will be met by European retaliation in the form of higher tariffs and lower quotas. World trade could then decline, harming everyone's economy. One major component of the Great Depression of the 1930s was fierce trade protectionism that

War Over Transylvania?

It sounds improbable in modern Europe, but war between Hungary and Romania over the plight of over 2 million ethnic Magyars in Transylvania is not out of the question. Transylvania has been a contested area for generations; both Hungary and Romania swear that historically and ethnically it belongs to them. During World War II, Hungary and Romania, both allied to Germany, verged on the outbreak of war over Transylvania. Hitler ordered this to be stopped. Hitler gave part of Transylvania to Hungary; Stalin gave all of it to Romania as Bucharest changed sides late in the war. Only the Communist regimes of both countries plus Soviet hegemony have kept the issue concealed for four decades.

As soon as Communist rule weakened, the Transylvania issue came into the open again. In 1988, the Hungarian Communist government permitted a major rally in Budapest against the Ceausescu regime for its persecution of ethnic Hungarians. At the time, it seemed like a clever way to deflect domestic Hungarian unrest against another Communist regime, but the rally was a mistake for the regime, because it got Hungarians acquainted with the idea of mass protest which they then turned against their own regime the following year. In 1988 and 1989, thousands of Magyars sneaked across the border into Hungary, and the Budapest regime received them as best it could.

The issue was an important one in the 1990 Hungarian elections, and the party with the strongest stand for helping Hungarians in *Erdely* (the Hungarian word for Transylvania) won big. The nationalistic Democratic Forum, now the ruling party, also notes that there are important Hungarian minorities in Slovakia and Yugoslavia. Romanian nationalism is also strong; no Romanian would dream of compromising on Transylvania. The fascistic Iron Guard was revived in 1990, and they hate Hungarians.

It is possible, but not likely, that highly nationalistic cabinets in both Budapest and Bucharest could find it convenient to deflect domestic discontent against foreign enemies who either covet or occupy sacred national territory. The European context would work against the outbreak of war, however. Hungary already wants to get into the EC, and Romania probably will soon. Brussels would not consider admitting either unless the Transylvania problem is resolved. Actually, EC membership for both lands might be a solution to the Transylvania question, for then Transylvanians of all ethnic background would be guaranteed the right to their own language and culture, and the right to free movement. Still, there are plenty of Yahoos on both sides.

only deepened and prolonged the economic downturn.

Americans look with joy at a United States of Europe—imitiation is the sincerest form of flattery—but must ask what kind of Europe will it be. Will it be one with few barriers to trade or many? Will a united Europe look inward or outward? We are happy to see East Europe escape from its poorly working Comecon bloc. Will they now become locked in another bloc? To be sure, the European Community is the kind of bloc they like. Even better would be a Europe that welcomes trade and competition with the world, not just among its members. A major American investment presence in East Europe would be one way to keep Europe relatively open to foreign trade. This, unfortunately, may not materialize.

2. The United States Fails to Invest in East Europe

American firms, who after World War II plunged into West Europe, are now slow and cautious about pursuing major investments in East Europe. From bold, expansion-minded risk takers, American capitalists have turned into timid pensioners. Much of the problem, of course, is that America doesn't have much capital to export. For some years, America has been a major capital importer as foreign investments have poured in to cover soaring U.S. trade and federal budget deficits. The world's biggest debtor nation is the United States.

The big investors in East Europe will be West Europeans, especially Germans, probably followed by the Japanese. Americans may come in a weak third. The reasons for the likely West European dominance in East Europe are clear: They are close; they have the capital; they are enlarging the EC; and they have much the same culture as the East Europeans. American businesspeople exploring East Europe for possible sales and investment found that the Germans were there ahead of them and in many cases had already wrapped up deals.

Is there anything wrong with this? Is it not the natural course of things? Maybe, but it contributes to the danger discussed previously, that a united Europe will form a protected trade bloc. Major U.S. investment would make East Europe a more outward-looking and open economy, exchanging goods worldwide, not just inside Europe. But at the present it doesn't look like there will be much U.S. investment.

3. Germany Takes Over East Europe

Unquestionably, a united Germany will be Europe's number one nation. It will have the biggest population (aside from the Soviet Union), the largest economy, the most skilled workforce, and the biggest trade surplus. East Europe, as we just mentioned, is its natural area for investment and trade. Between the two world wars, Germany totally dominated trade with East Europe, in part by a deliberate foreign policy. It is likely to do so again. After bringing East Germany up to West German levels of productivity and prosperity, Germany will naturally turn its attention eastwards, as it has done since the Middle Ages. The impulse for the *Drang nach Osten* (the "push to the east") continues in our day. To the west, as before, Germany faces strong and developed nations. To the east, as before, it faces weak and backward lands.

Would German dominance of East Europe be such a terrible thing? As long as it is purely economic, no. German capital and trade are likely the best and fastest ways for East Europe to rise economically. If it turns into something besides a free and fair economic relationship, though, the picture turns sinister. If Berlin in some future year starts talking about the recovery of lost lands, rigs trade deals, and uses East Europe for toxic waste disposal, we've got a problem. A thrifty, hard-working Germany could be a great benefit and example for East Europe. An arrogant and bossy Germany, however, could remind East Europeans of the Nazi vision of inferior and subservient East Europeans serving as Germany's slaves and victims.

This is why a U.S. presence in East Europe is important: It would be a counterweight to German domination. East Europe should not *belong* to anyone, not to Russians, Germans, or Americans. A middle-sized American presence— economic, political, and cultural—could serve to keep East Europe open and free. U.S. dominance, considering our present economic situation, is impossible. Our goal should be to get East Europe out of the pattern it has been trapped in for several centuries: caught between empires. Let us not cheer so loudly for the demise of one empire that we neglect to guard against the rise of another.

INDEX